HUMAN VALUES IN A CHANGING WORLD

ECHOES AND REFLECTIONS
THE SELECTED WORKS OF DAISAKU IKEDA

Showcasing some of the most potent and far-reaching spiritual works of our times, this major new series brings together – for the first time under the banner of a single imprint – twelve classic dialogues between modern spiritual master Daisaku Ikeda and a distinguished roll-call of discussants, who are uniformly thinkers of global stature and reputation. *Echoes and Reflections* ranges widely across the fields of religion, politics, economics, science and the arts, and in each instance puts a profound and searching new perspective on some of the most pressing issues of our age. Topics covered include: the search for worldwide social justice; the challenges posed by climate change and diminishing natural resources; the perils of religious misdirection; the urgent need for inner growth and harmony; the importance of learning and education; and, above all, the significance of the human quest for meaning and value in life.

Titles in the series:

Choose Life, Arnold Toynbee & Daisaku Ikeda

Dawn After Dark, René Huyghe & Daisaku Ikeda

Human Values in A Changing World, Bryan Wilson & Daisaku Ikeda

Search for A New Humanity, Josef Derbolav & Daisaku Ikeda

Before it is Too Late, Aurelio Peccei & Daisaku Ikeda

A Lifelong Quest for Peace, Linus Pauling & Daisaku Ikeda

Ode to the Grand Spirit, Chingiz Aitmatov & Daisaku Ikeda

Human Rights in the Twenty-first Century, Austregésilo de Athayde & Daisaku Ikeda

Dialogue on José Martí, Cintio Vitier & Daisaku Ikeda

Compassionate Light in Asia, Jin Yong & Daisaku Ikeda

Global Civilization, Majid Tehranian & Daisaku Ikeda

Moral Lessons of the Twentieth Century, Mikhail Gorbachev & Daisaku Ikeda

HUMAN VALUES IN A CHANGING WORLD

A Dialogue

BRYAN WILSON
and
DAISAKU IKEDA

Edited and Translated by Richard L. Gage

ECHOES AND REFLECTIONS
THE SELECTED WORKS OF DAISAKU IKEDA

I.B. TAURIS
LONDON · NEW YORK

Echoes and Reflections is a new series that repackages twelve classic dialogues held between Daisaku Ikeda and a variety of interlocutors, which took place from 1972 to 1996. The texts of these dialogues are presented in this series substantively in the form in which they were originally published. For the sake of verisimilitude, and to preserve the integrity of the series, the events, persons and dates referred to in the texts reflect the original periods and contexts in which the conversations were first held, and so have not been altered or edited to mirror subsequent developments in international affairs or the changed worldwide circumstances of later years.

Published in 2008 by I.B.Tauris & Co Ltd
6 Salem Road, London W2 4BU
175 Fifth Avenue, New York NY 10010
www.ibtauris.com

First published in English by Macdonald & Co (publishers) Ltd, London & Sydney in 1984
In the United States of America and Canada distributed by Palgrave Macmillan
a division of St. Martin's Press, 175 Fifth Avenue, New York NY 10010

ISBN: 978 1 84511 597 5

A full CIP record for this book is available from the British Library
A full CIP record is available from the Library of Congress

Library of Congress Catalog Card Number: available

Typeset by Initial Typesetting Services, Edinburgh
Printed and bound in Great Britain by TJ International Ltd, Padstow, Cornwall

Contents

PART III
The Problems of Organization

PART IV
Some Historical Perspectives

PART V
Matters of Mind and Body

PART VI
The Wider Ethical Perspective

Preface

During the winter of 1978–9, at the joint invitation of Soka University and the Institute of Oriental Philosophy in Tokyo, one of us, Wilson, visited Japan, and at the beginning of that visit was received at dinner by the other, Ikeda, the President of Soka Gakkai International. Our dinner-time conversation ranged over a variety of issues, and we sat far longer than either of us had perhaps expected, each finding stimulation in the other's very different, but by no means always divergent, perspectives. Explaining ourselves to one another, recognizing another world view and learning the subtleties of our respective positions destroyed whatever stereotypes we might otherwise have entertained – respectively, of a leader of a new religious movement, and of an academic sociologist. The spontaneous desire arose to meet again, to talk further and to exchange ideas on a wider spectrum of issues. We decided, there and then, to do so. Since that time, we have met on various occasions, both in Japan and in Europe, and have consolidated and extended our conversations with some lengthy written exchanges which, subsequently edited and reduced, have resulted in the Dialogue printed in the following pages.

There might be a temptation, after so long a series of exchanges, for the participants – like the participants in any correspondence in which friendship grows – to settle into the comfortable postures of mutual admiration and self-satisfaction in having "set the world to rights". Any such feeling could well have been reinforced by the pleasure of the exercise. We hope that we have not succumbed to such a temptation. Our conversations interested us, and we hope that they may interest others, but we are under no illusion that we have said anything like the last word. The issues all remain open issues. We are not experts on most subjects that engaged our attention, and on some we are very much laymen and amateurs. Thus, we are very far from supposing – jointly or separately – that we can pontificate on such matters. We both know the importance of keeping ourselves informed about what others think of all these things and, in our own distinct ways, we are both what might be called "people watchers", in the sense that we are eager to observe the climate of informed public opinion, to react to it and to comment on it. Clearly, some issues on which we touch have been the subject of much more prolonged debate and argument by experts in particular fields, but knowing this has not unduly inhibited us. Each of us occupies – from the point of view of Nichiren Buddhism or of academic sociology – a vantage point, albeit not by any means always a commanding view, from which to survey a wide range of contemporary concerns, and it is in the spirit of commentators that we offer our exchange of observations.

Our conversations have not concentrated on the details or technicalities of those fields in which we might each be said to have specialist knowledge. Our purpose has not been to provide the public with a comprehensive exposition of Mahayana or Nichiren Buddhism, nor to set forth the prospectus of the sociology of religion. For those who seek information on those subjects there are other places to look. We have instead discussed various ethical, philosophical, psychological, therapeutic, organizational and historical manifestations of religion – of Buddhist religion and other religions – as they impinge on vital human concerns. On these topics, the religious leader and the sociologist of religion, particularly in debate with each other, have special contributions to make. Our remarks are thus primarily addressed to what we may call the informed public, to laymen and to those who, in one or another field, are experts, since, outside that field, they are also laymen like ourselves. In the succeeding pages, the expert will learn nothing new in his own field, even if that field be Buddhism or sociology, but he might welcome broad, disinterested comment as a contribution to the democracy of opinions and the maintenance of public, not merely expert, debate. Certainly, the publication of this Dialogue expresses our belief that there is still room – and room there must remain – for the layman to express his views on contemporary and controversial subjects, from genetic engineering and abortion to religious freedom, parent-child relations and the nature of human-nature.

Long before we began our dialogue, we had each individually thought about most of the matters that we discussed, but making our ideas explicit and communicating across the considerable cultural divide that exists between Japan and the West occasioned for each of us a more searching scrutiny and a fuller reappraisal of points of view that, previously, we had allowed to go unchallenged. Now and then, no doubt, we may have talked past each other, not because our translators and interpreters were in any way inadequate – far from it – but because the extent and depth of cultural assumptions in any individual's discourse (on anything other than strictly mathematical matters) normally go unexamined, becoming apparent only when there has to be transmission to people from a different cultural world. The very exercise of translation, which might, initially, have appeared a stumbling-block, was in fact a stepping-stone to better self-understanding, requiring each of us to re-examine our premises and clarify our ideas. The rhetoric of any language allows the native speaker to avoid probing assumptions and issues that are ill-defined, ambiguous and inchoate and which it is all too easy to leave as such. At times, everyone uses "taken-for-granted" propositions, and the common ground within a culture is such that compatriots can be relied upon to comprehend, in however vague and intuitive a way, unspoken allusions and references. Translation has been a salutary experience: hidden cultural assumptions have had to be made explicit, and we have each gained from re-evaluating previously apparently self-evident notions. To the interpreters and translators who wrestled, not only with linguistic but also with cultural obscurities, we are deeply grateful. Ikeda wishes to express special gratitude to Richard L. Gage, who translated all of the Japanese-language sections into English.

We see our Dialogue not merely as a bridge between two cultures, between East and West, and more specifically between Japan and Britain – although we believe it to be that – but also as a sample of a type of discourse that, in the increasingly specialized social order of the modern world, has become something of a rarity. There was a time, not so long ago, when at least a few individuals commanded a wide range of knowledge and maintained close interest in quite disparate disciplines that, in the minds of these polymaths, became mutually informative. Such men widened their range of knowledge by engaging narrower specialists in the various fields, to which they themselves, by virtue of exceptional capacities, omnivorous intellects and much work, could make their own independent contributions. The day of the polymaths has gone, and neither of us remotely belongs to that extinct species, nor do we delude ourselves by seeking to imitate their range of competence. None the less, we should like to claim something of their spirit of enquiry: what neither of us could do alone, raising and re-examining subjects that otherwise might be taken for granted, we have sought to do together.

Obviously, the preoccupations of the world leader of a vigorous Buddhist organization differ fundamentally from the purposes, methods and assumptions of the sociologist of religion. The substantive matter of our discussion – the social role of religion – is, none the less, a deep concern for us both. We have tried to make clear, at various points in our talks, the premises from which we each proceed and, in some ways, this makes our discussion somewhat unusual. It is, of course, by no means uncommon for a sociologist of religion to hold conversations with religious leaders (particularly of movements that are objects of his academic study) but it is less usual for the sociologist to step aside from his active research role, or for the religious leader temporarily to relinquish his primary function as guide and counsellor of his followers, in order to discuss religious matters in a more detached way. For one of us, then, such a discussion represents a temporary disengagement from the empirical methodologically justified approach to religious matters when those phenomena are the object of ethically neutral sociological enquiry. For the other, the spirit of detached enquiry is adopted in the many exchanges in which there is no attempt to canvass the specifically Nichiren Buddhist position, even though that perspective clearly informs the values and concerns that are expressed. Thus, we have met somewhere in the middle ground, each contributing the insights that come from his own more usual activities. The encounter, then, is not based on an academic undertaking research or a Buddhist leader expounding doctrines. And this attempt to step out from our respective enclaves of special concern has been possible, we believe, without any suggestion of cynical disregard for our normal preoccupations and the values we separately cherish.

Some might suppose it difficult for a religious leader to espouse the idea of engaging in unconstrained debate with a religiously uncommitted academic who does not share his beliefs, and even more difficult since the record of their exchanges will pass into the hands of his own followers. Similarly, might not a sociologist of religion feel uneasy in discussing substantive religious matters in ways that might, at times, lead to outright value judgements? Such considerations gave no pause to either of us. The very idea of undertaking the dialogue was Ikeda's, and from the outset his intention was to make available the record of these conversations not only to the members of Soka Gakkai, but also to the public at large. Such an approach is its own testimony to the openness of the Buddhist position. For Wilson, a recognition of the importance of the issues persuaded him that there are times when sociological insights can properly and appropriately be used in determining one's stance on various human concerns. Manifestly, whatever the differences in our values – and some such differences emerge in what follows – we share the value of commitment to free intellectual exchange. The spirit of that value is embodied in our dialogue.

Western readers who are aware only of the other-worldliness of Theravada Buddhism, who remember the liturgical, soteriological, transcendentalist, and at times mythological preoccupations of Christianity, might mistakenly suppose a discussion of religion that focuses so centrally on its social role to be an explicit concession to the specifically sociological perspective. *Au contraire*, such is the essentially this-worldly orientation of Nichiren Buddhism that religion seen as a social phenomenon was readily acknowledged as common ground between us. The very character of Nichiren Buddhist thinking facilitates dialogue with the sociologist. Thus, although our opinions differ, our preoccupations are similar. We have not been concerned with narrow justifications for faith, nor do we seek to reach final evaluations about religion or religions: for one of us, such matters are already settled; for the other, they are not a prime concern. From the perspective of the influence of religion, we concentrate on the condition of mankind in a rapidly and radically changing world. Thus, we discuss such things as the nature of religious emotion, the character of miracles, the significance of ideas about life after death, mysticism, and the limits of rationality and its relation to religion. Some topics of a more or less detailed nature occupied a considerable part of our exchanges, and in consequence they occupy more space than might be expected in the following pages. On the other hand, certain fundamental issues were often taken for granted and receive no extended treatment. Such is the nature of genuine exchange: certain subjects touch off more vigorous trains of thought than are necessarily awakened by questions of the most abstract and general kind. We have been content to let such developments appear much as they occurred.

We have made some attempt to provide order in our discussion by treating distinct subjects under section headings, but it must be clear that in any set of talks there are likely to be both continuities and sharp breaks among sections. We have not tried to eliminate all of these perfectly natural manifestations of conversational exchange and believe the reader will wish to see how our interactions developed.

At the beginning, when we first decided to commit our exchanges to record, both of us must have wondered to what extent our views would widely diverge. We exercised no control or censorship over such a possibility and neither proscribed nor avoided any topics that appeared to be of interest. Indeed, the spirit of our exchanges encouraged each of us to open up particular issues on which our different perspectives might yield the intellectual excitement of real divergence of opinion.

Bryan Wilson
Daisaku Ikeda

PART I

Homo Religiosus

The Source of Religious Emotion

IKEDA: Anthropologists and archaeologists consider various markings and signs of ceremonial burial on human bones to be an indication of some kind of religious feeling. Certainly, such markings suggest awe in the face of death, awareness of the possibility of an invisible post-mortem world, and perhaps an image of what that world might be like. But, in spite of vague images, the world beyond death remains impenetrable; and perhaps respect for the unknown – a higher psychological function than raw, animal fear – is the true source of religious feelings. Reflections on the unknown and the rewards or punishments it may have in store stimulate man to re-examine his instincts and his actions with an eye to their control. Regulation of human action is one of the most fundamental roles of religion.

What do you consider the source of the religious emotion to be? Are we justified in linking burial ceremonies with its initial emergence? Do you think concern with death is always the most profound source of religion?

WILSON: Religious feeling, certainly as found among relatively unsophisticated people, appears to arise from a variety of fundamental emotions that are experienced in the face of uncertainty, the unknown and the untoward. The feelings that these phenomena engender stimulate dispositions of awe, fear, reverence and a desire to placate supposedly powerful forces. Dependence, helplessness and deep anxiety produce the need for acts to quieten involuntary emotions. Partly because they become familiar – at times almost habitual – responses, and partly by virtue of the objective effects that they are supposed to induce, these acts produce changes in subjective states. Ritual may be said to represent emotion recollected in tranquillity; ritual re-engenders emotions in a much modified and controlled way, hence providing men with the idea, perhaps at times the illusion, that they can control, or at least partially manipulate, outside agencies which otherwise might be harmful. As ritual becomes established as an appropriate response, so men may be sheltered from the direct and more forceful impact of their own emotions in the face of uncertainty and the unknown. By ritual, they may be able to "contain" the situation, to control themselves, and to experience, in refined and elevated form, emotions that might otherwise prove "raw" and potentially disruptive. We may regard these refined feelings as emotion filtered through an apparatus of religious ritual, myth and ideology. Undoubtedly, burial ceremonies were an important example of just such a social device, since bereavement is a condition in which every individual and every group faces the untoward in a particularly stark form. The experience is common, and yet it is always profound. Burial rituals represent a universal expression of the need to control hurtful emotions which, if unleashed, might imperil the surviving individual, the group, and even the fabric of social order.

This is not to suggest that burial (or disposal of the corpse) is always a focus of specifically religious concern in all human societies: but fear of the dead, apprehension about the changed condition of the living, and anguish about the possible power and vengefulness of the spirits of the dead, do vary widely in human societies, giving rise to the demand for some assuagement of the emotions that arise when men are bereaved. Bereavement is always a profound experience, but it might be an exaggeration to say that it was the most profound source of religious feeling. Religion is always concerned with the maintenance of man's psychic balance in the ordinary circumstance of everyday life, as well as on those occasions when he encounters death. Death represents an aspect of the unknown, but there are other forms of uncertainty. Men may regard power as manifested in natural objects (rivers, volcanoes, the sea); even the might of secular monarchs may induce powerful feelings of awe and reverence (which may be further stimulated by the need to placate such personages). Social situations of anxiety, as experienced in war, pestilence, famine and economic disaster, may engender vigorous responses which acquire a religious form. Yet, there are other sources of religious feeling. The celebration of the persistence and the renewal of the social group has often been recognized as a fundamental root of religious feeling. Coming together, men recognize a sense of social power, an almost mystical sense of enhanced social being, from which springs another source of religious emotion.

IKEDA: Yes, I see what you mean. My intention, however, was to seek the fountainhead of religious sentiment in the oldest possible primitive human relics, specifically in bones marked in one way or another for funeral purposes. If we look at humanity in its later stages of development, the possible sources you mention – natural forces, the might of secular monarchs, and social situations – must be taken into consideration. In his most primitive and undeveloped state, man is awed most by nature and by the unknown, particularly in the shape of death and the dead. In more advanced stages, social institutions, social bodies and monarchs to an extent stand between him and the unknown, which they in part usurp as a major object of awe and reverence. In other words, in more sophisticated circumstances, sources of the religious emotion diversify.

Over the passing ages, the philosophical regulation of these diverse sources and the abstraction of their major elements gradually resulted in the evolution of monotheism or of religions devoted to reverence for a universal truth. Belief in and respect (even aspiration) for something that cannot be directly perceived through the senses assists human beings in controlling and sublimating their desires and anxieties. As long as no drastic changes occur in human nature or the general situation in which man finds himself, I believe the emergence of religious emotion to be both inevitable and essential.

Anthropomorphism

IKEDA: The Judaeo-Christian and Islamic traditions posit an absolute anthropomorphic god who is the ultimate to which the whole universe is subservient and who has the same kinds of emotions – pleasant and unpleasant – as human beings themselves. In contrast, Buddhism is based on a belief in an all-pervading, universal, abstract and pure law. The law does not reward or punish in the same way as the Judaeo-Christian god, but human beings are both better and better off for living in accordance with it. Furthermore, it is accessible to all equally and has no so-called chosen people to whom it is partial and no specific promised land.

I should be very happy to hear your ideas on the differences between religions centred on anthropomorphic deities and those based on a law.

WILSON: The anthropomorphic god of the Judaeo-Christian-Islamic tradition is a highly concrete conception of the supernatural, which goes back to an era before the capacity for abstract thought had developed in the Middle

East. The supposedly powerful being whom the ancient Israelites regarded as their god, and who was supposed to guide the destinies of his people, was conceived in the image of man. As a result human attributes and, above all, human emotions were attributed to him. In all of this we may perceive the low level of sophistication of a primitive tribal people at the barbaric stage of development. Today, the idea of god as the tribal deity of a chosen race might be regarded not only as ethnocentric, but even as racist. As the religions which sprang from this tradition developed, and particularly in the case of Christianity, this anthropomorphism became qualified. Christianity originated in the apparent reinforcement of anthropomorphism, since it rests on the belief that god manifested himself in the flesh and, as Jesus the carpenter, lived among men. The idea is atavistic but, paradoxically, this recrudescent anthropomorphism opened the way for a more spiritual conception of deity. God might become manifest as a man, but he was a complex being beyond precise human conception, since he manifested himself also as the Holy Spirit. Subsequently – at least by analogy – his spirit was thought to be manifested in a wide variety of ways, both in human consciousness and in the objective world. Thus, while few Christians would deny that God had lived as a man, equally, very few would regard him as being confined to bodily form. To some, God is a person, but to most people he is abstract, ethereal and spiritual – although many are perhaps vague about just how God should be conceived.

The appeal of anthropomorphism is profound: men understand other men better than they understand any other order of being, and even in developed and intellectual milieux they sometimes revert, in their explanations of physical and social phenomena, to anthropomorphic models. In religious contexts, where such models are entrenched in ancient scriptures, even sophisticated believers relapse from more spiritual conceptions of deity and discuss the attributes and dispositions of God in terms of analogy to humans. Fundamentalist sects, in which a stark anthropomorphism is canvassed, flourish particularly in Anglo-Saxon countries.

Even so, Christians appeal to the idea of God's law and his transcendent grace, in which law has been metamorphosed from a concern for the particular and the concrete rule to the idea of the pervasive, abstract principle. Although, in orthodox Judaism and in Islam, the law is still a catalogue of meticulous rules, in Christianity the emphasis has shifted to participation in the spirit rather than obedience to the letter. Of course, the ecclesiastical history of Christianity saw a very considerable re-assertion of specific regulation, particularly in the development of Canon Law – a process which Rudolf Sohm characterized as a process "from love to law", or as Max Weber put it, from charisma to routine. Canon Law was sustained only in the Roman Church, of course, and in Protestantism, despite periods of Calvinistic rigour and the persistence of law-bound sects, the emphasis on God's grace may be said to have mitigated the force of slavish obedience to a code of regulations.

Paradoxically, while Christianity maintains concern for the importance of God's law alongside the existence of a god who is still sometimes conceived in anthropomorphic terms, Buddhism, although beginning with the statement of law, reverted in some of its forms to preoccupations with the idea of deity or deities, sometimes represented in the persistence (particularly in Theravada countries) of older gods or spirits, and sometimes, (and this is found in the Mahayana tradition) with the deification of the Buddha and his widespread representation by the image of a man. Clearly, even in a religious tradition in which the principle of deity is certainly not paramount, and is even officially denied, anthropomorphic conceptions of the supernatural still emerge.

There is an important difference between religions in which the origin is a tribal deity, the representation of which is only gradually universalized, and religions in which the original principle is a universal law, from which, because men look for more direct and personal reassurance, there is a periodic recourse to local spirits and deities. In part, the effectiveness of any religion depends on the means it evolves for the socialization of its members to its most developed mode of spirituality. Yet, it does appear that men find it hard to be satisfied with knowledge of a universal law or even of a universalized deity, and look for modes of reassurance which more closely approximate their human experience – in a local spirit, a merciful Buddha, or a compassionate, suffering Christ. In asserting universality, religion may have appeared to go beyond the experiential range of most men, and may also have become too impersonal for them to maintain its message in a pure form. Yet, as society itself gradually transcended its localism, the local, tribal and partial deities became increasingly anachronistic. The social order in the West steadily became more universalistic in its moral code, and more impersonal in its operation, and in religion the idea of conformity to the moral law became increasingly important – as in the Puritan reformation. That law was a moral imperative and not a means to salvation but a statement of man's duty. God, its supposed author, became of little further consequence to the operation. The sense of an impersonal law operating universally fitted well with the increasingly secular social order, and that conception persisted even when the religious content (the Christian inheritance of its anthropomorphic supernaturalism, its liturgy and its ecclesiastical apparatus) diminished in its social significance. Buddhism, in contrast, when purged of its sporadic deific accretions, might be better adapted to persist and to flourish in the context of a secularized society, and might be better placed to provide such a society with an appropriate universalistic ethic.

IKEDA: If I understand you correctly, the gist of your argument is as follows. Religions evolving from local deities like Jehovah can come to include elements of a universal, benevolent law, like God's grace. And religions based on law can come to include anthropomorphic elements.

This is no doubt true. However, a number of the points about the Judaeo-Christian tradition that puzzle me as an outsider shed light on the fundamental difference between the two kinds of religion. (Many of them deserve no more than mention in passing. For instance, if Lucifer was one of God's angels, why did God allow him to fall? When is God supposed to have made the angels? Why did God create the fruit of the tree of knowledge and then forbid Adam and Eve to touch it? Why did God put into the human mind the wilfulness to instigate rebellion against His own laws?)

But more important is the relationship between God and his creatures Adam and Eve, whom he expelled from the Garden of Eden for violating his command. According to this tradition, God's anger is the cause of all mankind's suffering. The great Mahayana scripture called the Lotus Sutra contains a number of parables, one of which presents a picture of parental attention very different from the one in the book of Genesis.

A certain good physician was called away from home on business. During his absence, his children, whom he left at home alone, mistakenly drank poison and fell into various states of distraction. Returning home and seeing the condition his children were in, the good physician compounded the right medicine to cure them. The ones who were still sound enough in their senses to understand took the medicine and became well at once. He used wise words to convince the children who were too far deranged to understand the importance of cure that they should accept the medicine. Not for a moment, however, did he reprimand or threaten to punish the children for having been careless. His sole concern was to see them well, and he was not wrathful because his children had done something they should not have done.

I am fully aware that God is a god of mercy as well as of anger and that he later sent his son Jesus Christ to earth for the salvation of man. None the less, the original relationship between Him and His believers was based on fear. And, although, as you suggest, Christian theology has tried to reinterpret God in terms of a law or something like a law, fundamentally He is imbued with very human elements of will and emotion.

In spite of the branches that seem to worship the Buddha himself as an absolute being, Buddhism is now, as it has always been, founded on the idea of an abstract Law uninfluenced by will or emotion. All things in the universe, even those gods that Buddhist sects have adopted from other religions, exist in accordance with this Law. And the Buddha himself is one who, having become enlightened to that Law, teaches it or applies the wisdom gained from his enlightenment in the work of saving other sentient beings. It seems to me that observing truth and putting the fruits of those observations to work in all phases of human life and culture are the best way for a religion to bring about, in your words, "the socialization of its members to its most developed mode of spirituality".

Syncretism

IKEDA: By the way in which it incorporates ceremonies and traditions of non-Christian faiths and makes saints of non-Catholic, local deities, Roman Catholicism offers a good example of religious syncretism of a more or less concealed kind. Similar borrowings and incorporations on a more open plane are found in Buddhism and probably in many other religions too, since even the most ungenerous and exclusive systems have often found indigenous customs and beliefs difficult to uproot and, when converting, have had to accept many alien elements into their fold.

Political leaders have used religious syncretism as a tool in controlling conquered peoples. For instance, the kings of Egypt and ancient India installed indigenous deities in their own temples to inspire goodwill and loyalty among the peoples over whom they had seized authority.

In the case of Buddhism, no attempt has ever been made to conceal the pedigrees of the alien divinities in the pantheon. Indeed, contrary to general custom – in most of its forms Christianity has always tried to veil its borrowings – alien gods have been permitted to keep their old, alien names.

Buddhism has opened its doors to gods of Aryan Vedic Indian religion as well as to those of the pre-Aryan tradition and has assimilated them, names and all, as protective spirits: Brahma, Indra, Surya, Candradeva and the four protector kings of the cardinal points, as well as such pre-Aryan demons as the *asuras*. Much later, when it arrived in Japan, Buddhism once again incorporated local divinities, including the sun goddess Amaterasu, and the god of war, Hachiman.

Not only full-fledged gods, but also figures from folk legend have found their ways into the immense Buddhist tradition. The Jataka Stories are said to relate the many lives Shakyamuni lived before the final one in which he attained ultimate enlightenment. In one of the stories, when the person who was later to become Shakyamuni was disciplining himself in a previous life in the form of the so-called Sessen-doji, Young Ascetic in the Himalayas, he agreed to allow a demon to devour his body if the demon would impart the teachings of the Law to him. In fact, the demon was none other than Indra, testing the sincerity of the Young Ascetic in the Himalayas. When Shakyamuni became a Buddha in his final life, it is said that both Brahma and Indra became his retainers and guardians.

Stories of this kind point out two important traits. First, Buddhism considers gods as one rank, in a system all stages of which are governed by the universal Law. Second, since gods are therefore not supreme, Buddhism has no difficulty in opening its arms to them, no matter what their origins.

What is your opinion of religious syncretism and what reactions do you think believers of a given religion experience when they suddenly discover, after years of ignorance, that old familiar ceremonies, saints or even gods are actually borrowings from alien faiths?

WILSON: The extent of religious syncretism in the case of Christianity would be difficult to over-estimate, particularly in its origins, but also in its accommodation to new environments both in the early centuries of its expansion and, conspicuously in Latin America, in more modern times. All of this is evident to the scholar, reticent as some priestly scholars have been to admit the full extent of religious borrowing in the up-building of the Christian tradition. In general, the Church has sought to conceal if not to deny elements of alien origin, which was easier when scholarship was itself subject to internal Church discipline and when historical materials were scarcely available to any but priests. The vast majority of practising Christians still have no notion of the extent to which the vital features of Christian mythology were common to alien and pagan traditions of the ancient Near East. The most significant Judaic elements in Christianity are disposed of by the assertion that Christians are the true and spiritual inheritors of the racial and material promises made to a chosen people who, as Christians have traditionally seen it, rejected and crucified their god when he appeared among them.

Subsequent syncretism became – not necessarily in a cynical sense – a matter of policy for the Church. The injunctions of Pope Gregory the Great in A.D. 601, to the missionary Mellitus, advising him to retain (but to re-consecrate) pagan temples and to permit the continuance (with a new *raison d'être*) of the festivals (erstwhile sacrificial feasts) of the people, make this plain. Shortage of priests and the consequent difficulty of effecting religious control of the populace may have dictated the policy of tolerance of thinly veiled pagan ceremonials in Latin America.

The need to conceal the syncretism of Christianity lies in the insistent exclusivity of the Church. No other gods could be tolerated by Christians, and all variants were suppressed wherever they might represent a challenge to the authority of the Church. Since, in practice, alien elements could not be easily eradicated (as Gregory noted) the policy was to incorporate them and bring them under at least the notional control of the Church. Unincorporated elements were assigned to the category of devil-worship, to which concept all manifestations of local magic and witchcraft were also relegated.

In general, the laity have not been aware of the extent of syncretism in Christian origins or history. Most committed laymen would, even today, refuse to believe that such things had happened. Protestants might be less embarrassed by such knowledge than Catholics, since Protestantism sought to reduce the sacerdotal, sacramental and ritualistic features of Catholic Christianity and, in so doing, not only reduced the evidence of earlier syncretism but also excoriated it as outside the pure tradition. Being more radically anti-magical than Roman Catholicism, the Protestant churches have made fewer concessions to pre-Christian magical ideas, both in their teachings concerning Christian origins and in seeking converts in missionary areas. Among scholars and better informed laymen, there have been attempts to reinterpret religious history in more relativistic terms. Whilst the practices and beliefs of other religions have generally been anathematized, these churchmen have sometimes allowed that some elements in non-Christian religions might be regarded as faint adumbrations in unenlightened minds, which were to be taken as precursors of the truths of Christianity. Thus, some Christian anthropologists, convinced at one time that primitives, because they knew nothing of Christianity, had no religion, later maintained that even the most tenuous conceptions of a high god, or a god of the skies, found among some primitive peoples, provided evidence of man's universal innate disposition towards belief in God and hence provided the basis for their gradual conversion to Christianity. Casuistry of this kind has facilitated some accommodation with the inconvenient facts of syncretism.

IKEDA: Although they pursue different courses I believe that, to a greater or lesser degree, outstanding leaders in all religions are seeking the same kind of truth. Consequently, it seems right for religions like Buddhism and Christianity to incorporate things from religions that came before them. (I am not, of course, talking about religious syncretism as a political expedient.)

Buddhism is concerned with life in all its manifestations and phenomena. Its field is immense and consists of a complex structure of overlapping, interlocking elements. The truths other religions have discovered about the phenomena of life can easily find a place in Buddhism as parts of the whole truth. The universal life is infinite in terms of both time and space; there is room in it for the gods that the Brahmans, for example, developed as symbolic representations of those parts of the greater life they examined and understood.

Yet, even putting aside the well-known inclusiveness of Buddhism, I cannot help feeling that an understanding appraisal of other religions is the best path to pursue in connection with cultural conservation and the broadening and deepening of the human spirit.

An entirely, and violently, exclusive religion that, upon moving into a new region, insists on destroying all traces of the culture, art and tradition of its predecessor religions is certain to stir up the most stubborn resistance, sometimes even amounting to war. Perhaps the Muslims, who reject the idea of any representation of god, felt religiously justified in shaving off the faces of the famous Buddhist figures in Gandhara; but no one can thank them for having destroyed part of a priceless cultural heritage. (The Christian mosaics on the walls of Saint Sophia in Istanbul fared better; they escaped with no more than a coat of plaster.) We have only to remember the damage Savonarola did to realize that the Muslims are not the only ones who have destroyed in the name of faith. There are many illustrations of this tendency in many parts of the world. It is important to notice that wherever it spread Buddhism never attempted to uproot the religions that had been there before, or to harm the physical cultures that had grown up together with those religions – even though those earlier religions were often much less gentle with Buddhism.

WILSON: No doubt the difference between Buddhism and Christianity in this matter reflects – or is reflected in – Eastern and Western conceptions of logic. The principle of non-contradiction in Western logic fortifies the idea of exclusivity: divergent or inharmonious propositions cannot be tolerated. This disposition is, of course, basic to Western science, and stands in sharp contrast to the poetic and religious mode of thinking in which ambiguities and multi-faceted propositions are not only accepted but are exulted in for their intrinsic richness.

Universality and Particularism

IKEDA: To appeal to the widest possible segment of mankind and to transcend its own historical time, a religion must have doctrines of universal applicability. As has already been said, Buddhism is highly inclusive. While preserving its fundamental doctrines unchanged, it has always permitted considerable alterations in minor matters to conform with the time, location and life style of individual peoples. Its teachings have been flexible enough to appeal to widely disparate national characters: to the Indians, who are contemplative and mystical; to the Chinese, who are rational; and to the Japanese, who are of a pragmatic turn of mind. How do you assess such flexibility and what are your views on religious universality in general?

WILSON: From their origins, Buddhist teachings in their pure form have been more universalistic than those of the Judaic, Christian or Islamic faiths, all of which are rooted in much more culturally and historically specific circumstances. The abstract metaphysical character of the Buddha's thought, and the absence in it of anthropomorphic conceptions of a deity, were factors which lent themselves to doctrines of a universalistic kind. In the Judaeo-Christian-Islamic tradition, the original conception of God as a tribal deity continued to exert its effect even after more universalistic claims had come to be made for him. Israel claimed and occupied a specific holy territory and awaited (and orthodox Judaism still awaits) a messiah of its very own; Christians claimed a special dispensation by which they were marked off from other men; and Muslims have a religion which is still deeply permeated by the particular characteristics of the circumstances of its origins. We have already discussed the incidence of anthropomorphism in the Christian tradition: the conception of a god-man is self-evidently highly particularistic. The adoption (and adaptation) of an administrative structure from the Roman Empire imposed another particularistic feature, despite its use by the Church to claim universality – a universality that owed much to the idea of political universality of empire.

Christianity and Islam have, of course, both expanded and sought self-selected adherents without regard to race or colour, and in this they have transcended the extreme particularism of the Judaic and Hindu traditions. Both have adapted, in some degree, to diverse national styles and cultures, even though their leaders have sought – particularly in the Christian case – to inculcate new populations with their distinctive beliefs, rituals and ethics. Diversity in national and regional styles has led to considerable diversification within the religious traditions of both Christianity and Islam, while variations in national temperament and character may themselves owe something to religion. In all such cases, we must suppose that a process of mutual interaction has always been in progress between national culture and character, on the one hand, and religious belief, practice and morality, on the other. If religion is to be effective it must, presumably, influence the life style and culture of its votaries, but the extent to which any religion effectively does this is always open to question. To what extent, for example, are the differences noted among the national personalities in countries in which Buddhism has flourished owed to Buddhism, or do they persist as entirely independent dispositions? If Buddhism is sufficiently flexible in its teachings to accommodate the contemplative and mystical, the rational and the practical attitudes of mind, does this allow that Buddhism itself remains the same in all these three different contexts? Or does Buddhism undergo some measure of internal differentiation, of emphasis if not of doctrine, in order to suit different cultures and temperaments?

In the long course of its history and expansion, Buddhism has obviously undergone considerable internal diversification. Such adaptations might be taken to indicate its capacity for universal adoption, but it might also be seen as accommodation to a context which threatens the idea of a universally valid ethic. Must a religion manifest internal unity and coherence if it is effectively to canvass concepts and precepts of universal validity? We have noted that central administration introduced one form of particularism into Christianity – at the level of organization. It was assumed that such organization was itself divinely inspired as the appropriate vehicle to promote the diffusion of universally valid teachings. If organization may be particularistic and owed to a specific culture and historic period, lack of organization may render a religion susceptible to atrophy in doctrine, practice and ethics. Like Islam, Buddhism has lacked centralized organization, and without such control the way has been open in each of these religions for the penetration of extraneous elements. Thus, the practice of Theravada Buddhism is, even today, often part of a wider spectrum of religious activity in which astrologers, diviners, healers and even, at times, Brahmin priests play a part, while Mahayana Buddhism has not escaped the infusion of elements of tantric magic and esoteric mysticism. Thus, Buddhism has been seriously affected by such alien particularistic accretions. Whereas Christianity broke down into a considerable number of mutually exclusive systems of belief, practice and organization, thereby demonstrating its own particularism, Buddhism may have suffered the opposite tendency of surrendering, in many diverse ways, its central concerns in tolerant compromise with indigenous religious traditions, becoming "all things to all men".

IKEDA: I prefer to view the situation from a different angle and to say that Buddhism is capable of being "all things to all men" because of its tremendous scope and inherent variety. During the 50 years of his teaching mission, Shakyamuni presented a staggeringly large number of amazingly varied teachings and methods of self-discipline. The world views and religious practices of various groups, all of whom call themselves Buddhist, depend largely on the particular teaching that group elects to revere above all others.

I agree that a mutual interaction between national culture and character and religious belief, practice and morality has probably occurred in the cases of the religions we are discussing. For example, while undergoing influences exerted by Indian society of the time of Shakyamuni, Buddhist thought exerted influence on that society too, by rejecting the discrimination of the caste system (at least within the Order itself). It seems to me that, in the cases of Islam and especially Christianity, it was local exigencies and life styles that accounted for internal diversification and not the scope and variety of the teachings as was, I believe, true in the case of Buddhism. (After all, Jesus actually taught for only a few years.) I further suspect that these same characteristics of simplicity and brevity made Christianity susceptible to centralized authoritarian organization and stimulated the unification of Christian doctrinal interpretations. Such unification is difficult to impose on a vast, multifarious body of teachings like those of Buddhism.

Obviously, the apparent vagueness of Buddhist doctrines has permitted various sects to systematize the teachings in their own ways. (One of those ways is the system worked out in the thirteenth century by the great religious leader Nichiren Daishonin. My fellow believers and I consider it the best system.) Since its fundamental aim has always been the development of man's inherent wisdom and the reinforcement of individual independence, Buddhism has not imposed life styles from without and has never striven for cultural or any other kind of overall uniformity. It has, therefore, as you point out, been open to the penetration of extraneous elements. This accounts for the striking differences in Buddhist art styles, depending on the historical period and the location in which they were evolved. A little training enables anyone immediately to distinguish Indian Buddhist art from Chinese Buddhist art and to differentiate them with equal speed from Japanese Buddhist art. However, my firm conviction is that, in spite of "penetrations" from without, in most of its manifold forms, Buddhism has preserved its original core of distinctive doctrine.

Are the Religious Emotions Universal?

IKEDA: Current astronomy substantiates the possible existence of intelligent life on other planets somewhere in the universe. Although there seems to be little chance of it in the immediate future, the likelihood of contact with extraterrestrial living beings will probably increase as man makes new technological advances or as those beings attempt to get in touch with us.

If and when we do make contact, we may find that they are on a level of development as high as, or higher than, our own. In what fields do you think we may be able to achieve some understanding with them? Perhaps we will share an interest in natural science, since the phenomena of physics and chemistry are probably similar throughout the universe. Mathematics too is a possibility. Some scientists claim that, in intercourse with intelligent beings from outer space, mathematical codes will of necessity replace verbal communication. Do you think we can achieve mutual understanding with such beings in terms of a religious emotion? In all probability, as thoughtful beings, they are fully aware of their own existence and have a conception of the nature of the universe. This may enable them to ponder the mysteries of birth and death and of other things beyond their ken. And, as we have said, contemplation of the unknown can be the starting-point for religion.

WILSON: Whatever may be the nature of the intelligence of beings on any other planet, it is difficult to conceive that scientific and mathematical formulations alone would be adequate for them to communicate within their own society. Of course, one is aware that the very terms *society* and *communicate* may be altogether misleading for the structure of relationships that prevail among them, and yet it seems clear that human beings on earth could have no possibility of rapport with such beings if their social organization were entirely rationally coordinated. Unless such creatures were possessed of human emotions – love, fear, doubt, anxiety, self-interest, altruism and the rest – it is difficult to see that any contact could be effective except for the exchange of strictly scientific information, and even that might be found to be more culturally (and planetarily) relative than we might suppose. Mathematical codes might suffice for the communication of strictly factual information, but they would not lead to any empathic understanding, and if that were so, then no relationships based on respect, trust or affection could develop.

Yet if, as you suggest might be the case, they were thoughtful beings, then we must suppose that they would respond to the circumstances of their own existence. If we were to assume that they were subject to birth, growth, decay and death, then they must react to the traumas involved in such experiences. If such were the case, then I would agree that this might lead them to what we call a religious interpretation of being. The demand for answers or at least for guidance would then almost certainly lead to concern for the meaning of life and to bodies of teaching concerning it and the individual's comportment; and that, as you say, would be a starting-point for religion.

Mystic Elements

IKEDA: To one extent or another, all religions include elements that are mystical and defy theoretical explanation. Indeed, delving into what can be called the mystical sets religion apart from non-religious philosophy. But mystical elements do not always work for good. In this, as in most other things, moderation is best. Over-emphasizing mysticism robs religion of its actuality, whereas under-emphasizing it removes the sense of mystery that generates faith.

By its very nature, religion deals with those things that are beyond human comprehension. Buddhism always stresses rationality, but the great universal Law that is its foundation lies beyond the powers of the human mind. In other words, it is mystical. What interpretation of the mystical have you evolved as a result of your examinations of many of the religions of the world?

WILSON: I concur entirely with your view that all religions, in their nature, embrace elements that are mystical: even the most rationalistic branches of religious traditions come to a point at which they grapple with un-explained elements, or with the final question of "why should these things be?", to which any answer is necessarily mystical. Indeed, it appears that when, within a religious tradition, rationalizing tendencies occur and the effort is made to make religion entirely "reasonable", then there is a risk that the commanding appeal of the faith will be lost. One sees, for example within the later development of Puritanism, how the Unitarians, rejecting the mystical doctrine of the trinity, sought a "reasonable religion" consonant with the spirit of the age of reason in late eighteenth-century Europe. But in so far as they succeeded in making their religion rational, they left their followers with little to feel particularly religious about. Eventually, they had to content themselves with becoming high-minded humanitarians with strong ethical preoccupations. The whole history of Protestantism suggests that the road that leads away from mystical faith towards reason has few satisfactory stopping places, until the point arrives where men completely rationalize their experience and lose their faith.

Of course, all the more advanced religions – that is to say, those within which religious functionaries have acquired scholarly dispositions and have developed an intellectual apparatus for the exposition and systematization of teachings and the capacity for self-criticism – contain a body of rational discourse. This is sometimes developed by a process of increasingly well-ordered and rationally conducted debate and enquiry, in which the central issues of teachings are freed from contradictions, refined, coordinated and given a sub-structure of rational justification. Yet, despite such tendencies, the unexplained mystical items remain, and to grasp them the devotee is called upon to make a leap of faith, to give his mind, to abandon the restraints of intellect and experience, and to acquire a subjective disposition in which to unite himself in the central principle, being or performance, in which, at the core of that religious system, salvation is said to be found. Nor is this mystical element merely the object of special devotion by those virtuosi of religion whom we describe as "mystics", and who practise what is called "mysticism". Such devotees of the mystical are a special, and usually a very tiny, class among believers, but they become recognized and celebrated as people of illumination and saintliness and even as guides for the devotional life of the majority of worshippers who can themselves never aspire to such intense religiosity. The mystical may have more profound meaning for such *mystics*, but the focal point of religion for all believers is a sense of truth that transcends mundane experience and that, at least for this reason and perhaps for others, is mystical.

IKEDA: I think we agree then that the mystical is essential to religion but is not sufficient in itself. The important thing to keep in mind is this: do the mystical elements within a religion comply – as much as possible – with rational thought and, most important, do they contribute to the maintenance and development of the best of man's spiritual capabilities?

For the evaluation of any religion, Nichiren Daishonin worked out three criteria that are of the utmost significance since, if applied, they can protect believers against the use of a cloak of mysticism to conceal the true nature of teachings that are conducive, not to man's spiritual improvement, but to his spiritual degradation. First of all, in dealing with Buddhist sects, Nichiren Daishonin said that doctrines must be judged according to whether they are truly founded in the recorded teachings of Shakyamuni: that is, in general, doctrines must be in line with the thought of the founder of the religion in question. Second, he insisted that doctrines agree with reason and good sense insofar as they are submittable to the judgement of human ratiocination. Finally, he required that, in actual affairs, doctrines bear the kind of fruit they promise to be able to bear.

Interpreting the Miraculous

IKEDA: The numerous aspects of religious teachings that are not part of ordinary experience are often perplexing. For instance, in a part of the Lotus Sutra, an immense treasure tower rises to hover in the air as the ground trembles in six fashions and a throng of people float above the surface of the earth. Of course, other religious classics, including the Bible, contain their share of miracles.

Although it is unwise to regard all miracles as unvarnished fact, it is equally ill-advised to discredit them all as hyperbolical fiction. Scientific discoveries in later times have often shown that earlier religious mysteries are rationally explicable and even significant. Like other mystical elements, miracles must be neither overvalued nor undervalued. We must attempt to plumb their profound meanings without being distracted by their apparent aberration from reality. In short, miracles are a language of symbols, the accurate interpretation of which brings us closer to a religion's true wisdom. What is your opinion of the optimum way to interpret the miraculous?

WILSON: From an external perspective like my own, reports of the miraculous are seen not so much as claims to be proven or disproven but as evidence of the commitment of believers. What is considered a miracle is always subject to the interpretation of those involved: the commonplace of today's science would have been the miracle of a thousand, or even a hundred, years ago, and the miracles of those times might now have acceptable scientific interpretations. The more important aspect of the miraculous is its significance for believers. Miracles were themselves rarely regarded as sufficient proof of religion. A faith resting only on the miraculous would be magic and not religion. Nor have miracles been seen as reasons for men to become believers; the great religious teachers often demurred when asked to work miracles solely to induce men to believe. Miracles were aids to existing faith, acquiring meaning from a coherent philosophy or doctrine. As you point out, they conveyed a symbolic or poetic truth which was quite incapable of rational appraisal. Religion necessarily deals in symbols; in communicating attitudes of mind; in awakening consciousness, sensitivity and humane dispositions; in stimulating in men an awareness of their group responsibilities and allegiances; and in cultivating, assuaging and regulating the emotions. These functions of religion cannot be easily delegated to specifically rational agencies, nor are secular authorities capable of assessing society's needs with respect to such matters. In part, individuals must become aware, for themselves and for those around them, of the importance of the cultivation of mental and emotional dispositions. Among the symbols that religions deploy towards the attainment of these ends is the idea of the miraculous. It provides an allegorical statement of possibilities, or of the extremes of possibilities. It represents the ideal of perfectibility, of restoration, of social order and of the transcendence of evil. If the idea of the miracle has *also* catered to a literal-minded hope of expectation that evil can be eliminated at a stroke, disease healed and death overcome, this represents the many-sidedness that we can observe in a wide range of religious phenomena. Religion is, after all, the most ancient human institution, and it would be surprising were it not to embrace ideas, beliefs and practices that might be differently understood at different levels of consciousness – some of them primitive, literal and magical; others elevated, spiritualized and symbolic. It is the ambiguity and flexibility of religious symbols, the fact that they cannot be equated with a constant mathematically expressed value, which is the source of their richness and their durability. Such symbols simultaneously communicate not merely, nor chiefly, the factual, but also the evaluative and the emotive. Religious language and concepts, including that of the miraculous, not only transmit information, but also simultaneously evoke response. In consequence, from a strictly rational perspective, this language is always elusive, volatile and poetic in its multi-faceted quality. Because it deals in values and emotions as well as in references to empirical reality, it defies systematic analysis and formal logic. The miracle, then, is not an event for which specific scientific appraisal is required: it is the idea of transformation, of power, of mystery, which gives to the miraculous its importance within religion. The miracle performed without the religious context is, of course, merely a pheno-menon, perhaps even a trick; placed within the context of a world- view, a call to belief and behaviour, it becomes the symbol of what might be wrought in the believer – the objective and apparently tangible expression of the subjective transformation of consciousness which religion seeks to bring about.

IKEDA: Your idea that the miracle is a "call to belief and behaviour" and "symbol of what might be wrought in the believer" is interestingly consonant with the attitude of Nichiren Daishonin. In a letter to one of his own believers, he explains the appearance of the immense tower – said to be equivalent in height to the diameter of the earth – in the Lotus Sutra as symbolic of the enlightenment to their own immense Buddha natures experienced by the people who heard the sutra taught. Nichiren Daishonin consistently related such other symbolic language in the Buddhist classics as heaven and hell to the human psychological condition. Certain traditional Buddhist sects insisted that heaven and hell are actual places – either in the infinitely remote west or under the earth – to be desired or dreaded as external, objective realities. In contrast to this, Nichiren Daishonin taught that all such things and places exist within our own minds. The universal life, of which we all partake, is limitless and universal even in individual manifestations, and consists of a complexity of entities, including the polarities of good and bad. This inclusive approach finds room for both the traditional Christian idea that God made man and the modern European interpretation to the point of a total shift in emphasis from religion to man – an emphasis that limits man to the functions of his desires and his reasoning power – and a rejection of the importance of religion. As I have said, the teaching of Nichiren Daishonin is that human life is inexplicable in rational terms because it is universal in expanse and infinite in complexity. He founded a religion on the belief that this life, in its undifferentiated state and in its individual manifestations, deserves ultimate reverence.

In my opinion, it makes no difference whether miracles and the miraculous are viewed as external or as violations of scientific reason. I agree with you that the miracle "is not an event for which specific scientific appraisal" is needed, though many people today might find this statement unconvincing.

The Rational and the Irrational

IKEDA: Science is developing now and will probably go on developing. Some day things that are currently inexplicable scientifically may become part of common scientific knowledge. Practically all the knowledge we possess at present pertains to things that were unknown at one time or another; thus it is rash to condemn as false and thus to reject ideas, doctrines, teachings or goals because science has not yet endorsed them. In other words, ideas that cannot be explained by science at any given stage of its development are not necessarily erroneous.

The teachings of religions deal with issues transcending the realm of rationality. In assessing them, it is important to discriminate between the truly irrational and those things that, although mysteries to science now, may become easily explicable at some future date. We must neither attempt to justify the truly rationally unjustifiable nor glibly dismiss everything that does not immediately respond to the power of reason. (Obviously things which have been scientifically proved to be impossible ought not to be accepted as fact, though they may have a symbolic role to play, as we have already commented in connection with miracles and the mystical.)

What are your opinions of rationality in relation to religious teachings? To what extent do such teachings need to be submitted to scientific verification?

WILSON: Before the development of systematic empirico-rational enquiry into natural, social and psychological phenomena, religious systems represented, within their own cultural sphere, the sum total of knowledge, encompassing, in the case of Judaism and Christianity, a cosmology and a theory of creation and, in the case of Buddhism, a psychology and something approximating to a theory of matter, besides the more central doctrines of a spiritual and ethical kind. The growth of empirico-rational enquiry and the systematization of findings have resulted in the development of what we regard as objective science (even though one must allow that there are various philosophical reservations about the status of scientific knowledge and the basis of its social origins and acceptability — matters which we may surely leave aside). Today, even in our non-scientific concerns, people who have no real scientific knowledge are thoroughly accustomed to assessing empirical evidence, to judging matters of cause and effect, to regarding empirical tests as valid procedures and to accepting as common sense the canons of pragmatism. These dispositions have all been acquired as a concomitant of the growth of science. As a mode of thought, scientific reasoning and experiment stand in sharp contrast to religion. Scientific knowledge is always subject to doubt and criticism, whereas in religion knowledge rests on faith and devotion. Science puts forward hypotheses to be recurrently tested by validated procedures: its propositions are always in principle falsifiable, in contrast with the unfalsifiable assertions of religious truth. The scientific attitude of mind admits error and expects development, in contrast with the tendency in religion to suppose that all wisdom has already been enunciated.

IKEDA: I should like to make a comment on what you call "unfalsifiable assertions of religious truth". Since religions begin with acts of faith, they sometimes require that their believers accept everything in their doctrines and question nothing. Ironically, but undeniably, such inflexibility often leads to religious decadence. This is particularly true when the religions demand blind faith in connection with all aspects of their teachings related to scientific knowledge, even when faith and scientific truth are at odds with each other.

Antagonism between faith and science no longer affects whole societies as it has in times gone by, when a number of scientists were sacrificed in the name of a kind of truce between the two camps. However, other factors have also played a part. First, religious faith no longer holds as powerful a hold on societies as it did in the past. Second, the power of men of religion has dwindled, and their scope of activity has narrowed. This means that, even in the case of the Roman Catholic Church, people are freer than ever before to question religious doctrines in the light of reason. In addition, they must constantly question to ensure that they do in fact conform with truth and with the spiritual best for mankind.

When accepted blindly and unquestioningly, religion can lead to the kind of tragedy experienced by the members of the People's Temple, who died because of tenets imposed on them by one tyrannical man.

It is precisely because they all inherently contain the danger of such a tragedy that religions ought to submit their doctrines to judgement and verification, and people in general should come to look on religious doctrines as subjectable to testing. I believe this approach would work to the good of the religion and help protect society from religious tyranny.

WILSON: It would be easy to contrast the opposition of scientific and religious pronouncements, and in Christian cultures there is an acute awareness of the steady retreat from erstwhile religious orthodoxy in the face of scientific advance, in such matters as creation and evolution, in astronomy, geology, biology and psychology. The conflict of the Roman Church with those who experimented in science, from medical investigations to astronomy, is but a further illustration of the opposition between science and religion which late nineteenth and early twentieth century Western intellectuals tended to regard as inevitable. Today, when religion has retracted much that once it claimed, it is still true that many claims made for religious belief and practices could scarcely be successfully put to the scientific test, and scientists have often been dismissive of religious phenomena – from claims to healing, visions and spirit possession to religious doctrines and philosophy.

It would, however, be easy to overstate the antagonism between science and religion, particularly if too much attention were paid to the case of Christianity, with its emphatic dogmatic system and its specific time-bound utterances about creation. It has to be remembered that modern science had its roots in earlier systems of knowledge which were invariably religious. That is to say, earlier philosophies offered interpretations of both the natural and supernatural worlds, not always distinguishing between them. There are, after all, therapeutic procedures even in primitive religions; Buddhism embraces a theory of matter which is not at odds with scientific explanation; medieval Christianity facilitated the development of older systems of logic; the Puritan reformation encouraged the practical mastery of the material world and was a direct stimulus to scientific enquiry. In Christianity, a process of steady rationalization may also be discerned and, in so far as the founded religions all militated against local magic and incoherent, random and arbitrary claims, they can all be seen as having promoted rational systems of knowledge.

As we have already discussed, there is a limit beyond which the application of reason to religion cannot go, if the core of religious belief and practice is to remain intact. Reason does not dictate ultimate goals. Indeed, by rationality we mean the process by which contradictory elements are eliminated from any system of goals (social or personal) and by which less efficient means to attain those goals are always displaced by more efficient means. The goals themselves are not dictated by reason, but once those ends are given, then rationality inheres in the process by which they are most quickly and efficiently attained. Clearly, the specification of goals may itself change, and the given ends of action at one time may later become the means to yet further ends, but if we may postulate ultimate ends, then, we may say that they transcend rational choice. Science constitutes a rational system of enquiry and of the organization of knowledge. As such it has very limited value premises, and these are predominantly of a procedural rather than of a substantive kind. It is, of course, true that ultimately the choice of issue into which scientific investigation will be pursued is a matter of value judgement, but beyond this the choice of means is always rationally determined. It is generally true to say that the canons of rationality apply to *how* things should be done, and not to *what* shall be done.

If this is so, then we can admit a separate domain in which certain values have an autonomy from scientific enquiry or test, and certainly from scientific determination. We may say that religious values exist at this level. Religion always offers men propositions (stated as truths) and requires activities (which we call rituals) in the light of which to lead their lives. These teachings and requirements, whatever their specific content, respond to the human need for peace of mind, for psychic balance, for reassurance, for harmony in relationships and for positive attitudes to life and work. The satisfaction of these needs, in their complexity and subtlety, is an ancient human concern which quite transcends the possibilities of science. They are facets of salvation from evil for the individual, his community, nation and the world. They are prospects of wholeness which can be entertained by poetic imagination rather than by empirico-rational procedures. As these goals are stated within any given religious tradition, whether as Nirvana, life after death, resurrection or the transmigration of souls, they constitute hypothesized spiritual states, the attainment of which passes beyond the rationally constructed means of science. The goals, and therefore also the means, are super-empirical. If, let's say, peace of mind is a transcendent human goal and aspiration, and is acquired by contemplation of, for example, the kingdom of heaven, and destroyed by, say, an accurate analysis of the physical constitution of the body and its inevitable decay, then what can science offer towards the attainment of peace of mind?

IKEDA: I am in general agreement with you when you say that the value premises of science are procedural and not substantive; that is, they concern how something should be done and not what should be done. I also agree that the rational goals of science and the goals of religion belong in different domains. Scientific knowledge and the technology born of it can help support human life and make it more pleasant, but cannot give human life significance or goal orientation. As you say, setting goals of this kind is the work of religion.

But, if when you say the goals set by religion are super-empirical you mean that they need not be tested against actual human experience, I cannot agree. In selecting and abiding by a set of religious doctrines, the individual must always be free – religion enforced for national or political reasons is unacceptable – and must thoroughly examine the kinds of effects faith in that religion can have on his actual experience. Failure to do this can be disastrous. Beginning in the late twelfth century, in Japan, the Pure Land Buddhist sect became immensely popular. A basic tenet of this sect is the notion that invoking the name of the Buddha Amida guarantees rebirth in the Sukhavati Paradise (Pure Land) in the west. Times were hard in Japan then and many people found the idea of paradise so seductive that they resorted to suicide to accelerate their attainment of its blessed state. In other words, they adopted a religion without carefully investigating the effects it would have on their actual experience.

People must always examine religious teachings empirically and, as rationally as possible, try to select a path that promises consonance with the best of human nature. The dangers arising from neglecting to do this are greatly multiplied in the cases of large organizations which restrict individual freedom of action and threaten mass fanaticism.

WILSON: The types of religious goals that I call super-empirical are such things as reincarnation, resurrection or the everlasting life of the soul. The hope of attaining such a state may make men happy, and the prospect of earning it as a reward for present behaviour may make them good; but neither their happiness nor their moral rectitude proves that their belief is true. What is beneficial need not be true and what is true need not be beneficial. One remembers the Psalmist who, observing that the wicked prosper "like a green bay tree", consoled himself with the conviction that in due course justice would be done. The Judaeo-Christian tradition relies considerably on unprovable assertions that *in the end* the righteous will be rewarded even though their experience of this world is that of a "vale of tears". Meanwhile, it cannot be said that those enjoying life to the full are thereby proving the validity of their religious faith (whatever it might be). There is a difficulty, as I see it, in using human experience as a source of consistent empirical evidence for religious truths.

The Idea of an After-life

IKEDA: Many religions reject the idea that individualized life ends at the demise of the individual; that is, they refuse to believe that life is an ephemeral, one-time-only occurrence. Buddhism, for example, teaches the doctrine of transmigration; and Christianity, that of life everlasting. As you know, the Buddhist theory is that a current of cause-and-effect relations is manifested in the sentient being (including of course human beings) of the moment and this current links present life with lives lived in the past and with others to be lived in the future. A poor performance in the present life is the outcome of actions in former existences. Acts perpetrated now will affect future existences favourably or adversely, depending on their quality. The ethical implications of such a system derive from pure practicality: it is wise to act now in ways that will not lead to misery in a future life. The Christian view is the personal one of God's reward in heaven for good deeds now and punishment in hell for present malefactions.

In short, regarding life as continuing, in one way or another, into eternity can have ethical implications for the way people use their allotted spans on earth. Considering life a one-time matter can also have ethical implications. For instance, the man who refuses to recognize both future reward and future punishment may live the hedonistic life of his choice. What difference can it make if there is nothing beyond death? I should be very happy to hear your thoughts on the concept of the after-life.

WILSON: The higher religions all offer men the prospect of believing that life is not confined to their present experience: clearly man's attachment to his loved ones, to his social involvements and activities, is such that he finds it difficult to relinquish them. That such things should be enjoyed for the span of only one life-time is an uncongenial idea wherever men reflect on their own circumstances. Of course, there is but slender empirical evidence of continued or renewed life in other spheres, by reincarnation or by resurrection; those who endorse it do so as an act of faith.

In all religions, however, this promise has been made only conditionally. The possibility of further life, or of life in agreeable circumstances, is usually tied to demands for moral performances during this life-time. This promised balance of performance with appropriate reward or punishment provides a system of social control and the maintenance of moral dispositions, characteristic of the advanced religions. The extent to which an individual may at any given time influence his future is also tightly hedged about by other provisions, for, in all the higher religions, the ledgers of merit and demerit are complex (and there is the extreme case of Calvinism, in which the possibility of influencing such matters is ruled out of court). Simply stated, the great religious teachers respond to the widespread demand from humans that they should be given some reassurance concerning future life, but they do so while simultaneously making demands about human behaviour.

In the modern, secularized world, belief in the old religious formulations concerning future life has manifestly declined but, certainly in the West, it has done so very unevenly. We know from public-opinion polls that far more people believe in heaven than in hell, whilst a growing number apparently believe in reincarnation (quite independently, as far as can be seen, of any direct influence from Buddhism). What appears to be occurring is that the implications for social control of the former ideas on eternal life are being abandoned, whilst belief in the prospect of such a future life declines much less quickly. The moral economy of the old formulations is rejected, even though the attraction of continuing or renewed life persists. The negative idea of *hell* is less congenial in the modern world, in which hedonism is a very widely canvassed value, powerfully advocated by commercial interests and disseminated through advertising. For this reason, the idea of *heaven* endures better, and the idea of reincarnation (without the complex theodicy of Buddhist morality) leaves many Westerners with the notion that they may return again and lead another (neither necessarily better, nor necessarily worse) life at some future time. Perhaps in the background is the fact that whereas, in past ages, life for the majority of people was full of hardship, illness, pestilence, famine and grief, modern life, at least in advanced countries, is much less bedevilled by all of these. Thus whereas in the past another round of existence seemed like a prospect of torture, today it seems more like a renewed prospect of pleasure. In consequence, the ethical significance of these doctrines diminishes, at least in Western countries, where the causal links between present acts and future rewards or punishments are much less readily accepted.

As aids to social control, the vigour of doctrines of an after-life was derived principally from their negative, retributive aspects – men were enjoined to behave well in order to avoid the unpleasant after-life consequences of immoral acts. Once belief declined in the (certainly very complex) idea that moral acts here and now had strictly empirical consequences in the shape of rewards or punishments hereafter, the utility of these teachings as an agency of social control greatly diminished. Science has led to the diffusion of cause-and-effect reasoning, but this reasoning is essentially concerned with empirical and not with moral issues. Moral dispositions appear to be increasingly irrelevant to the way in which the physical, biological and technical world works. Modern man does not believe that the moral status of an act induces a specific morally retributive consequence – unless society so decrees by designating the act a "crime", and by instituting agencies of detection and punishment. Given the loss of their ethical significance, the doctrines concerning future life become increasingly gratuitous and sometimes self-indulgent speculations, which appeal to hedonists more than to moralists.

IKEDA: Instead of the decline you observe in the West, in Japan in recent years, especially among the urban intelligentsia, belief in the super-empirical and in the after-life seems to be on the rise, though the interest has to a great extent been sparked by fascination with so-called super-sensory abilities and by books written in the West which supposedly recount the after-life experiences of people who have been recalled from the verge of death. (Apparently none of these reports of the after-world has any connection with cause-and-effect relations and none describes suffering of any kind; they all talk of entering a realm of light.)

Like the Christian tradition, that of Buddhism incorporates the idea of a hell, which is to be avoided by doing good for others during this life. But people today, as you point out, disregard the punishments of hell in favour of the idea of coming back to a life very much like the one they lead now. Since I believe that religions ought to impart hope and tranquillity, not terror and anxiety, to the human heart, replacement of the threat of hell with the, as you say, "renewed prospect of pleasure" is not necessarily bad. The important thing is to find something that, replacing the fear of hell, none the less cultivates high ethics and morality in current human life.

It would be excellent if reason alone could accomplish the task; but, unfortunately, the desires and impulses of the human mind do not always submit to reason's guidance. In traditional Buddhism and Christianity, fear of hell restrained desires and impulses on levels where reason's voice was ignored. Agreeing with you that hell no longer functions satisfactorily in this way, I see a pressing need for some other kind of control system. Nichiren Daishonin's teaching of hope for the after-life, based on independence resulting from the cultivation of wisdom in each individual human being, seems to me to offer an excellent way of combating unruly desires and impulses.

Lives Past, Present and Future

IKEDA: As I mentioned in the preceding section, Buddhism teaches that, in an infinite series of transmigrations, living beings have already had vast numbers of past existences and will have vast numbers of future ones. The idea of transmigration, as you point out, is today welcomed by some. Many others, however, ridicule it as superstition on the basis of a total lack of evidence to the effect that anyone has ever recalled a past existence. Still, I have heard that hypnosis enables people to travel back in time to become the individuals they were in former lives. How do you evaluate reports of this kind? Is it true that some pre-Christian teachings resemble Buddhism in connection with continuity of life from the past, through the present, and into the future?

WILSON: The idea of reincarnation is certainly widespread, not only in the East, but as an appealing, if often lightly entertained, idea among many people in Western countries, and is found as an element in the thinking of some relatively undeveloped peoples. Apart from the idea itself, certainly many curious and unexplained phenomena, which some might be inclined to relate to reincarnation, occur not only as private intuitions among highly reflective people in the West, but also as cultural phenomena among tribal peoples, for instance, the Dogon. From a scientific perspective we have, however, no hard evidence. The unexplained paranormal phenomena that are observed – and they are of many diverse kinds – are sufficiently unspecific to be marshalled as supporting evidence for a wide variety of beliefs concerning what we may, for brevity's sake, call the supernatural. Thus, Christian spiritualists believe that they have evidence of life "beyond the grave", on the "other side", and although a considerable amount of what they have sometimes accepted as "evidence" has been shown to be fraudulent or illusory, there is still an abundance of the unexplained. The Christian Church, in both its Roman and Anglican branches, retains rituals for the exorcism of demons, whilst instances of the activities of poltergeists are not infrequent in Western countries. Reincarnation is a more difficult concept because the lives of a reincarnated being must be distributed through time and, probably, also through space. In each life he would need to learn a new, and presumably usually quite different, body of social knowledge, including language. Since no individual is ever born with any signs of such past learning we may suppose – and the question of language is crucial – that his thought processes are incapable verbally of transcending the divisions between one life and another. Thus he has no direct recall, whilst the evidence from hypnotism, dreams, the experience of *déjà vu*, or the inexplicable affinity felt for earlier times or for particular places, is difficult to assess. In strictly scientific terms, I think that we must keep an open mind. Believers may feel that they need no evidence. Between these two positions, it would take a bold man to deny entirely the possibility that the individual may have experienced numerous previous existences.

Hinayana and Mahayana

IKEDA: Some of the teachings of Shakyamuni insist that ordinary human life is a futile round of sorrows from which the individual should try to escape by various methods designed to induce the state called Nirvana, in which no sorrow exists. Others of his teachings centre on the ideal of the compassionate bodhisattva, who finds true Nirvana by plunging into life for the sake of bringing salvation to others. Believers who emphasized this practical and compassionate course of action called their form of Buddhism Mahayana (the Greater Vehicle, capable of carrying all to salvation) and dubbed the Buddhism of the advocates of the more self-centred system Hinayana (the Lesser Vehicle). Mahayana Buddhism found its way from Central Asia to China and Japan, whereas today Hinayana Buddhism is mainly practised in the nations of South East Asia.

In the past, Western scholars have frequently concluded that Mahayana Buddhism is not Buddhism at all and does not represent the teachings of Shakyamuni. As a follower of the Buddhism of Nichiren Daishonin, whose basic religious text is the Mahayana classic called the *Sutra of the Lotus of the Wonderful Law*, I frequently encounter criticism based on this Western interpretation. People who adopt this view assume, but have never proved, that the Lotus Sutra is not a teaching of Shakyamuni. Even if it were not one of his direct utterances, this would be beside the point. Its contents are none the less great; its influence on millions of believers has been none the less immense. For these reasons, I conclude that, no matter who the originator (or originators) of the Lotus Sutra, he, she or they could have been nothing less than profoundly wise. I should appreciate hearing your views on whether Mahayana is or is not truly Buddhism.

WILSON: Knowledge of Buddhism was first developed in the West largely through colonial connections with Theravada countries, and in particular with Sri Lanka (Ceylon). When Western scholars came to study Buddhism, they assumed, not surprisingly, that what they learned from their first contacts was indeed the basic, true and orthodox form of Buddhism. Such an assumption is understandable, and there have been parallel cases in history; the version first met with is taken as the norm against which later discoveries are measured for their deviance. Western knowledge of Buddhism developed as European scholars studied and translated Pali texts, and published works on the history of the Buddha and the doctrines of Buddhism, as they learned of these things in Theravada countries. When Western scholars gradually became more aware of other developments in the Buddhist tradition, many of them were disposed to regard these other developments as deviant forms; they projected the sequence of the Westerners' process of discovering Buddhism on to the history of the religion itself. The Pali texts were taken as the original, and Sanskrit and especially translations were viewed circumspectly on those matters in which they departed from the knowledge acquired from the Pali. In consequence, Mahayana Buddhism, less well-known, encompassing much larger populations, exposed to wider and more diverse influences in its transmission through Tibet and China to Japan, came to be seen as a transmuted form of Buddhism. If this appears to be an arbitrary judgement, one might imagine a parallel in which Eastern scholars, having become acquainted with, shall we say, Coptic or Monophysite Christianity, regarded that form as normal and, subsequently, on discovering the Orthodox, Catholic and Protestant variants of Christian teaching, chose to regard them as deviant. In more recent times, Western scholars have accorded wider recognition to all traditions in Buddhism, and the influence of the Modern School has been to accord equal recognition to the Hinayana (including Theravada) and Mahayana traditions.

As to the Lotus Sutra, I am sure that the point you emphasize is the one which really matters. Questions of absolute proof of the authorship of materials as old as this must remain a matter for specialists, even if their perspectives may sometimes be rather narrow. Perhaps it is a peculiarly Western obsession to be concerned to establish just who wrote what. That scholarly concern grew up in Christianity, in which doctrinal niceties, precise formulations, and the elimination of contradictory elements became indispensable to the faith. (Since the Christian deity was believed to have spoken directly to his disciples, the various versions of what Jesus said became subject to much contention; unapproved "gospels" exist, and those that the Church has accepted are now generally acknowledged to contain items that were added by later scribes.) For Buddhism, with its very different conception of the person, and with its less localized, less particularistic conceptions of truth, disputes about authorship are less important than the acceptability and coherence of the teachings themselves and what those teachings offer for the salvation of mankind.

Ultimately, the important judgement of religious truth is perhaps less a matter for textual analysis, whether it be concerned with the attribution of authorship and the historicity of manuscripts or with the contextual plausibility of ideas, than for the appraisal of what that truth offers to men. Religion is, after all, a social phenomenon – and one may assert this without prejudice to the idea-content of any religion, and without attempting to assess (even if anyone could) its ultimate truth. If religion is a social phenomenon, then what must matter to mankind is the purport of teachings and their influence on the lives of believers. As a sociologist, in studying that influence, I try to maintain a detached objectivity in which detachment is always balanced by human sympathy.

Existence and Non-existence

IKEDA: Within its rational framework of measurable space-time and clear-cut opposites, Western scientific thought finds itself incommoded by the idea that something can simultaneously exist and not exist in a state transcending the duality between existence and non-existence. The Buddhist doctrine of Sunyata, however, is based on just such an idea. Sunyata, though sometimes translated as "void", means limitless potential for existence. The philosophy based on it rejects absolute dualities and is, admittedly, difficult to comprehend on the basis of scientific concepts of space-time alone. It is, as you know, essential to the theory of transmigration, in which, when an individual human being dies, his life is thought neither to exist nor not to exist, but to become part of a limitless potential for existence. Though people trained in the Western way of thinking condemn the approach as vague and incapable of verification, I think it explains much that is inexplicable by means of clear-cut distinctions between being and non-being. Do you agree?

WILSON: There is a real difficulty for those nurtured in the Western system of thought, with its strong principle of non-contradictory, mutually exclusive and exhaustive logical categories, to grasp a concept like that of Sunyata. Whilst the Westerner may acquire a notional understanding of such an idea, he needs both time and perseverance fully to enter into its intellectual and cognitive significance. The dominant orientation of thought in which contemporary Western intellectuals have been trained, and especially so in the natural and social sciences, has been to preclude metaphysical elements, and to admit non-empirical references only with the utmost circumspection. The problem about concepts defined as the "potential" for something is the specification of the conditions for the realization of that potential. Until realization occurs, it is not easy to indicate potential: once realization has occurred, potential becomes a retrospective category of limited utility. Of course, as an empirical generalization and by analogy, one may say that since so many acorns have become oak trees, each acorn has the potential to become an oak tree. However, the acorn is a physical entity, and when we say "potential" we refer to an empirical probability. Where we have no physical entity to allude to, the concept of potential becomes more tenuous for the Western mind to grasp.

The concept may, of course, be much more readily understood by those whose experience has been filtered through literary images and ideas, where empirical rigour is less demanded than spiritual or poetic insight. The religious mind, whether trained in Buddhist thought or not, may embrace the idea of Sunyata more readily than the mind trained in the sciences. Again, since the concept has a central part to play in the Buddhist interpretation of life and transmigration, it becomes comprehensible from its context of discourse. Perhaps, given its role in such a discourse, it is a mistake for an outsider to attempt to understand the concept in isolation; its meaning comes from its association with, and its relationship to, other concepts and teachings, and in that context it may become less problematic. The practising Buddhist also has another means of apprehending such an idea, since the concept has played a part in the mental structuring of his own experience, and has meaning in the system of ritual activities in which he is regularly engaged. Faith in a certain pattern of realities, in an order that may be partly perceived and partly intuited, provides an important structure of association which confers meaning on each given element within that structure.

In common with many Western observers, and particularly with those who have a background in the broadly scientific method of enquiry that characterizes the major disciplines of contemporary thought, I have difficulty in grasping the full meaning of Sunyata, but any enquirer into man's religious beliefs must acknowledge two things. First, he must recognize that the categories that we inherit from our cultural tradition are always far from exhaustive of natural or human phenomena; and, second, he must accord that, by imposing our rigorous thought structures on nature and experience, we may shut out certain things just as surely as in so doing we illuminate and control others. Above all, I feel that it is vital for the sociologist to accept the testimony of religionists with regard to their own intimations of the universe and its operation. These intimations are the necessary data in terms of which the sociologist must understand and interpret the world-picture and the thought processes of other men. Thus, even though I do not fully comprehend the meaning of Sunyata, and do not adequately penetrate the system of meaning embraced within the concept, none the less, I must respect the integrity, intelligence and life interpretations of those who do, and try, as far as I can, to understand what such a concept means for them.

IKEDA: I realize that Sunyata is incompatible with the Western way of thinking (though recent subtle developments in Western science seem to me to facilitate an understanding of it); but, as I have said, this does not negate its value or reduce its interest. Buddhism teaches that not only life after death, but also current life and all other phenomena require more than the categories of existence and non-existence to explain them.

The fundamental Buddhist doctrine of causal origins interprets all things as temporary aggregations of elements instead of as immutable essential entities. (Interestingly enough, the doctrine shares points in common with both modern physics and the philosophy of Democritus.) All things depend on causal relations that bring them together, and their aggregation results in a different entity that is more than a mere sum of its parts, just as water is something very different from its components oxygen and hydrogen.

But the aggregation is a state and not an entity and thus exists and at the same times does not exist. Similarly, the aggregation of oxygen and hydrogen, the *sine qua non* of water, can be called neither existent nor non-existent but must be described as Sunyata or potentiality.

The situation is obviously much more complex in cases of living organisms like the human body, which is composed of an immense number of aggregations of organic materials. In the processes of metabolism, these organic materials are ceaselessly being broken down, eliminated and replaced. Yet the individual's fundamental characteristics remain relatively stable and on many different levels his existence is supported by the operations of the life manifest in him. Because of its tremendous complexity, the human mental, psychological and emotional composition is more difficult than the physical body to explain in terms of *is* and *is not*.

Faith and the Fruits of Commitment

IKEDA: Faith has enabled apparently hopelessly ill people to overcome sickness, has pulled others through financial crises, and has been a source of mental help for many more. These effects are admittedly often psychological. The efficaciousness of medical therapy is also frequently affected by psychological factors. For example, group experiments have shown that mere nutritive tonics are more helpful in curing colds when administered to people who believe them to be medicinal. None the less, after all the psychological and accidental elements are eliminated or accounted for, religion still proves helpful for human beings. What do you think is the source of such help? Is it coincidence? Auto-suggestion? Or the opportunistic use by religionists of fortuitous, circumstantial phenomena? If religion's helpful influences are adequately reinforced with sound doctrinal teachings their value ought to be recognized. Do you agree?

WILSON: It seems to me to be an incontestable proposition that religion has positive social and psychological functions. Traditionally, the social (as distinct from the psychological) functions of religion have been recognized in the reinforcement that religion has given to the moral life of society; in the support it has lent to agencies of social control; in its effect in promoting social cohesion and a sense of allegiance and identity; and in legitimizing authority and policy. Many of these social effects have, of course, waned in the modern world as the organization of society has become increasingly conscious, instrumental and rational (even though serious social problems have also arisen from this process of change). In contrast, many of the psychological functions of religion have continued. Religion has remained a source of strength and a reinforcement of commitment for many people. The sick have indeed recovered, as you say, and the bereaved have been comforted, and some have attributed their capacity to overcome other kinds of misfortune to religion. One cannot simply explain away such experience as coincidence or accident. Believers may sometimes deceive themselves about the source of benefit in their lives, but I do not doubt that religious commitment is a potent source of powerful consequences.

Of course, although individual believers ascribe benefit to their own religion, to their god, their system of meditation, their ritual or creed, in practice we find that many very different religions, with different doctrines and explanations, appear to be more or less equally effective in bringing about consequences that believers regard as beneficial. Within Christianity, for example, people testify in the utmost sincerity to healing experienced by quite divergent practices and beliefs, from Roman Catholic miracle shrines to the emotionalism of a Pentecostal prayer meeting, or the silent affirmation of a Christian Science practitioner. Yet, these styles of religiosity are remote from each other, and their votaries are sometimes quite dismissive about the claims of any faith other than their own.

What all this suggests is that the important feature may be the sincerity of beliefs and practices, rather than their substance. Obviously, no religion succeeds in all cases; were it do so, its results alone would quickly induce many more people to adhere to it. On the other hand, no religion is likely to offer itself solely for the material and psychological benefits that adherence might confer. Religion is offered because it claims to be the truth and to be the appropriate moral guide for believers. Sometimes its truth is said to be proved by its good results, and particularly by peace of mind, but it does not offer itself merely as an agency for the production of miracles. Men take up a religion because it claims to be the truth and not because it claims to "do you good"; at the same time, religious men are receptive to the idea of receiving blessings, and learn to count their blessings and express their gratitude. Believers are usually prepared, sometimes without too close a scrutiny of cause and effect, to testify to the benefits they have derived from their religion. This is not to say that such benefits are not real, but only to acknowledge that devoted adherents are likely to attribute all manner of good experiences to their religion.

There is an intimate connection between faith and the fruits of commitment. Since these fruits are felt by believers, we may certainly say that they are real, at least psychologically real. The believer has embraced a faith, felt its power, satisfied himself as to its validity and attained a more contented state of mind, and he may have experienced positive physical benefit as well. Obviously, if a man's claims were to become too discrepant with reality, his faith might be dangerous and he might deceive himself (as in the case of faith-healing and mind-healing cults in which people proclaim themselves cured when, by all objective evidence, they are still manifestly ill). Such cases aside, however, the generally beneficent effects of religious belief are well attested. These effects of religion, which are often a powerful reinforcement of commitment, undoubtedly work towards the greater good of humanity.

IKEDA: In saying, "Men take up a religion because it claims to be the truth and not because it claims to 'do you good'", you have underscored the most essential element of religion. Nichiren Daishonin said, "Whatever obstacles I might encounter, so long as persons of wisdom do not prove my teachings to be false, I will never yield!"

But ordinary human beings find it difficult to fathom great religious profundity or to discern truth from falsehood in a religion. Consequently, for such people, present advantage is often the easiest approach to greater truth. In this connection, Nichiren Daishonin said that the actual effects religion has on human life are more important than all theoretical or documentary evidence. For this reason, my fellow believers and I emphasize the importance of actual and advantageous effects as a method of teaching the Buddhism of Nichiren Daishonin, in order to bring happiness to people burdened with troubles they cannot understand, no matter how hard they try.

Since the individual life to which happiness can be brought in this way is finite, the practical advantages it bestows are not a religion's most fundamental truth. They can, however, serve as an expedient leading people to an awareness of that fundamental truth. And this is their importance. In other words, the value of these blessings is less what they contribute to the happiness of the moment than the enlightenment they inspire with the knowledge that the individual life is one with universal, ultimate life and is therefore eternal and indestructible. Some religions concentrate solely on sophisticated philosophy and lose their holds on the hearts of ordinary people. Other religions attempt to win men's minds by ignoring philosophy and promising all kinds of blessings in this life. Surely, the best approach is a balanced combination of philosophical inquiry and concern for the improved mental and physical conditions of believers?

PART II

Reason and Responsibility

God's Will and Human Reason

IKEDA: It seems to me that philosophy – that is, the rational attempt to explain the universe and man's place in it – plays a much smaller role in the theistic religions than in Buddhism. Sometimes, in religions demanding submission to the will of an absolute god, the questioning reason is regarded as dangerous or heretical. Shakyamuni came to enlightenment as the result of deep intellectual effort and meditation, and the religion he founded urges other people to attempt to do the same. In what ways is the differing emphasis on theistic and philosophical thought reflected in religions themselves and in the attitudes of religious believers?

WILSON: It would, I think, be perfectly true to say that, whereas Buddhism began as a philosophical system, Judaism and by extension Christianity and Islam have their origins in an essentially primitive conception of a world ruled by the arbitrary decrees of an anthropomorphic god. In this dispensation, as *originally* conceived, there is clearly very little room for philosophical debate or speculation. Old Testament Judaism and Koranic Islam, in particular, were concerned more with the specification of the laws of public and personal comportment than with abstract propositions or philosophical interpretations of life and the universe. But, in all three traditions, the faculty of human reason steadily acquired a larger part in the maintenance of the faith. The Diaspora providentially freed Judaism from its sacerdotal and sacrificial origins and, although concrete rules persisted as a primary focus and as a major concern of Jewish everyday life, philosophical ideas gradually developed among the more intellectual rabbis (just as highly superstitious and magical systems developed among less elevated intellects). The medieval period, receiving a renewed impetus from Greek thought, saw the flowering of Christian philosophy, even though its problems were all conceived within the framework of Christian dogmas as the Church derived these from the scriptures. The roots of modern Western philosophy go more directly to the Greek traditions, side-stepping the adaptations Christian thinkers made in the light of their theology. Islam, too, despite its highly legalistic formulations, gave rise to prominent schools of logic and mathematics and to something approaching the type of university of learning that eventually achieved fullest and freer expression only under Christian and post-Christian auspices.

The philosophizing of the Judaeo-Christian tradition was of a different order from that of the Hindu and Buddhist traditions. The existence of a powerful Church in the Christian case certainly imposed limits on the range of speculative philosophy in which the clergy might engage, and some clergymen fell foul of the Church authorities for their philosophical formulations. There were, of course, prominent mystics, but the expressions of mysticism – often suspect – had to conform to dogmatic expectations to win the approval of the Church hierarchy. In general, as Western philosophers freed themselves from the specific theological preoccupations of the Church, their thoughts turned more to problems concerning the material world and its explanation, and a significant branch of philosophy developed in relation to more practical arts and empirical methods of enquiry. Under the impact of Puritanism, a concern with the mastery of the universe gave a distinctly practical bent to philosophical enquiry and an impetus to the growth of modern science and technology.

IKEDA: As you say, once freed from theological preoccupations, Western philosophers turned to an examination of the physical universe. It seems to me that this emphasis on the physical, sometimes to the exclusion of the spiritual, is a point of primary interest in distinguishing between the general Judaeo-Christian and the Buddhist approaches.

It is only natural that Western thought should concentrate on the finite space-time world – that is, the physical universe – since the Old Testament tradition on which it partly rests is characterized by, first, the will of an absolute God and, second, by the highly limited universe God is believed to have created.

When outstanding Christian minds set out to acquire an accurate understanding of the universe, they were motivated not only by pure intellectual curiosity, but also by the desire to prove somehow that God was both right and mighty. In other words, they were acting in the fervour of faith. But, ironically, the more objective their examinations of physical facts became, the more they tended to disprove venerable traditional beliefs, like those connected with the Creation and the structure of the universe. To appreciate the problems this stirred up, it is necessary only to recall the furore that surrounded the question of whether the earth moves or the stars in their appointed spheres move.

The Buddha was unconcerned with abstract examinations of the origins and structure of the physical universe. His sole interest was in bringing relief from the suffering that human beings experience in actual life. Although ancient Indian learning had a branch of astronomy, the Buddha passed it by in his concentrated concern with inner psychology. And Buddhist priests and sages of later ages have by and large continued in the same tradition. For instance, some Buddhist sects have evolved a subtle analysis of the human mind that covers nine (in some versions eight) mental stages from sensual perception to the deep subconscious, which is similar in many respects to the theories of Carl Jung. In brief, I believe that whereas the Judaeo-Christian and Islamic traditions turned to philosophy after being liberated in one way or another from theistic and sacerdotal concerns, Buddhism concentrated on philosophy and psychology from the very outset.

Art, Religion and Inner Realities

IKEDA: Art must never be forced to serve the propaganda purposes of any ideology or religion. When a given religion controls art, the people engaged in creative activities within the limit of orthodoxy may flourish, but all outside – dissident – art will be excluded. This is wrong. Art has a right to exist for itself and should not be made a means to ends extraneous to its nature. I do believe, however, that when a religion has convincing power to attract faithful adherents, its teachings will naturally and inevitably be reflected in the works of artists who accept its teachings. What are your opinions on the correct relation between art and religion?

WILSON: I concur entirely with your point that it is inappropriate for art to be forced into the service of a particular religion or ideology. Indeed, when that occurs, we tend to see a breed of self-serving artists in whom genuine vision is displaced by stylized forms and dictated content. The artist becomes a mere technician, interpreting ideas that are handed down to him. The possibilities for such a development have, of course, expanded in the modern world, where ideological systems have grown more powerful in their methods of social control and more pervasive in seeking to influence the minutiae of everyday life within totalitarian societies. In such systems, art is entirely dominated by official patronage, and the attempt is made, by the state or the party, to enforce unity of perspective on all agencies of communication, including the most individual forms of expression.

At the same time, many of the greatest works of art were brought into being in cultural contexts in which there was a high degree of value-consensus within each given society and in which the artist expressed – at best with his own idiosyncratic touches – the dominant values, often for patrons who were princes or religious authorities. Some artists were themselves men of considerable religious commitment, but others merely accepted the themes of the times in which they lived and of the culture in which their own artistic genius was fashioned. Yet other works of art were no doubt the result of the well-organized labour of craftsmen, not all of whom necessarily shared the religious dispositions of those whom they served (as we can see from the occasional evidence of *joie d'esprit* in the decoration of religious monuments and, at times, from covertly expressed pagan sentiments, even in the carvings of some cathedrals).

Many artists have been neither devout men nor men inspired by religious morality. Some artists of the highest talent often led reprobate lives, and others were indifferent to religious ideas in their own lives, even though they interpreted religious themes with daring and imagination. As manifested in past centuries, the successful artistic spirit has often been independent and wilful, whilst many devout men who have wanted to create art inspired by their religious convictions have signally failed, their work often lapsing into the sentimental and banal, and becoming the model for religious kitsch (for which there has been an extensive popular market in Europe).

There is, however, a deep affinity between the artistic imagination and the religious view of the world. Just as the religionist sees a world impregnated with values and meanings, resonant with symbolic elements, which are to be discovered as much in everyday activities, commonplace objects and trivial events as in great scenery and exceptional deeds, so the artist may perceive deep significance in phenomena that others dismiss or fail to notice altogether. Both the religious man and, traditionally, the artist live in a world suffused with meaning, in which a wide variety of things may stir the emotions and in which implicit values reside. Their world-views may not coincide, and their values may diverge, but they are of a similar kind. They contrast fundamentally with the positivistic attitudes and material interests that tend to prevail among other men. For both art and religion, the world is not to be taken at its face value.

IKEDA: You are quite right: art and religion do – and must – go beyond face values. In this and in other respects, they share elements in common on a very deep level, as René Huyghe and I agreed during a dialogue we conducted not long ago. Religion provides human beings with a frame of reference for spiritual and moral value judgements. Art gives the artist a similar frame of reference in aesthetic matters. Both religion and art are rooted in the inner world and colour the individual's whole view of the outer world.

The inner and outer worlds are not isolated entities but mutually interpenetrate each other. (There is a Buddhist doctrine, summarized in the Japanese term *esho-funi*, to the effect that the environment – *e* – and the living being – *sho* – are indivisible – *funi*.)

A Buddhist scripture contains a passage stating that the mind is a skilful artist. In other words, no artist creates without filtering the outer world through his mind or his own inner world. This concept applies to both people who produce realistic representations from actuality and people who produce versions of deities and fantastic creatures – dragons and so on – that have never existed in actuality. In both cases, the artist's inner and outer worlds mingle to result in the artistic creation. Similarly, in the case of the man of religion, the inner world of belief and the outer world of daily life co-mingle to result in a kind of work of art called the life based on faith.

WILSON: Yes, in other words, religion and art interact with phenomena and seek, not clinical objectivity, but emotional rapport. Whereas the scientific tradition demands objectivity and detachment, both religion and art demand an apprehension of inner realities and make a commitment to sub-jective discernment and to personal interpretation in which involvement rather than detachment is the essential. For them, the world is drenched with meanings that lie below the surface of things and beyond the possibilities of mere scientific measurement.

In the great religious traditions of the past, the artist, even when he himself was not a strong believer in the prevailing religious ideology, was at least aware of the same resonances and had a similar intuitive grasp of the world. He received the same cultural intimations, and that religious culture provided him with the stories and characters, symbols and motifs to embody in his artistic creations. In contrast, in the modern world, where free societies encompass a plurality of values, artists lack the significant cultural themes of the religious *Weltanschauung* of the past. In consequence, art itself becomes less coherent, more dispersed in its subject matter and divergent in its values, and hence less readily comprehended by ordinary people. One danger is that art becomes excessively personalized. Artists, who must seek a style since the culture lacks sufficient coherence and continuity to provide them with one, become idiosyncratic and unduly self-conscious. They sometimes take on a style, for a time, as if donning a suit of clothes, later to replace it with another. Their art ceases to come from an inner integrity of the person; rather, it is derived from the fashions or fads of the (temporary) times.

When men lack a coherent value-system in society there must be profound consequences for, among other things, art. The public then views art with a considerable and by no means unjustified scepticism. In this sense, then, whilst art can be rendered unduly subservient to religion or ideology, it is paradoxically also the case that when society comes to lack an integrated sense of values, the artist has difficulty, beyond the purely personal level, in communicating anything of general value to society or indeed in doing more than exercising his technical skills. Such is the openness and pluralism of modern society that even skill may no longer be a requisite, when some artists profess to believe (to my mind nonsensically) that art and accident converge.

Suffering and Blame

IKEDA: Although it is possible to explain logically why a certain family is poorer than others, why a nation prospers or does not, or why natural disasters strike in some zones with greater frequency than in others, from the subjective viewpoint, the individual sufferer is able to find no satisfying explanation of his plight. Simply saying that such is the lot of man is insufficient. Failure to be satisfied with fate leads some people to act in ways detrimental both to themselves spiritually and to the community at large. They may come to hate and to act wrongfully under the deluded conviction that society, political factions or isolated individuals are actually the cause of their hardships. Although a case may be made for animosity against people who are indeed sources of wrong, nothing can be said to defend sufferers who take their ills out on people completely unrelated to the issue in question, as is often the case with social and political radicals determined to destroy the Establishment, on which they load the blame for all their woes.

The Buddhist view is to interpret external causes and effects in ordinary phenomena as secondary to true karmic causes, which can be traced to the past part of the present life or to previous existences, though the impossibility of demonstrating rationally what has taken place in earlier lives makes reliance on such karmic causes a matter of faith. The great advantage of belief in karmic causation is that it places the responsibility for good or bad fortune squarely on the shoulders of the person experiencing it. And this in turn cultivates both profound independence and trust and respect, instead of suspicion and hatred, in human relations. No one who realizes that what happens to him, for better or worse, is his own responsibility can reasonably thank or blame anyone else. Furthermore, the awareness that what one does now will have an effect on the future inspires men to act in such a way as to generate good, not evil, karmic causes. And this cannot fail to have a salutary effect on the welfare of others and on social harmony. Do you agree with me that we must do as Buddhist teachings advocate and look for the causes of our suffering within ourselves?

WILSON: The human ego is always affronted by suffering. "Why is this happening to me?" is the universal question posed by sufferers, and in Christian, and perhaps also in Buddhist, cultures, the question easily becomes, "What have I done to deserve this?" implying a sense of moral cause and effect. In the Christian case, when this is said cause and effect are assumed to have been linked within the same lifetime; in the Buddhist case, moral failure in previous lifetimes provides an explanation. Yet, the question and the search for an answer are not confined to men brought up in sophisticated religious traditions. Exactly the same enquiry stimulates speculation about witchcraft among undeveloped peoples. The late Professor Evans-Pritchard recounted a question asked by the Azande tribesman: why were the foundations of his house eaten by termites? The Azande tribe knew that termites were the cause of house-collapse, but this knowledge in itself did not suffice to answer the question of the individual Azande: "Why *my* house?" Seeking to reconcile objective knowledge about cause and effect with the essentially subjective response to such a process prompts men to ask questions that can only be answered in religious terms. Men are not subjectively content with an answer that is objectively adequate. An answer that merely recounts how things happen is not enough for most people: they want an answer to the question of why something happens, and above all – such is their involvement and their lack of capacity for detachment – they want an answer to the question "Why does it happen *to me?*"

Although in general we may recognize the circumstances prompting such a question, from a strictly scientific point of view it might be said that the question cannot be given a convincing answer. What is perhaps of greater moment is the quality of the answer that a given tradition or a given culture leads men to expect. The answer of the Azande is ultimately a destructive answer, leading men to suspect each other of malice and evil-doing by clandestine means. The answers that have been traditional both in Buddhism and in Christianity are more elevated, in the sense that, even if no actual relation between immoral cause and evil effect can be demonstrated – and certainly, in no way that would meet the requirements of science – at least these religions put responsibility firmly on the shoulders of the individual agent himself.

In certain respects, this makes the burden of suffering easier to bear: when we know that something is our own fault, at least we recognize that it is pointless to wreak our anguish on others. It also provides us with the moral lesson that we must be responsible for what we do and teaches us that actions have consequences. In the religiously prescribed economy of morals, which in broad outlines works in a not entirely dissimilar way in the great religions, it is maintained that we help to ensure our own well-being in the future (whether in a future life or in a post-mortem condition) by moral behaviour here and now. Whether or not this is so – and it is certainly not possible to put it to rigorous test – at least such an idea of an *Ausgleich* has beneficial consequences for mankind in general. A man may refrain from wrongful deeds to avoid untoward consequences at a later time. He may be correct or mistaken in believing in the imputed relation-ship of cause and effect, but by believing in it, he does at least acquire a certain respect for his fellow men. This belief, therefore, has the latent function of helping to maintain the moral standards of society, on which we all depend, and of protecting one's fellow men from the evils that one might otherwise perpetrate against them.

Fate and Karma

IKEDA: Biology and genetics can explain some of the many differences that distinguish individuals from each other, but determining why a certain person should have his own unique genetic composition is beyond the powers of science. Fate, which seems to be the only answer, plays a striking role in non-hereditary aspects of individual human lives as well. Christianity envisages fate in the person of an omnipotent, anthropomorphic God and creator of the universe.

The Buddhist interpretation is of an unbroken continuum of life from the limitless past to the limitless future. In that life, each person has created a karmic account as a result of past actions. This account determines the fate of the person in the present. There is a certain amount of latitude, since the way the person lives at present can alter the karmic load his life has borne from the past. The late Arnold Toynbee interestingly compared the human karmic situation to a banking account in which entries are always being made in the debit and credit columns to alter the balance, which is the fate of the individual life at any given moment. Buddhists believe that what Dr Toynbee called the karma balance sheet continues in effect after death and into coming lives. How do you view the Buddhist interpretation of karma?

WILSON: Man always seeks an explanation for his circumstances, and often what he has not been able to explain by reference to empirical observation (or what he has not been prepared to accept as the consequence of his own doing) he has explained as due to supernatural causes. In the Christian case, he has sometimes regarded his fate as "the will of God" and particular events as "acts of God" – a phrase still used in English law for otherwise inexplicable accidents. In Buddhism, the notion of karma represents a more significant element of personal responsibility, but since the cause of present circumstances lies in earlier lives that he cannot recall, the individual's immediate sense of responsibility is somewhat muted. Perhaps the idea of karma operates effectively in giving people warning, in the shape of present sufferings, of what they might be laying up for themselves in the future if they fail to conform to the moral demands of the present. In this sense, karma might be represented as a socially functional agency of control, or as a way of inducing men to cultivate self-control.

Although the idea of karma embraces powerful intimations of determinism, this type of theodicy clearly admits the operation of free will, if not as the influence decisively affecting the present, as least as a powerful agency in the determination of the future. What is, is already settled; what will be (in future lives) men may yet influence. Thus the debilitating effect of total fatalism is escaped, even though the individual may absolve himself from immediate and present responsibility for his current sufferings. The rewards of moral conduct now are envisaged as something that will be realized only in – possibly remote – future lives (and indeed, since there is no continuing consciousness between lives, the differences in the interval between cause and effect is both incalculable and inconsequential).

Sociologically, karma operates over an apparently longer interval than is envisaged in the traditional Christian conception of reward and punishment for sins in some immediate post-mortem circumstance. Whether the threat of hell-fire has been more effective as an agency of social control than the prospect of creating bad effects in future lives is not easy to assess. Christians were once powerfully affected by fear of hell and hopes of heaven. Perhaps those emotions were strongest and, because they were subjected most effectively to control, the effect greatest during the period of early Calvinism and in the Puritan and Pietist movements that followed. At that time men began to look for immediate consequences of moral and immoral acts in the course of their actual earthly lives, at least by way of intimations of their post-mortem prospects. The strength of self-control of the emotions that were attached to these utterly serious concerns led to new type of effective regulation of conduct in society. The growing individualism of the period entailed that men should take on responsibility for their own consciences. Since they had more opportunity for individual action and were less bound by local traditional custom, which had kept men safe within the confines of conventional morality, their concern with sin and rectitude was intensified.

The philosophical implication in the doctrine of karma is thus not one that is altogether alien to the thinking of Western peoples – namely, that there should be a balance between cause and effect, between one's dispositions towards good and evil, and the consequences that follow from such dispositions. Despite their differences, Buddhism and Western philosophy embrace a not dissimilar moral economy. There appears to be an implicit attraction in the natural justice of a cause-and-effect programme, even though the time-span of the Buddhist conception of things and the discontinuity of individual identity are difficult elements to comprehend for minds wholly formed in the Western tradition.

IKEDA: Yes, I see what you mean by a common moral economy. In the Christian belief, people who act according to the will of God go to heaven; those who disobey God and do evil go to hell. This is certainly similar to the karma system and, in some interpretations, makes allowance for the element of independent will, since human beings may decide on their own whether to follow the good or the bad path. Calvinistic predetermination, however, although a logical outcome of the belief that, since God is omnipotent and omniscient, he has already drawn up an unalterable schedule of fate for everything and everybody, leaves no latitute for free will.

The classical Christian predicament is the contradiction between the belief that man is free to act and therefore responsible for his actions and the dogma of an omnipotent, omniscient God who, having predetermined everything that has and ever will happen in the universe, is himself responsible and thus ought to lift the burden of moral blame for ill from man's shoulders.

WILSON: I take your point: there is an inherent contradiction in the Christian depiction of God as both omnipotent and omniscient. If God were omniscient he would know everything, and would know it in advance. Such knowledge would, however, preclude his being simultaneously omnipotent since he would no longer then be able ever to change his mind. Theologians have, of course, wrestled endlessly with the problem of free will and determinism, and the issues still occupy contemporary philosophers, and can scarcely be explored here. In fairness to the Calvinists, however, it must be acknowledged that their commitment to the doctrine of predestination did not preclude free will, it merely challenged the idea of cause and effect within this sphere. Although they believed that God had already decided who should have everlasting life and who should be damned, without allowing man the possibility, by his own conduct to influence that decision at all, Calvinists none the less taught that man had to choose whether to obey the moral law. They urged upon men their duty to obey that law, because that was what God wanted and not because they could expect to benefit from their obedience in the afterlife. Theirs was, in that sense, a very elevated ethic – man should be moral without believing that he could by virtue of that fact claim any reward. He must not doubt his post-mortem prospects, but equally he must not presume to know with any certainty what his after-life condition would be. The choice of obeying God's law, however, was an aspect of his free will.

IKEDA: In spite of the supposed all-pervading knowledge and power of God, other elements of Western thought and practice demonstrate a similarity with the concept of karma. For instance, personal responsibility for action is the basis of all Western criminal penal codes. Furthermore, most people in the West accept the idea that effort (cause) produces rewards (effects). In short, the Buddhist law of cause and effect seems to agree with what human beings everywhere experience in actual practice; and, although actual karmic links are often very difficult to demonstrate, awareness of a degree of connection between his actions and their outcomes can inspire man to strive to be and do better.

Individuality and Universal Life

IKEDA: Believing that life is a one-time affair followed by nothing at all, some people feel justified in pursuing extremes of either hedonism or pessimism. Others think that, since they are unique and finite, they ought to do their best to make their lives as meaningful as possible for contemporary mankind and for posterity.

People who trust in continued individual existence beyond the grave often posit places of reward or punishment – sometimes elaborate hells, purgatories, and heavens like those described by Dante – to which people must go to get their just deserts or from which they may be excluded until they have shaken off all lingering connections with humanity – just as Hamlet's father's ghost is compelled to walk the earth a little while longer.

The Buddhist interpretation lays less stress on the individual life, which is believed to blend with the universal life at death and later to resume individualized form as the outcome of karmic causes in a limitless stream of births, lives, deaths and rebirths called *samsara*. I should be interested to hear your assessment of the effects that belief in a melding of the phenomenal life with the universal life has on men and their communities.

WILSON: The Buddhist conception of life, and of individuality and collectivity, represents an intellectual tradition standing in stark contrast to the very strong sense of individual identity that pervades Western, Christian, and most especially Protestant, thought. The individual ego is much more sharply delineated in the Christian scheme of things. Given this powerful sense of self prevailing in Western thought, it may well be that, once the idea of a super-empirical system of rewards and punishments after death ceased to command credence, the underpinning that had sustained morality in personal behaviour was very much weakened. The pervasive preoccupation with personal salvation in the after-life was eventually transformed into a search for personal gratifications in one's present life, and this became the dominant motivation in Western society. The Western social system today is characterized by the supreme value of individual profit and individual pleasure which are to be sought in as systematic and rational a way as possible. These values have come to constitute the common-sense logic of Western life, and social organization operates on the assumption that all individuals are motivated primarily by the systematic acquisition of wealth and welfare. Relationships are contractual, and contracts are made in total self-interest. The state holds the ring for free enterprise, interfering as little as possible in economic matters and steadily abandoning what remains of the earlier, more religious and more substantively moral system. The actual operative values of the modern world are increasingly dictated by technical and instrumental considerations, rather than by any intimations about the substantive or intrinsic quality of acts. We may say that the value system of this type of society is egocentric and that its moral norms, which are necessarily an expression of the collectivity, none the less urge upon individuals the importance of self-interest rather than communal responsibility. It is not surprising that the peoples of so many Western nations (certainly the Americans, the Scots, the English, the French and the Italians) pride themselves on the strength of their individualism – even if that individualism often appears most markedly as a negative egocentricity excusing men both for competitive aggressiveness and from the need to make sacrifices for the collective good. In contrast, one observes in a Buddhist country like Japan the extent to which, in factories, schools, universities and civic communities, there is a vigorous collective commitment and a willingness to moderate selfish and egocentric behaviour. Might this facet of Japanese culture, which so readily impresses Westerners, stem from the Buddhist conception of the blend of individual lives with universal life?

IKEDA: I am afraid not. You see, the idea of blending the individual life with the universal life is not recognized as a fundamental tenet by all Buddhist sects. As you know, primitive Buddhist scriptures advocate self-discipline for the sake of attaining the state of total extinction called Nirvana. There can be no thought of melding with the universal life something that has become totally extinct. The concept of the union of the individual and the universal lives is set forth most clearly in the philosophy of the *Sutra of the Lotus of the Wonderful Law.*

In my opinion, quite different factors account for what you call the Japanese "collective commitment". First, competition is so fierce in our society that people are forced to rely on groups for the sake of survival. Second, from childhood, we Japanese are surrounded by a psychological environment in which subordination to the group is praised as good and conspicuous individuality and rebelliousness are condemned as bad. Third, hierarchical structures still dominate Japanese society; people on the lower rungs of the ladder follow the rule of obedience to those farther up. Regrettably, I must say that the Buddhist concepts of the continuity of all life and of karmic causation do not function as foundations for living and acting for most modern Japanese, not a small number of whom have no idea what basic Buddhist teachings are like. In short, the Japanese communal commitment is more social than moral and has no religious reinforcement.

WILSON: In the West, the idea of an individual after-life was a powerful reinforcement of the social demand for moral conformity but, once belief in the after-life diminished, what had been a support for moral conduct appears to have become a millstone round its neck. If post-mortem benefit was the main reason for being good, when men came to believe that they had only one life there were fewer arguments for not seeking the maximum pleasure (in whatever way pleasure might be conceived) during the course of that life. It would be facile to attribute the changing pattern of morality in Western countries solely to the decline of belief in heaven and hell; that belief was only one reinforcement of morals. However, since moral conformity was closely tied to a religiously defined idea of profit-and-loss accounting in the after-life, the decline of belief in the after-life may have contributed to the decay of morality and to the replacement of the moral values of work, willingness, service, communal responsibility and personal moderation by the quite different values of hedonism and extravagance.

Today, many men feel that to commit an immoral act is of no consequence (as long as they can get away with it), and the tide of hedonistic thinking therefore steadily rises. Because consumption is so important to the operation of the modern technological social system, we are all encouraged to consume as much as we can of the so-called good things. Our societies all sustain an elaborate advertising industry, the sole aim of which is to persuade us to consume. Today, advertising is perhaps the most powerful disseminator of the relentlessly hedonistic social values pressed upon us, subtly and blatantly, systematically and urgently, morning and evening, from our births to our deaths. The same values become the staple fare of the entertainment industry, by which, ironically, they are presented without the same ulterior commercial motives, as *the* values of modern life. A pop song of a few years ago summed it all up, when it urged: "Enjoy yourself, enjoy yourself: it's later than you think." The message is that life does indeed end at the grave.

Antidotes for Suicide

IKEDA: The members of the Judaic religions, including Christianity, assume that shortening life wilfully by the act of suicide runs counter to the will of God and is therefore wrong. Other philosophies and religions have viewed suicide in other lights. Regrettably today – especially in Japan among the elderly and even among children – suicides are numerous. Though some Buddhist sects have approved of suicide when life is deemed meaningless, the Lotus Sutra insists that life is intrinsically worthy of the greatest respect and that the ability to live it out determines the value of the human being. Consequently, severing even one's own life ahead of time is tantamount to denying the dignity of life itself. Buddhism based on the Lotus Sutra not only condemns suicide, but also strives to revive the courage and strength to go on living in people who have been driven to emotional extremes. Karl Menninger, the American psychiatrist, argues that a confusion of desires is at the bottom of all suicides: the desire to kill, the desire to be killed and the general longing for death. I believe that one important role of religion is to sublimate these desires and channel them in the direction of strength to live. How do you view the issue of suicide?

WILSON: We know from sociological studies of suicide that the individual's hold on life depends on an appropriate measure of social support. In modern Western societies, the increase in the rate of suicide has generally been attributed to the intense individualism of modern life and to the failure of the local community to survive the effects of the modern technological order. In an increasingly impersonal society, in which large urban agglomerations, commuting, mass-media and role relationships dominate everyday life, many individuals come to feel isolated and in despair. Beyond these general conditions, there are times when social values break down or are thrown into confusion, when the norms and mores of society are obscured or uncertain – a condition known to sociologists as *anomie* – and in those circumstances, the rates of suicide tend to rise, sometimes dramatically. On the other hand, it has been suggested that, in intense traditional cultures, such as characterize Asia and particularly Japan, the very strength of social pressure on the individual, the demand for performance and conformity in the acquisition and maintenance of social honour, might produce circumstances in which the individual feels that he cannot live up to his obligations and so might be induced to commit suicide. In such a case, the force of social norms and values is such that the individual's life is devalued for their sake. The traditional case is of less moment today: in modern societies, even though the moral order is often permissive, a high premium is frequently placed on individual success in narrow intellectual or economic terms. Highly motivated people who find the pace too hard might be induced to suicidal tendencies, either because they count themselves failures or because they have too strong a sense of shame in the presence of contemporaries, peer-groups or kinsfolk.

Very often it is either those undergoing difficult adjustments to the expectations of new roles who appear to be at risk, or those whose roles are ill-defined and whose social bonds are loose. Old people sometimes find it difficult to come to terms with modern life, feel neglected and simultaneously consider themselves nuisances. Students too, of whom much is expected and who are less tightly bound to their families as a consequence of their new roles, are very much at risk, especially when they are highly, but all too narrowly, motivated. They tend to have a very restricted idea of what constitutes success, and it is one of the tragedies of the intense specialization of our social system that things such as sound character, human warmth, a capacity for generosity and affection, and a wide range of amateur skills are not more positively evaluated. From talents such as these, which were once highly esteemed in everyday life, individuals could derive alternative or diverse understandings of personal worth and dignity. Such alternative foci of self-appraisal might protect men both from undue emphasis on mere intellectual or mere economic success and the feelings of shame, isolation or worthlessness from which suicidal tendencies often stem.

It has generally been a function of religion to encourage in men a sense of hope and potential worthiness, and for many people, even in the secularized societies of modern times, it may still play a part in encouraging positive attitudes and alternative measures for appraising human qualities. No doubt we must seek through our educational institutions to provide people with the opportunity to recognize their own potential and their own inner resources from which a sense of worthiness can develop. Religion has perhaps the greatest opportunity to promote such a goal and to sublimate the aggressive dispositions that appear to lurk in the human psyche.

IKEDA: You are certainly right to point to large urban conglomerations and an impersonal society – on an immense national and industrial scale – as causative factors in the growing suicide rate. On a deeper level, I believe men kill themselves when they fail to understand the worthiness and value of persevering in life. Goals for achievement and ideals to realize stimulate human beings to go on, no matter what hardships and sufferings they encounter. Yet not all people have goals and ideals of this kind. Some flounder in frustration when they have achieved one set of aims and realized one set of ideals without finding new ones to take their place.

A sense of being trusted and needed by other people may be a great incentive to go on living when times are dark. The power of this sense of being important burgeons as the individual deliberately strives to make himself useful to his fellows.

As you point out, religions generally function to encourage in men a sense of hope and potential worth. Some religions have established goals to be attained – Nirvana for some Buddhists, heaven for believers of the religions of the Judaeo-Christian tradition – and teach the possibility of finding meaning in one's own life through altruistic service for others. Not all religions, however, share such lofty and encouraging elements, which might indeed serve as a useful criterion of judgement of a religion's value.

The Value of Human Life

IKEDA: Buddhist teachings condemn the taking of life, the most precious of all things. Christians condemn taking life sometimes – that is, when they assume that it is contrary to the will of God and therefore evil – but condone or even applaud it when the persons to be destroyed are deemed to run contrary to God's will. I assume the wars of religion, the Inquisition and intolerance of heresy are outcomes of this approach. At present, when absolute faith in Christianity is on the wane in many parts of the world, nationalism and various ideologies have inherited the role of justifying staggering atrocities in the name of glowing, often ostensibly enlightened, doctrines. However, in attempting such justification, they lapse into a state of moral darkness no better than those displayed in the worst excesses of religious and political oppression.

Until profound respect for the dignity of life is implanted in the minds not only of ordinary people, but also of political leaders in national states, murder – and by extension war – will not be eliminated. It seems to me that the Buddhist doctrine of respect for life could be useful in turning the minds of men away from the irrevocable destruction of irreplaceable lives.

WILSON: In the long course of Western history, Christian ethics have been invoked to support widely divergent, and at times quite contradictory, propositions. Jesus commanded men to "turn the other cheek", a formulation that implies both pacifism and passivity, and to forgive one's brother "70 times seven". The Church, however, at the most vigorous periods of its history has required that men be prepared to kill in the cause of just warfare and especially in defence of the Church and Christian monarchs. Executioners were to accept their task as a duty when required to act by judicial procedures which the Church had either instituted or sanctioned. To kill in these various circumstances was held not merely to be justified, but also conceivably to benefit the souls of those who were to be killed. When the Church became strongly identified with particular monarchs or with national states, the religious legitimation of killing was sometimes harnessed to purely political ends.

There have always been Christians who have stood out against this development of the religious legitimation of warfare and judicial killing, but they were certainly not very influential in the past. In more recent times, the growing separation of Church and State, the diminished reliance of modern nation states on religion for their sense of legitimacy, and the general decline of Christianity have all occasioned the growing abandonment by Christians, and even by the churches, of those earlier attitudes of tolerance for (and the sanctioning of) violence towards the person. Today, Christian believers and church authorities – because they are no longer trammelled by the need to support political systems – can return to the simpler, absolute moral prescriptions of Jesus. It is now easier for them to condemn murder and warfare, and many of them do so. On the other hand, for the same reasons, they have a weaker voice in the affairs of their nations and increasingly become little more than an unrepresentative minority. The state proceeds in its purposes with diminished reference to ideological justifications, according to what is perceived as the constraints of political necessity.

For my own part, since I am not a Christian, I have no doubt that the inculcation of a positive respect for life has an important part to play in effecting a restraint on violence of all kinds. The legal codes of Christian countries are today based on the positive respect for life and do not designate crimes by reference to the will of God. Given that in Western countries not all men are Christians and that many of those who accept that title are apathetic or indifferent to Christianity, it seems vital to me that the conception of what is criminal should not rest on religious interdictions but should rest on propositions that command the assent of the vast majority of civilized and human people. Neither rudimentary Christian ethics, as expounded in the Christian scriptures, nor the elaborate codes evolved by the Roman Catholic Church are likely to prove adequate for the exigencies of modern life. This is because those codes were first articulated in conditions very different from those of the present and in societies in which social and human problems were both quantitively on a different scale and qualitatively of a very different kind. In pluralist societies, men have widely divergent religious beliefs which, even among believers in the same religion, are held with widely differing measures of intensity; and there are also some who reject all beliefs. In these circumstances, it seems essential to base social ethics and the criminal code on propositions of a broad humanistic kind to which, whatever religious preference they may have, men can give general assent. The worth of the human being is clearly a starting-point for such an ethic and one that can usually be supported by men of widely diverse religious creeds.

IKEDA: The worth of life – not only that of human beings but of all other living creatures as well – is the crux of the issue. The story goes that, in a former life, the Buddha, who was called Prince Sattva at the time, went with his brothers into a forest, where they came upon a tigress unable to feed her cubs because she was on the verge of starvation and her teats had dried up. The cubs too were not far from death. Seeing this, all the young men except Prince Sattva returned home. Prince Sattva remained and gave his body to the tigress to eat so that she could regain strength and rear her offspring. Another story tells of an ancient king who once tried to protect a pigeon from the attacks of a hawk. Frustrated in his efforts to obtain food, the hawk said to the king, "You wish to protect the pigeon and in doing so condemn me to death from hunger." The king reflected for a moment and then cut off some of his own flesh as food for the hawk.

These tales are intended to point to the preciousness of all life. The famous Indian king, Ashoka, demonstrated an understanding of this by founding veterinary hospitals in his kingdom.

But killing is a built-in part of the circumstances under which all animals – including man – must live. We slaughter animals for food, just as animals kill and eat each other. We destroy creatures we consider harmful or disagreeable annoyances. None the less, in spite of a certain amount of apparently unavoidable killing, we human beings must always remain aware of the dignity and value of life and be deeply grateful for the lives we take for the sake of our own sustenance. This is the message of the Buddhist legends of Prince Sattva and of the king who gave his flesh to feed a hawk. An ingrained awareness of the dignity of all life, if widespread among mankind, could lead to the elimination of murder and of war – which is murder on an immense scale.

Capital Punishment

IKEDA: Arguing that it is morally wrong for human beings to take the lives of their fellows, even after trial and judgement for a crime, and insisting that its abolition will inspire no increase in serious malefactions, many Japanese humanists plead for the elimination of the death penalty. Opponents of their view argue in favour of retaining capital punishment which, they believe, significantly deters criminals. Because of my own conviction that life is worthy of paramount respect, I am opposed to capital punishment. Life must not be manipulated as a means to an end, even the admirable one of restraining crime. Evidence has not conclusively established the effectiveness of capital punishment as a deterrent, but I cannot imagine that its power to intimidate criminals into refraining from wrongdoing is as great as the moral evil of taking life. Certainly, capital punishment as retribution in the name of what is called teaching criminals a lesson must not be condoned. What is your stand on the issue of capital punishment?

WILSON: Most of the arguments that favour capital punishment now appear to rest on its possible deterrent effect on criminals. The actual evidence of deterrence is difficult to assess. Certainly, crimes of passion would appear to be uninfluenced by the scale of punishments. Crimes committed in the pursuit of illegal gain might be affected, if robbers recognized that not to carry weapons is a way of escaping more severe sentences if they are caught. Murder statistics are unfortunately difficult to interpret with respect to this one specific influence, but overall there is no doubt that the likelihood of arrest is a more significant deterrent than the type of punishment if apprehension is unlikely.

Retributive justice has become intellectually unfashionable in Western countries, where most of those who engage in public debate on the matter are men of refined sensibilities for whom the idea of retribution is certainly unattractive and at times incomprehensible. I have considerable sympathy with them for wishing to believe that mankind has reached a point of civilization at which the demand for retribution has been generally transcended. I am inclined to believe, however, that there is still a considerable demand for retributive justice among the public at large and, even though I do not myself support the motive of revenge as an appropriate basis for legal sentencing, I do not think that these popular sentiments can be entirely ignored. Western countries operate systems of democracy in which the public will is, theoretically, implemented by politicians. Many issues are too technical for the public will to be easily interpreted, but in this case the issue can be made relatively simple and could easily be subjected to public referendum. I do not think that those who proclaim democratic values can very readily escape the obligation to take into account public opinion on a matter of this kind, even if, at the same time, they seek to promote educational processes that might induce the public to reconsider its attitude to the matter of capital punishment.

IKEDA: Public opinion is powerful and, as you say, must not be ignored. But it is all too often – especially in this time of mass communications media – emotionally manipulated. For instance, radio and television report on murderers the horror of whose crime seems mitigated by circumstances, and the public is mercifully inclined towards them. Other murderers who have acted in a calculated and cold fashion incur public ire. The prevailing opinion in cases of these kinds is to reject capital punishment for the first kind of killer and urge it for the second.

Punishment for crimes is established by national laws and implemented by the appropriate officials. The judges who hand down sentences are fallible humans who, aware of the possibility of error, are saddled with the onerous duty of deciding whether the human being in the dock must live or die. The likelihood of influence by emotionally impelled public opinion or the ordinary element of human error on the part of judges casts grave doubt on the wisdom of inflicting capital punishment in any case.

Still another point against capital punishment is the finality of death. An executed criminal can never repent or try to make restitution in some way for the wrong he has done. A criminal who repents of rash or wicked acts, perhaps perpetrated in the recklessness of youth can, if allowed to live, even in confinement, make a positive contribution to society and ought, it seems to me, to be allowed to atone for his wrongs in this way.

I am fully aware that many people fail to share my views. I realize that it must be difficult for the families of murder victims to be forgiving towards the killers. A large number of survivors probably suffer such anguish and grief at their loss that they would prefer taking revenge on the murderer with their own hands to allowing the state to try and sentence him. These emotions of vindictiveness and hatred are part of the numerous aspects of human nature which demand deep-reaching correction.

WILSON: The sentiments that favour capital punishment for murders are perhaps intensified by two sets of factors. On the one hand, many people believe that prisons are becoming increasingly comfortable for convicts. Regular reports in the press suggest that prison life is not nearly as rigorous as many members of the public feel it should be. On the other hand, in recent years, Western countries have seen some extraordinary instances of both gruesome and wanton murders. In the United States there have been several cases of multiple murders committed either for purely sadistic reasons or in connection with extraordinary sexual activities. In Britain, we have at present in prison people who have plotted together to murder several small children. As I write, the police are hunting a man who has savagely and brutally killed several young women, putting a city of half a million people in terror. There are men who hire themselves out to commit murder for a fee and who have killed innocent people, including a child, because he was "in the way". We have a number of terrorists who, merely for purposes of political propaganda, have exploded bombs without regard to the destruction of innocent lives, which they have wantonly sacrificed in the vanity of their cause. For all of these types of crime, the public in Britain, perhaps overwhelmingly, would like to see the restoration of the death penalty, which was abrogated some years ago.

IKEDA: This underscores the point I am attempting to make. The British public would "perhaps overwhelmingly" like to take the lives of criminals as payment for their crimes. It is my belief that all people must come to see that life is too precious to be taken, even as punishment for evil.

Japanese history offers an illustration of the kinds of steps that might be taken. During the age called the Heian period (the period of peace and tranquillity, though this is more a hopeful than an accurate label), which lasted from the late eighth to the late twelfth century, capital punishment was abolished throughout Japan. This is not to say that murders and crimes did not take place. They did, and warring broke out from time to time as well. Yet the general tone of the civilization of the age was set by the Kyoto court aristocracy, who were in many cases devout Buddhists. The prevailing feeling was that man should not punish malefactors during this life since they inevitably must face justice in the next and will probably be sent to hell for what they had done. Unfortunately, when the elegant court aristocrats lost the reins of power and the warrior class assumed pre-eminence, the Buddhism-based pacifism of Heian times gave way to bitter fighting and cruel punishments, which only bred more crime, leading to still further punishment.

Respect for the sanctity of life is the soil in which a more healthy, more humane society of the kind envisioned, if not realized, in Heian times can grow. Obviously, the needed improvements in human attitudes and actions cannot be effected overnight, but effort in the right direction would undeniably benefit all.

WILSON: Your strong commitment to the view that life should command paramount respect is one that I deeply appreciate. In most matters, I should want to associate myself fully with efforts at all genuine life-enhancement and with whatever promotes the human-ness (as distinct from the animality) of man. I find myself deeply concerned, however, about the type of murder that is committed in the pursuit of gain, about murder committed by terrorists, and by what I shall call wanton and sadistic murder (which would need to be rather carefully defined). It is with regard to these types of murder that I think the public feels the need for stronger measures than those that are available in countries in which, as in Britain, the death sentence has been abolished. The paramount respect for human life must extend, I believe, to the protection and reassurance of potential victims even more than to the preservation of convicted killers. If the death penalty has any degree of deterrent effect, or even if the public at large believes that it has such an effect and takes comfort and reassurance from it, I think that capital punishment for the three types of murder I have mentioned might be justified. Some have suggested, and it is a point that deserves to be considered, that a sentence to life imprisonment with no prospect of release, which would in itself be a living death, might indeed be a more effective denial of all that we mean by the enhancement of life than the swift execution of the death penalty. Be that as it may, there may be times when the question we face is not life versus death, but whose life and whose death. If that is an effective choice, then I should like to choose life for the innocent.

Gandhi's Principle

IKEDA: As is well known, Gandhi advocated non-violent resistance to tyranny in his drive for Indian independence from British colonial rule. Other great leaders in East and West alike have adopted a similar course. And, although the followers of these men have sometimes sacrificed their mentor's lofty principles in the name of ensuring their own personal power, the attempt to save humanity from misery and destruction by means of a spiritual victory over material power – like the one Gandhi can claim – is of the utmost importance. What is your interpretation of the value of Gandhian non-violent resistance?

WILSON: The merit of passive resistance is surely that it calls for a very high measure of self-discipline, impartiality and objectivity on the part of those who seek to promote a particular cause or who seek to register a protest. A fundamental problem with all forms of political protest is the tendency for those who feel strongly that they are right to allow their emotional commitment to lead them to acts of violence or destruction, sometimes even to action that directly contradicts the aims they are supposed to be pursuing. If those who are struggling for their freedom, for independence from alien governors, for basic human rights, can so regulate their responses that their resistance remains non-violent, then the virtue of their restraint must in its own right lend moral weight to their cause. The cultivation of such self-control is difficult even for cultivated men educated in a climate of reason and tolerance; it is very much more difficult for the uneducated, who may have a sense of oppression that eclipses all other values and to whom their own passion appears to justify any means used to realize their goals.

One sees how certain men – Gandhi among them – attain greatness and elicit reverence by virtue of their austere self-restraint, and they stand out from among the many other popular and political heroes whose advocacy included resort to violence. Those who admire and eulogize these self-restrained leaders are not, of course, always men who can themselves summon the same high-minded moral courage or virtuoso performance. The "saint" so often becomes less the model for emulation than the owner of a name evoked as a slogan for action which, in every particular, conflicts with the values for which he himself stood.

The importance of Gandhi for me is as an exemplar not so much in the art of political and moral protest, as of a certain type of supremely civilized self-restraint. To attain detachment from our own emotions requires a quality of self-criticism and self-disdain as well as of self-control. It demands recognition of the need for order, decency and respect for others as the essentials in the conduct of human relationships and for all social development. To be able to stand back from those things that concern us most deeply, to acquire the forbearance, patience and inner resources to put oneself in a position where one takes the risk that the strength of one's commitment might even fail to be appreciated is the attainment of a very high degree of civilization. Stable, persistent and relentless concern expressed without emotional involvement is a peak of moral performance. How we comport ourselves when our deepest feelings are stirred is a measure of our civilization.

IKEDA: The Indians certainly felt very deeply about their independence. No doubt some of them believed they could not obtain satisfactory vengeance for what they had suffered under the British Raj without resorting to violence. And, in spite of an extensive recognition that the British, who were more skilful rulers of colonies than most others, had done much that was useful for India – the introduction of railways for one thing – colonial status was undoubtedly so difficult for the proud Indians to endure that Gandhi must have had a very hard task indeed convincing his compatriots of the importance of non-violence. Achieving his end among people driven virtually to despair by a long period of humiliation and misery must have forced Gandhi to battle with himself in the hope of attaining the self-control that you say is difficult even for cultivated men educated in a climate of reason and tolerance. However, he faced that challenge and became – once again to borrow your words – an exemplar of supremely civilized self-restraint.

If more people followed Gandhi's example, many evils could be eliminated. I believe capital punishment would no longer be necessary. It is likely that both domestic and international disputes could be solved peacefully. On the other hand, if we do not strive to produce a civilized society of self-restrained people, we will never divest ourselves of our long human tradition of solving problems by violence – which is never a solution at all, as countless examples from human history all too painfully reveal.

I realize that attaining the state of spiritual power that Gandhi achieved is nearly impossible for most of us. None the less, we ought to try to come as close as possible to it in all our daily affairs and in larger cultural and political efforts, too.

Religion and Politics

IKEDA: The intimate relationship that has long persisted in human civilization between politics and religion has had some good effects but has so often resulted in grave trouble that today, as a general rule, most modern states prefer to pursue a policy of separation between religious and political matters.

The followers of a religion can use their faith to do either good or harm. They can employ it in altruistic service for others, or they can strive to use it as an authority by means of which to interfere with or compel others to do as they wish. Both the good and the bad aspects of religion are amplified when allied with political power. To suppress evil and encourage good for the sake of society, politicians who are men of religion must never attempt to force their faith on others but must work in the best spirit of altruistic service. I am certain that your wide knowledge and experience in these matters has enabled you to form valuable opinions on the optimum relationship between religion and politics. I should be very happy to hear some of them.

WILSON: In the modern world, there are very few countries in which either the institutions of the state or the politicians who attain authority within it require the kind of legitimation that it was once an important function of religion to provide. In the formation of state societies or in the earlier building of empires, it was almost always the case that political expansion and the claims of leaders to legitimate authority required the endorsement of supernatural powers as vouchsafed by the leaders of organized religion. Chief priests placed the crowns on the heads of emperors, justified the wars they fought, validated the titles they assumed, endorsed the policies they pursued, claiming the mandate of heaven for whatever was done in the ruler's name. Not infrequently, political leaders, discontented with mere monarchy, claimed divine status for themselves – so frequently, indeed, that we can recognize a distinct trend towards deification of secular kings. In recent centuries, these associations between religion and political agencies have grown weaker. The voice of the people has replaced the voice of heaven as the source of legitimacy for the heads of modern states, and now the trend is common to the world's two largest countries, atheist

Russia and secular America (where religion still flourishes, of course, but as an essentially private matter separated from all involvement in state or federal agencies). In Europe, lingering associations persist in the established churches of England, Scotland and the Scandinavian countries; but even in these cases the association is between religion and monarchies that are purely constitutional and titular, no longer a focus of real political power. The association might be said to be one between two purely symbolic manifestations of the sacred.

As the state has grown stronger, religion in Western countries has lost influence in public affairs, even though, in some European countries, political parties explicitly declare themselves to be committed to Christian values. In practice, such a commitment appears to be little more than a token gesture of only historic significance, reminding voters that the party opposes various secularizing measures and in general supports the Church. There are somewhat more fluid and less formalized relationships of what might be called an elective affinity between the right-wing in American politics and the inclinations of many "born again" American Christians. In Britain, religion is generally regarded as being beyond and above the political arena, and this is in spite of – perhaps because of – the lingering connection of Church and state. If the monarch is to be temporal head of the Church, then the Church, like the monarch, had better remain aloof from political entanglement. The English spirit of compromise and relatively more tolerant attitude towards religious dissent than that which prevailed in France, Italy or Spain, rendered unnecessary in England the type of liberal, rationalist, free-thinking political parties which acted to reduce the influence of the Church and which became vehicles of anti-clericalism in those countries.

Perhaps, however, the wider implications of the question you raise are essentially ethical. To what extent can the principles of truth and altruism, which the higher religions have generally promoted, inform political expression and action? Political parties, because they are organized with power as their goal, probably attract men who are interested in power. Power in the national arena is the ultimate goal, but a subsidiary goal – power in the party – almost inevitably arises. The possibility of goal displacement, the process in which the long-term ends become obscured and more immediate goals are substituted, is one to which political parties are probably particularly prone. Some politicians become mere organization men, loyal to the party rather than to the principles for the attainment of which the party originally came into being. Others use the party as a vehicle for the furtherance of their own careers, or develop entrenched interests and use power in the party to secure or confirm their own ends, whatever these may be. Beyond this is all the dealing and the compromises that characterize modern politics, as alliances of convenience are made and unmade by men seeking short-term advantages at the cost of long-term high ideals.

If religiously committed men form a "religious" party for action in the political sphere, they must recognize that in so doing they run the risk of jeopardizing their own principles, since the roles and rules of the political arena are alien to their religious experience. The political context has its own tensions, its own demands and responsibilities, its own relationships and patterns of social action, and its own ethics. Since they are involved in the political process, religiously committed politicians learn the terms of the political struggle and operate in a social space different in every way from that of the religious sanctuary, and on assumptions made by men whose concerns are defined by quite different priorities. The politicians of other, non-religious parties become their reference group to whose expectations and standards they must respond. In such conditions, the original vision of altruistic service may be difficult to maintain.

Of course, some religionists have learned this kind of political behaviour even within their own religious bodies. In all hierarchically organized and centralized systems in which there is real power at stake and even in some which are less formally structured, power struggles can occur, despite the emphasis on piety and obedience which so often characterize religion. Religious bodies have a political side, not only with respect to the secular society, but also in their own internal management and public self-presentation. The more centralized and formally organized, the more pronounced such a political aspect is likely to be. It was perhaps most conspicuous in the Roman Catholic Church. Since that church was so heavily involved in the legitimation of secular power, the secular power acquired an interest in maintaining the spiritual monopoly of the Church and in the credibility of the Church authorities: at the apex, religious power and secular power were mutually reinforcing in the promotion of bigotry, intolerance and religious persecution.

IKEDA: You are quite right to say that religiously committed men who participate in politics run the risk of jeopardizing their principles or of being contaminated by lust for secular power. And this danger pertains not only to individual human beings, but to whole religious organizations as well.

A still more pressing danger today, however, is that politicians of religious convictions may lose sight of the goals that all political parties and politicians ought to strive to attain: peace and the welfare of the people. I believe that these goals can only be achieved on the basis of a spirit of compassion. I realize that cynics will deride the very idea of politicians who resist the temptations of power in the name of the general welfare. I know that politicians of this kind are very hard to find. Nor has a shift in political system from despotic monarchies to more liberal elected democracies – whether of the direct American variety or the party kind as found in England and Japan – resulted in ideal, altruistic politicians. Quite the contrary, modern political systems have led to tragedies more horrendous than anything known under the despots of the past.

The key to the problem is the inner spiritual revolution, both of the public and of the politicians. In our Buddhist view, the accomplishment of this tremendously difficult inner self-perfection is to be achieved by what we call the human revolution. While knowing that the self-perfection process may require a lifetime, we insist that everyone must make the effort and that if everyone does so, altruistically oriented political parties, enthusiastic for the good of their people and immune to the allurement of personal power, are possible. (Although it is independent from our organization, Soka Gakkai, the political party called the Komeito, which we Soka Gakkai members support, is dedicated to peace and the general welfare and to politics, not for power, but for the people.)

PART III

The Problems of Organization

Fellowship

IKEDA: Apparently the most familiar characteristic of the organizations of religious sects is a feeling of togetherness with the group. From personal experience, I know that this feeling cannot be ignored. The traditional oneness inspired by family and geographical relations has now lost much of its strength. To replace it, people try to form ties on the basis of common interests or proximity, but the resulting sense of communality has none of the unifying power generated by common religious faith. How can this be explained? My own opinion is that religion reaches the deepest levels of human life and that religious activities create a sense of togetherness by conquering all superficial differences among individuals.

WILSON: Religious sects generally appear to fulfil for their votaries the important function you describe as the feeling of togetherness. Whatever the diversity of their ideologies and despite their very wide range of organizational structures, sects in general demand a high investment of individual commitment, provide a strong sense of identity for those who belong, and involve these participants in a community that draws together the like-minded and creates a primary focus of allegiance with more than merely earthly or temporal implications. Sects certainly command more persistent and unequivocal support than do groups that arise simply as interest associations. Trades unions and property-owners' associations are vehicles for those who have one specific, often narrow, instrumental purpose in view. They entail no personal commitment, no sense of attachment other than what one can "get out of" being in the movement or what can be achieved in a quite material sense by unity of action. Such unity is brittle and purposive; it rests on a very different basis from the diffuse and pervasive sense of unity of the sect.

IKEDA: A sense of unity with something is important to human beings, and religions derive most of their influence over the human mind from teaching how to achieve union with the profoundest, most fundamental origins of the universe.

Of course, the human being is born into the world as an isolated individual. The entire process of maturation is one in which the characteristics of the individual are manifested and fulfilled. Yet, since individualism can be so lonely that it leads to despair, human beings long for a sense of togetherness with something inclusive and fundamental. Though it is impossible to return to the womb, religions teach that it is possible to return to communion with universal origins. Because it is instinctive to hope for such union, human beings inevitably turn to religions that promise it.

Interestingly the word *religion* derives from Latin roots meaning to tie again; that is, to re-establish bonds with the ultimate. The Chinese characters with which the Japanese word for religion *shūkyō* is written mean teaching about the origins of things.

Although tribal cults confine themselves to a prescribed realm, religions like Judaism, Christianity, Islam and Buddhism are concerned with effecting unity between their believers and the entity they conceive as behind the whole universe, whether it be a creator God, as in the Judaeo-Christian tradition, or a law, as in Buddhist philosophy. It is usually believed that such union establishes proper balance between the isolation inevitable for the individual and communion with a greater entity and that this balance alleviates the insecurity of feeling alone. Fellowship in a body of people who believe in the same ultimate entity further reduces the insecurity of the individual and creates goals that are, as you say, more than earthly or temporal.

WILSON: The character of the bonds of relationship that prevail within a sect reflect the strength of the transcendent goals of a deeply committed community. Like those goals, the bonds become total, over-riding and all-encompassing. The sect is not just an association of the like-minded: it moulds the minds of its constituents, shapes their moral apprehensions, and conveys a sense of transcendent purposes that pass beyond precise specification and that collectively become something more than the mere sum of the purposes of the individual adherents. The sect tends to become a surrogate community. As such, it is all the more vigorous precisely because the natural communities of past history, of the times when men lived their lives solely at local level, have now largely broken down. The fellowship of a sect is not merely one set of relationships among many, within which a given individual may participate. Rather, it is an all-determining involvement, in relation to which all other life activities and associations are themselves measured. The strength of the bonds prevailing among sectarians may often be reinforced by family and kinship allegiances, of course, but there is abundant evidence that, when religion and kinship conflict, sect allegiances are often stronger.

In the advanced countries of the world, natural communities have virtually ceased to exist. The process of urbanization, the increased mobility of modern populations, and the reorganization of economy and industry at the societal level have steadily undermined the strength of local communal life. Other social institutions have ceased to have the local community as their obvious locus and have become increasingly integrated at the societal (usually the national, but sometimes even the international) level. Politics, law, education and recreation are all departments of life in which such a process might be easily illustrated. Mass markets and mass communications now treat even those who remain as villagers as if they were a mass public. In consequence, the old communities have lost their vigour even where they continue to exist, and with the vigour have gone the intrinsic values of local allegiances and the strong reinforcement they provided for individuals. Even entertainment is increasingly organized in ways that make it less dependent on local effort and local associations, and all of this means that, in their emotional responses, and in their sense of kinship and obligation, men, even though they live closely together, acquire a sense of being further apart.

IKEDA: As you may have noticed in your visits, modern Japanese certainly live very much apart and have been growing farther and farther from each other since the end of World War II, and especially since the period of high-rate economic growth that took place in the 1960s. In big cities like Tokyo and Osaka, huge numbers of families live in blocks of flats without knowing the names and occupations of their neighbours. Sometimes school children of the same age form a link among mothers in an apartment building; but husbands, who usually work till late, take no part even in this meagre community life.

The situation was different in the past. Traditional wooden Japanese architecture is much more open than the modern apartment block. People aggregated in smaller numbers and in more manageable community units.

Families knew their neighbours, and people freely borrowed from each other when the bean paste or soy sauce had run out and it was inconvenient to go shopping. The flood of urbanization and great modern mobility bring people together from all over the nation, to live for a period in homes and apartments that are virtually no more than places to sleep, and then perhaps to move on to another city or neighbourhood where they are as much strangers as ever.

In other words, people today do not take root in any one place long enough to develop themselves as total persons. They perform as cogs in the wheel on the job and return at night to houses, not homes. It is difficult to estimate the depth of mental insecurity and irritation that life without community contacts engenders.

WILSON: Indeed, and as a consequence of this way of life, people become more used to dealing with others as if they were mere "role performers", rather than as total persons. Thus, even for those who live in what appear to be communities, the strength of communal life has been sapped by the diffusion of values and attitudes that are modelled on quite different patterns of association from those of a real community. But in the religious group, the nature of these primordial ties of human affection can still find appropriate expression.

We may note that not all religious bodies provide a sense of deep communal involvement. In the West, certainly, the larger established churches and the major denominations, while they may contain within themselves cells of dedicated religious specialists (of which monastic communities are the major examples), mainly serve to provide facilities for the coming together of a wider public, among whom many are only nominally, notionally or intermittently committed. For such a public, the sense of community arises, if at all, in only a dilute and attenuated form. The constituency of these religions is often amorphous, heterogeneous and only randomly and haphazardly associated in religious activities. It is a constituency often linked solely for social, traditional or sometimes political reasons, or through the force of inertia. It is among the distinctive ideological minority movements, which make stronger demands on their followings, that the more powerful benefits of communal association are most readily seen. The very strength of collective identity, and the meaning which the individual acquires for his own life from his involvement, may at times alarm those outside the group, but the benefits to participants in the sense of belonging, of being loved and of having a transcendent purpose can scarcely be gainsaid.

Community Values in the Modern World

IKEDA: Although they are weakening today, close family ties and the blood relationship were afforded the greatest significance in societies of the past. There were a number of reasons for this: natural affection, religious concepts and economy. Once, psychological elements, like love, duty and obligation, were intimately associated with economic considerations, such as preservation of the family wealth – a not infrequent cause of disunity as well as of unity. Together, these dispositions and the benefit of safety in numbers maintained the family as a basic unit of material production. Together, such families formed the local community.

Today, however, the family is no longer the basic unit of material production. In pursuit of wealth, society now turns its eyes away from the local market and the cottage industry to immense, international fields of production and trade, where there is no room for the warmth and intimate contact of the old ways.

In a sense it is true that Japan is slightly exceptional in this connection. There are still many more small farms and businesses in Japan than in other parts of the industrialized world – small concerns are said to have vanished almost entirely from the United States. It is also true that many Japanese factories operate on a somewhat family-style organizational basis. But here too great pressure is being exerted on the middle and the little men by the big men at the top. The Japanese are known for their love of belonging to groups. Perhaps this in part accounts for the enthusiasm with which they work when they have been accepted into a group, in the form of the business concern that hires them. However, for all its famed assurance of lifetime employment and security, Japanese big business does not hesitate to say a quick goodbye to employees who have reached retirement age. Here, as elsewhere, the technological age is creating an impersonal world where warmth and amicable contacts count for much less than speed, knowledge and efficiency.

The loss of community life with all it stood for causes human beings insecurity and mental anguish. What is your interpretation of the importance of the old-fashioned community? Do you agree with me that religion and membership in religious organizations can fill the human need for familiarity and warmth that was once satisfied by the local community?

WILSON: Human beings need warm emotional attachments. The human infant, after all, takes much longer to nurse and nurture than do young animals and depends much more than they, not only for food and sustenance but also for emotional reassurance, on intimate relationships with his own kind. The pattern is thus set in biological factors from the very outset of a human's life, and virtually all humans reveal, to a greater or lesser degree and at least at certain times in life, emotional dependence and the need for affective security. In the past, the local community was the normal source of such emotional and social support, and men still yearn for contexts in which they are valued, not for what they have or own, or even for what they have achieved, but simply for their own sakes. This is not to imply that the emotions involved in community life were always positive: jealousies and hatreds occurred as well as love, as in all human contexts, but generally such antagonisms were contained within a framework of on-going order and mutual dependence and were controlled by settled procedures and constraints. Local custom and myth, often embraced within what we may call a religious context of thinking, assuaged the potentially more dangerous emotions of acute fear and anguish and provided devices for the management of passions and tensions.

The modern world rests on quite different premises. Status has been replaced by contract; folkways and mores, by bureaucratic regulations; personal allegiances and loyalties, by impersonal association; total persons, by role performers; traditional customs, by rational planning; community, by organization; localism, by internationalism. The autonomy of local life has been invaded by increasing interdependence among localities, regions and even nations. People in regular social interaction with each other do not nowadays necessarily know each other as persons, but only as role-players. The structure of the system is no longer dependent on individual goodwill and affection, but only on the adequate performance of roles by well-trained occupants of each position. In consequence, rules for personal moral comportment give way to regulations of an essentially technical kind.

Religion, I believe, has its natural and original locale within the local community, where it unified men by bringing them collectively to a consideration of more solemn concerns, entities or objects, and communicated more serious purposes which transcended their day-to-day interests and activities. Beyond this, it provided men with a shared sense of necessary moral performance, of mutuality of obligation and of the wider ends of life. Although the great religions came to extend throughout much wider societies, some of them acquiring immense influence over secular rulers, it was, none the less, at local level that the indispensable functions of religion – the provision of reassurance for laymen – were fulfilled. The organization of modern social systems is no longer rooted in local communities, and religion has much less significance within these systems. It is no longer regarded as necessary for social functioning. Its rituals and doctrines are regarded as irrelevant to the assumptions on which a contemporary social system operates. Whereas religion served to solemnize and sacralize the rhythms and routines of the relatively settled agrarian life of the past, no such requirement is made for the rhythms of industrial and technological society. It is not only that modern man regards religion as irrelevant in his daily concerns – this may or may not be the case, since individuals may still manifest strong religious predilections – it is rather that the operation of the social system proceeds without specific regard to religion. For man in technological society, religion becomes a private choice, whereas for man in agrarian society it was part of the warp and woof of everyday life and social order.

It would be all too easy to derogate modern society in order to enhance the obvious attractions of traditional community. Perhaps because so many modern men lack the warmth and affectivity of community, there is a powerful disposition for us all to dwell on its evident virtues. We must, however, also remember the narrowness of life in the community, the absence of intellectual stimulation, and the dangers that men faced when they moved beyond its confines. For those within, there was security and affection: for those without, there was hostility and fear. Not to be part of the community was, at best, to be a stranger; at worst, to be an inferior being or an enemy. The old German saying, *Stadt Luft macht frei*, asserts the point that men gained an extension of freedom by getting away from the local community.

IKEDA: You are quite right. Although the old local community affectionately enfolded them, it imposed upon its members the imperative requirement to abide by a strict set of rules and traditions. Like an embryo in the womb, the person who docilely complied with that requirement felt totally safe and at home. For the man who insisted on asserting his individuality and who could not compel himself to follow the rules to the letter, the old local community could be a cruel prison.

It is interesting to reflect that, today, the person who expresses the greatest nostalgia for the community of the good old days is exerting individuality in doing so. Set down by some miracle into the community of the past, where individuality was less welcome than it is today, that same person would most likely be highly dissatisfied.

Resuscitation of the old local community would be preposterous, even if it were possible, since it would be tantamount to renouncing all the liberties modern man has won by breaking down the undesirable restrictions imposed on freedom by many of the old-fashioned political systems.

In the long run, it is neither the community nor society that must be reformed first; it is we members of the social body. Unless we become aware that society exists within, not without, us and is therefore the result of our actions, we will never attain the ideal community that is warm and human yet free as well.

WILSON: Modern man finds himself torn between the need for the reassurance provided by the local community and the desire to be treated impartially and equally in any situation. Although, in the impersonal contexts of the modern city, men are often dealt with almost as if they were instruments, as if they were mere means and not ends, at best they are treated with a certain minimal dignity as human beings and so may comport themselves in the knowledge of impartial justice for all. On the other hand, at times men wish to be treated as more than impersonal equals. They like to enjoy a context of affectivity and special regard; to be favoured; and to move among people with whom they experience deep rapport and share values, goals, mores, customs and a general world-view. While we appreciate the objectivity and fairness of universalistic ethics, at times we all demand situations in which particularistic values – particular to us and our kin or our kind – receive full expression. Predictably, as the social environment in which we lead our lives grows increasingly impersonal, as reflected in the growth of cities, bigger factories, bigger schools and hospitals, and by the extension of the mass-media, the search for warm and affective human contexts grows in urgency. As many of our social involvements become governed by integrated, rational and technological prescriptions, so men may increasingly seek the benefits of community life.

Perhaps the only agency capable of implementing community values in the modern world is the religious association, and particularly the religious association of intensely committed people – namely, the sectarian group which consciously stands apart from the ordinary and unthinking patterns of everyday life. Such groups, however, have to function within the wider social framework in which quite different ground rules for moral and social action prevail. The tension between the impersonal and secular social system, with its technical routines, and the affective religious community remains unresolved. Such communities are not easily established or maintained in the modern world, in which the demands of work, modern social, economic and political organization, education, welfare and recreation all operate according to assumptions that are antithetical to communal particularism. There has been an observable tendency for religious movements to accommodate themselves to the forms of organization and structure prevailing in modern society. The trend is clearly evident in the United States and has been referred to as a process of the internal secularization of religion. Yet, if authentic religious elements are to persist, there is, I believe, a limit beyond which such a process cannot go. Religion today faces the rationality of the technological world along an uneasy frontier of tension; as yet we have no way of knowing how that tension might be resolved.

Organization – Means or Ends?

IKEDA: Some people feel that organization is inimicable to true religious faith. Undeniably, large, powerful organizations have a way of running on their own and for their own sakes at the expense of the needs and rights of individual members. Religious organizations which develop in this way betray the goals for which they came into being.

However, organization *is* necessary. Although a few truly remarkable people with firm convictions can maintain faith unaided in the face of all difficulties, most people are too weak to emulate these stronger individuals and require the kind of support organized religion offers. I suspect that the majority of us need such help. It seems preferable to make maximum use of the advantages organizations provide, while constantly keeping in mind and striving to rectify their faults.

WILSON: Since religion is a social activity, some measure of organization is essential to its very existence. The solitary individual living a life of faith makes no impact on society until his knowledge, values and example are communicated to a wider public. Once such communication begins and once others are drawn into his religious beliefs and practice, a measure of organization occurs. There is little organization that is specific to religion in those relatively simple societies in which religious activity is implicit in the social relationships of everyday life, and in which the social community is itself a religious community. In the modern world, however, religion is of necessity separately organized and takes its place among such other major social institutions as politics, law and education. All activities have become specialized, requiring their own pattern of organization, type of facilities, rhythms, distinctive training and specialist functionaries. Religion is no exception in these respects. Whereas it was once scarcely distinguishable from many other social involvements, religion today is a separate activity, clearly distinguished from other institutions, and as such it has its own organization. Today, when every area of life has a distinct form of organization and when, apart from the major institutional activities, all manner of voluntary commitments, from ecological protest movements to folk-dancing clubs, are consciously organized, religion has had to acquire organizational form. Despite the resistance to organization shown by some highly spiritual religious leaders, all persisting religions have had to come to terms with the need for rules and regulations, no matter how minimal.

IKEDA: It is true that some highly spiritual leaders have strongly resisted organization. Interestingly enough, Buddhism tends to welcome it. Indeed, the Order, or *Sangha*, the organized body of priests and the faithful, is numbered among the Three Treasures (the Buddha, the Law and the Order) in which all Buddhists profess faith. This is because, unlike religions that are concerned primarily with post-mortem salvation, Buddhism is most interested in the development and elevation of the individual during this life and in making contributions to peace and the welfare of all society. For this reason, Buddhism has included, instead of resisting, the element of organization.

    None the less, it is often difficult to keep even organizations formed on lofty principles operating on a high level of morality and spirituality, since the act of organizing automatically involves authority, which in turn generates desire for advantages and fame. In spite of the need to ensure that only the noblest and wisest achieve them, places of great authority are frequently secured by persons whose sole motivation is the desire for power or glory. In religious organizations, vying for power at the top has a detrimental effect on the spiritual level of the general membership. It is all the more important to train members and officials in the highest spirit of morality and devotion, since large bodies of believers can neither exist nor develop unless they are organized.

WILSON: I quite agree. As a voluntary activity, religion persists only if it co-ordinates the resources – time, energy, money and action – of its votaries. Any religion has to have means of retaining support; winning new adherents; disseminating its values; training its members (and most particularly its officials); promoting and publicizing its concerns and achievements. All this implies organization. Such organization is necessarily somewhat specialized. The organizational structures that religion requires are not, ultimately, like those required for, say, a health service or a sporting activity. It is different – because more pervasive in its concerns – from a trade union or an insurance company. Religions have, therefore, evolved their own somewhat distinctive form of organization. Even if, in certain respects, there are similarities to aspects of the organization of other agencies – for example, in the increasing dependence on a trained bureaucracy of officials who administer the movement's property and legal concerns – none the less, there are also distinct differences, since the religious administrator is not merely doing a job, but is also promoting a cause that, in the nature of religious activity, is undertaken not solely for personal gratification and certainly not solely for monetary reward.

We can, therefore, recognize certain similarities in religious and other organizations, but we also need to recognize that, because of the nature of the intrinsic ends religious action pursues, there are certain distinctive differences. Over and above all such distinctions, however, is the fact that religion could not make its presence felt in the modern world without organization. All too often, its organization has been less than effective, and certainly often less effective than that of other agencies with which it competes, in certain respects, for time and interest. In part, this has been the case because religion has its roots in the past, in practices and attitudes that were organizationally scarcely differentiated from other facets of communal life. These traditional patterns themselves often became sacralized, even though they were the means of religious practice and not its necessarily sacred ends. Such sacralization may itself have been a way in which life became suffused with religious values, but it was also an impediment to the deployment of more effective techniques and patterns of organization when these evolved and were available for other social purposes. Thus, it has been a commonplace in the world to see religions that have been unable to divest themselves of ancient customs and traditional procedures of a purely customary kind, even though these have clearly been a hindrance to the diffusion of the religion's teachings.

On the other hand, what I have already referred to as an uneasy frontier exists between the arbitrary or supra-rational ends of values of religion and the rational and bureaucratic organizational techniques by which those values might be disseminated. Religion cannot be run like a business. It has no productivity level that can be assessed by strictly rational criteria. Spirituality is an indivisible ultimate that cannot be measured in discrete particles. Therefore some techniques relevant to enterprises that can be run according to strictly instrumental and pragmatic values simply cannot be adapted to the needs of religion, since religion deals in the intrinsic quality of life, which remains beyond quantitative measurement. Thus, beyond a certain point, it is impossible for religion to become rationalized in any way that modern organization demands of business concerns, or even to the extent to which such rationalization may be adapted for politics, the administration of justice, or the procedures of education or of medical welfare.

There is a continuing and irresolvable tension about the appropriate extent to which religion can be organized. Of course, that tension is felt differentially by different groups within a religious movement. There will always be those whose specific activities cause them to put strongest emphasis on the intrinsic quality of spiritual experience. Others will at times feel that spirituality may be expressed in ways that prevent them from doing what they see as best for the organization. The balance is often a delicate one.

As you so rightly say, organizations can come to subvert the ends of the spiritual system they come into being to serve. Sociologists call such a process "goal displacement" – the original religious goals become obscured by the preoccupations of maintaining a properly functioning organization and by concern for techniques, procedures and effectiveness. These purely procedural concerns may be pressed so strongly that the pristine quality of religious truth is no longer recognized as the end for which the organization was itself brought into being. The organization may then come to live entirely for itself and not for the goals for which it was established.

Clearly, modern techniques of organization and the rational co-ordination of effort become indispensable for religious movements, as for all other enterprises that seek to maintain a societal or international presence in the modern world. On the other hands, these techniques and procedures must always be seen as no more than means towards goals given from outside the rational system of the organization itself, and those goals must remain to inspire and purify the minds of persons committed to the faith. Experts in the means sometimes lose sight of the ends for which those means are employed; people preoccupied with the ultimate ends may sometimes need to be reminded about the utility of the means. Given the broad tendency in the modern world for purely instrumental and procedural values to subvert absolute and substantial values, one must perhaps emphasize the fact that the development of elaborate organization in a religious movement demands constant vigilance to ensure that the means do not subvert the ends.

IKEDA: I agree entirely that the real danger is stressing the means and forgetting the goals. I can call to mind relatively few instances in which people have become so engrossed in the goal itself that they have entirely overlooked the means required to achieve it. Perhaps the Chinese priest and founder of the Tiantai school of Buddhism, Zhiyi, (538–97) is one of these rare cases. He was totally absorbed in plumbing profound Buddhist truth and in developing a method of discipline and training in connection with it, and neglected to seek means of ensuring the endurance and prosperity of his teaching by taking it to a wider audience. As a result, no more than a century after his death, his doctrines were embraced by only a few priests living in remote mountain villages. (They were subsequently brought to Japan, however, where they have had tremendous influence.)

I suspect that cases of man's neglecting the means because of overwhelming interest in the ultimate goal have always been rare and are, if anything, growing rarer now. Lamentably, in too many religious organizations, the means – and specifically the means of sustaining one's own position of power and influence – have become all-important and they sometimes totally obscure the organization's original aims. In saying that a religious movement demands constant vigilance to ensure that the means do not subvert the ends you hit upon a truth that all leaders of such groups must constantly bear in mind.

Teaching Individuals, Not Courses

IKEDA: The problem of education is one of the most important that mankind faces. In the case of religious education, as with all other kinds, personal teacher-pupil relations almost inevitably develop into an educational organization, which is excellent as long as all the members of the organization remain guided by the desire to lead their pupils to an understanding of the material under discussion. Enthusiasm and purity of intention in this matter cannot be overemphasized.

When educational zeal flags, teachers become aloof from their students and allow their attention to be diverted by such considerations as protecting their position within the educational organization, gaining additional authority if possible, and jealously guarding what they have managed to acquire. If this occurs in religious groups, the students cease to grow and therefore fail to attain the knowledge, commitment and self-confidence needed to carry on the work of their faith. Perhaps even more serious, lack of stimulus from instructors can delude the members of a faith into believing they have already gone as far in learning as they need to go. Such complacency can spell the direst consequences for a religion. In my view – and this is an issue that has caused me much personal suffering over the years – to prevent this, religious educational organizations must keep ultimate goals before the eyes of students of all ages at all times.

WILSON: The maintenance of religious commitment is a perennial problem in all faiths. It is particularly manifest in the self-righteous attitude that arises among some who are, as we may say, inured in the faith. Some years ago I recall hearing an interview with a self-made business man, who was asked if he was religious. "Oh yes," he replied. "So you go to church a lot?" asked the radio interviewer. "Oh no," said the man, "I don't need to: you see, I'm religious already." The problem becomes more acute when a religious movement relies on its lay members to become the teachers who then disseminate its teachings to newcomers, since, as you say, if teachers become self-satisfied or preoccupied with their own superiority, the processes by which the faith is transmitted and by which new generations of members are socialized break down.

The problem arises quite widely even in the sphere of secular education. Teaching is of necessity a largely repetitive activity. There is a certain basic body of knowledge that a pupil must learn. A good teacher knows that each pupil must be brought along from the point at which he has arrived. The teacher's task is not to assert his superiority, but to recognize the pupil's potential; the pupil, after all, may one day surpass the teacher. Nor is his task to "put over" as much as he can, but rather to ask himself constantly, "How much of this can the pupil make his own?" Some pupils may need to be taken slowly and repeatedly over some of the ground, but may then break through and learn quickly. If the teacher disdains a pupil when he is slow, the breakthrough may never come. A teacher requires constant self-criticism, sensitivity to the needs of others, discernment among individuals, awareness of their differences, and above all dedication to the goals of teaching. Unfortunately, the sheer repetitiveness of the teaching work comes to bore some teachers, partly because they see themselves too much as "teaching a subject", and not sufficiently as "educating an individual". They become too discipline-orientated and insufficiently pupil-orientated. They tend to dwell too much on the overly familiar subject instead of on the challenge of the unfamiliar pupil.

To put the matter like this may be to risk sounding high-minded and pedagogic, but I believe that teachers have to remind themselves of these things in an age in which there is rapid social change in the type and quantity of information being disseminated. The modern mass media stimulate a persistent demand for novelty. They cannot risk boring their public, and so they claim to offer something new all the time. They try to persuade their audiences that what they have to offer is "the latest", the most sensational, the unprecedented and the exclusive. Against such a background – and we must remember that many, perhaps most, children, at least in Western countries, now watch television for more hours in a week than they are actually exposed to their school teachers – the feeling that teaching, meditation and ritual are in some way an old-fashioned waste of time, boring, tedious and repetitive, is intensified.

IKEDA: As you suggest, teaching a subject is much less important than educating an individual. But modern society demands that teachers offer pupils the latest from the kaleidoscopically changing spectrum of technical information; and teachers often forget about the individual needs of their pupils in their eagerness to satisfy this demand. Unfortunately, this backfires because today's latest data are outmoded tomorrow. Before much time has elapsed after a student has finished a course, he finds that what he learned is already old-fashioned; as a result he loses confidence in the educators who passed the no longer useful information on to him. (I cannot remember where I heard it, but I am in full agreement with the opinion that education is what remains when you have forgotten all you learned.)

Knowing how much of the immense amount of available information a student can assimilate determines whether a teacher's efforts are well or ill spent. Forcing a child with a weak digestion to eat too much of even the most nourishing food is likely to lead to a stomach upset instead of to sound growth. Similarly, teachers must know how much knowledge students can make their own and not, as many today seem to do, content themselves with covering a prescribed amount of material within a set period, taking no consideration of students' assimilative capacities.

It seems to me that educators too frequently lose sight of the most basic elements of their role, while desperately attempting to keep pace with the dizzying advances of technology and the equally bewildering increase in information associated with those advances. As we have noted, the most up-to-date information will be out of date in practically no time at all. Education ought to concern itself, at least in part, with things that last longer.

The Buddha's way of teaching was always gauged to evoke and develop the potential of the individual, as the following anecdote reveals. One of his close associates and disciples, Shariputra, had spent a long time trying to impart wisdom to a smith and a laundryman. In working with the first, Shariputra had concentrated on a method of meditation called Contemplating Impurities, whereby the student is taught to concentrate on the uncleanliness of the physical being and in this way to find freedom from delusions. In working with the laundryman, he had employed a system of stimulating mental concentration by counting breaths. When the Buddha noticed that Shariputra's teaching was making no headway, he suggested that he reverse his procedure and teach the smith, whose trade entailed such actions anyway, to count breaths for the sake of concentration and to allow the laundryman to study by Contemplating Impurities. Shariputra followed the Buddha's counsel, and his pupils soon found the wisdom they had sought. Nichiren Daishonin also adapted his teaching to the personality and needs of the pupil of the moment, explaining difficult, obscure doctrines to some while guiding others by means of tales and homely parables. Called teaching in an expedient fashion, this method suggests a course all educators ought to consider: respect for the individuality and possibilities of each pupil and the desire to guide each person to improvement and wisdom.

WILSON: Spiritual and moral wisdom are qualitatively different from technical knowledge. Technical procedures are constantly being superseded, and long years of experience in the technical field, which was so highly valued when industry was a matter of craft skills, is today less important than knowledge of the latest technological devices. Indeed *long* experience may even be a handicap: the experienced man becomes, in the technical sphere, a *has-been*. In contrast, moral wisdom and spiritual awareness are not subject to these processes of social change in the same way. They are only slowly acquired as the individual matures. There are no quick methods and electronic gadgets like those that constantly supersede one another in the technical sphere, by which a man may gain moral sense and humane values. There are no effective electronic calculators for the moral calculus. In a world increasingly dominated by technology, the idea of necessarily slow processes of socialization and the cultivation of a moral self becomes more alien to many people. We live in a world with a profound imbalance between the technical and the moral. In such a situation, all manner of dubious agencies arise offering short cuts to wisdom, mastery, intelligence, and emotional and mental health. That they are spurious must be recognized when we remember that these personal attributes grow slowly and must be patiently planted in the individual personality and cultivated by dedicated teachers. These things cannot be bought like a suit of clothes to be put on at will, they must be part of the man himself.

The congeries of influences arising from the media, from advertising, from technology and from the purveyors of quick-cure nostrums make the task of the teacher more difficult to perform. However, these are only the external threats to his commitment. You mention the internal ones – the fact that teachers are prone to develop vested interests in the perquisites of the role and jealousies about status and authority. Maintaining the freshness and the dedication of teachers appears to require first the intensive socialization of those who will later become teachers. Their future role must be anticipated from the outset, and the teachers who draw this to the attention of their present pupils will, by anticipating that pupils will one day be teachers, reinforce their own commitment to do the teaching task well. Periodically, perhaps more than most others, teachers need to return to being students. Reversal of roles can be a stimulating experience, re-kindling dulled perceptions, and reminding teachers of what being a pupil is like. Perhaps the solution of the problem lies in teaching and re-teaching the teachers. Teachers need to realize that they too are still learning – sometimes from their pupils.

Organization and Commitment

IKEDA: I think we have already established the need for organization, in religion as in other fields of society, to compensate for the weaknesses of individual human beings in order to achieve generally accepted, higher goals. Undeniably, however, organizations sometimes grow so powerful that they trample on the rights of members in ways inconsistent with those goals. Efficiency of operation demands a degree of subordination and the exercise of authority. This in turn demands caution to prevent authority being abused. In my opinion, one of the most hopeful ways of making the best use of the advantages of good organization, while minimizing the evils inherent in the application of authority, is to decentralize and grant maximum autonomy to subdivisions.

WILSON: Formally structured organizations and movements are characterized by differential authority. Sometimes that authority is hierarchically arranged and finely differentiated, but we may broadly distinguish between those who exercise authority and those who are subordinate to it, between the professional personnel and the clientele, the specialists and the laymen, the organizers and the organized. Despite the primacy of overriding spiritual concerns and, sometimes, the demand that all should be equally devout, new religious movements, as they acquire stable organizational form, reveal themselves to be by no means immune to this general division of authority. However, the nature of the attachment of the adherent to a religious movement differs from that of the subordinate individual within most other bodies. In modern societies, religious adherence is a voluntary act: men may join a movement or leave it as their conscience dictates. Consequently, religious authority can operate only within the confines of commitment and consent. This implies, and the point is worth noting, that there is some special merit in making the free choice of being committed to a religion; in most religions in the modern world that very choice is in itself regarded as a spiritual act.

Thus it becomes offensive to the public, and often contrary to the laws of society, when evidence emerges of religious constraint, whether it takes the form of social or psychological pressure on prospective converts, financial exploitation of adherents or the use of the power of a religious organization for ends that are not easily identified with its explicit religious goals. The idea that men may be unduly constrained to make a religious choice, or be subject to undue influence within a movement after they have made that choice, appears to arise from the differential commitment that religion summons among men, and this becomes most evident in pluralist cultures in which religions are, in some degree, in competition with each other. Since men are differentially committed and since religions compete, some religious officials try to bolster the faith and to re-invigorate the commitment of laymen. This is perfectly understandable, and most modern religions expect, or even require, that their dedicated members, or some special department of their professional personnel, will devote themselves to diffusing doctrinal knowledge, summoning positive response, re-activating dormant members and seeking to attract new ones. The line between enthusiastic encouragement and undue techniques of persuasion or coercion is not always easy to draw, as has been evident in the many legal cases in Western countries in which outsiders have sought to prove that their kinsfolk (usually their children) have been subjected to excessive pressure in making religious choices.

Part of the authority problem within religious organizations, and particularly for religions that are in a vigorous phase of growth, is that their personnel and more committed laity are likely to be amateur enthusiasts for the faith whilst being less than wholly "professional" organizational men. That is to say, they are likely to use organizational authority in ways that are quite uncharacteristic for professionals in other organizations, in which impersonal authority is used to regulate the performance of role-players. Within religious movements, the zeal of those with some authority may exceed appropriate organizational comportment. The diagnosis of this difficulty lies in the differences in the nexus of authority in different types of institutions. In some it is frankly coercive – in prisons, for example. In most organizations it is contractual: the subordinate contracts to fulfil specific obligations, usually for a specified reward. In such circumstances, the super-ordinate official knows the limits of the extent to which he can command the skills and time of the subordinate. He is not, for example, empowered to command the purely incidental and uncontracted competencies or time of the subordinate. If your junior clerk is an excellent violinist, he cannot, as an employed clerk, be required to perform musically, since this lies outside the contract. The nexus of authority in religion is of a different order. It is voluntaristic and normative. The super-ordinate may indicate what a faithful believer should do, or indeed must do, if he is to remain in good faith. All the subordinate's skills and abilities are to be used in the cause to which he has committed himself. He puts his entire self under authority in a certain sense. It is the quality of this bond of authority that renders religious organization vulnerable to disparities of religious commitment.

The problems of religious organization are intrinsic, arising from the disparate nature of the necessarily non-rational religious ends and the deployment of increasingly rational means. How are efficient organizational means to be prevented from sullying the spiritual ends? Perhaps the answer lies in the cultivation, at all levels, of an awareness of the tensions and dangers of organization. Officials need to be recurrently sensitized to the delicacy of their task; laymen need to be awakened to the difficulties under which officials labour.

IKEDA: I agree that the two needs you cite are pressing and, going still one step further, believe that mutual understanding and respect are the essential foundation on which to satisfy them.

Unfortunately, however, as organizations grow larger and more centralized, they come to regard individuals as no more than role-players in the greater machine, and therefore tend either to ignore or eliminate the aspects of their members that are not directly pertinent to roles in the organization. In smaller – especially regional as contrasted with urban – organizations on the other hand, members at all echelons of authority tend to share common experiences and backgrounds, providing a wider basis for association and thus reducing estrangement from society, into which religious groups are prone to fall, and abuse of authority. In other words, the members of the organization constitute the majority of the society in which the organization exists and, perhaps familiar with each other from childhood, realize that, even when tempted to do so, the power-greedy cannot get away with as much high-handedness as they might if they were dealing with a group of strangers. For this reason, in Soka Gakkai I strive to minimize centralization of authority while giving maximum authority to regional subdivisions.

WILSON: Decentralization may indeed be a way of preventing the ossification from which organizations often suffer, particularly if local leaders are constantly induced to invigorate an active response from local lay people. The effectiveness of decentralization can perhaps best be ensured by a diffusion to local leaders of those qualities of sympathetic involvement with, and the interpretative awareness of, the needs of the laity. A programme of systematic but humane re-dedication of local leadership appears to be a contingent requirement of such a policy. Obviously only a well-organized religious movement can actively promote and sustain such an effort, but then, the continual re-socialization and re-humanization of adherents is very much the core of what a religion is generally concerned to achieve.

Authority and Democracy

IKEDA: Whereas the Roman Catholic Church has traditionally adopted the orthodox, authoritarian, pyramid organizational structure, believing in the equality of all men in the eyes of God, Protestant sects have usually employed more democratic organizational patterns. What is your opinion of the relative merits of the two approaches to authority?

WILSON: It might not be an exaggeration to say that the accidents of history that influenced the organizational structure of the early Christian Church were perhaps the determining factors in its stability, endurance and resilience. The congregational form of worshipping groups was acquired from the model of the synagogue (not, notably, from the temple) of Judaism. This pattern of meeting regularly contrasted with the client mystery-religions of the times, in which regular congregational involvement was usually lacking. The early role of bishops and presbyters is not entirely clear, but the founder of the faith certainly did not institute a sacerdotal priesthood of the kind that gradually evolved in the early Church. Of greater organizational importance, perhaps, was the endorsement of Christianity by the state, from which the Church inherited the administrative structure appropriate to empire. Thus it acquired the capacity to encompass large numbers of adherents within one integrated system. The authority structure acquired from the empire ensured the permanence, integration, co-ordination and increasing unification of Christianity, until the great schisms broke it asunder. The Roman Church took on the socially instituted pattern of authority of the times of its establishment and growth, eventually setting into the feudal mould of medieval Europe. Bishops became the clerical equivalents of princes, and priests of knights or sergeants, maintaining a spiritual system which duplicated the pattern of secular feudal hierarchies. This was a structure of authority appropriate to the age, and it probably served the Church better than any other conceivable pattern of organization could have done.

Protestant movements generally emphasized the priesthood of all believers, and the implications of that doctrine have certainly legitimized various forms of organization. Protestantism emerged at a time when feudalism was already in partial dissolution. Incipient nation states were acquiring their early form. Individualism was finding new opportunities for expression. Changes were occurring in the pattern of the individual's own self-control and in the organization of social control, as some of its elements were increasingly formalized under the new political agency of the state. New models of personal self-awareness and of social responsibility were coming into being, both of which Protestantism very much intensified.

Since the Protestants had rejected and rebelled against the prevailing authority of the Church, they needed to invoke their radical beliefs to legitimize an alternative system of authority. The process was not altogether easy: extreme rejection of all authority led to social unrest and to scandals among the most radical groups of reformers. Eventually, the churches that arose from the Reformation adopted either a modified ecclesiastical structure derived from the Roman Church (as in the case of the Church of England) or a more democratic, if incipiently bureaucratic, system. The most radically democratic groups, such as the Baptists and the Congregationalists, emphasized popular congregational control and sought to facilitate a high degree of ordinary lay participation, at least in local church government. This policy was one in which effective co-ordination among congregations was difficult to achieve, however, and these movements remained relatively weak at the top. The Methodist Church, which emerged much later, was granted a much less democratic structure by its founder, and he and his successors often behaved with authoritarian vigour.

Reform movements in religion always have the opportunity to reject traditional styles of leadership and organization. In doing so, they have often manifested a more systematic and rational approach to the organization of the facilities and activities of religion (as the very name "Methodists" itself implies). New movements that arose in the nineteenth century often condemned traditionalism and, despite the tension between rational organization and sacred values, they found it possible to adopt more rational strategies and structures and so to maximize the co-ordination of their concerns in such matters as securing higher degrees of individual involvement, publishing, fund-raising, regulating missionary activities, training ministers, and so on. We have already discussed some of the difficulties inherent in the adoption of rational systems to religious ends, but the advantages of rational techniques for growth, order and effectiveness are apparent. The nineteenth-century movements, like their predecessors, were utilizing the secular forms of organization and the secular knowledge available in their own times. Orthodox and traditional religionists often fail to recognize that new movements – far from being merely vehicles of emotionalism and fanaticism – are often inspired by the obvious benefits of applying up-to-date techniques of organization. In eliminating or truncating ancient rites, which have frequently become encrusted with an excessive sentimentality for the sacred and invested with a (sometimes far from intrinsic) patina of sanctity, these movements have opened up the way for the adoption of much more systematic routines and pragmatic procedures.

It cannot be categorically maintained, however, that traditionalism is always a hindrance of a handicap to a religion. In the highly routinized modern world, tradition has its own special appeal for many people since, in ancient symbols and ceremonies, myths and practices, they see something which they recognize as authentic. In an increasingly programmed society, in a world in which there is a great deal of drab and routine activity, tradition appears as something curiously real, outside of, and perhaps above, the normal round, transcending the purely rational, which has increasingly come to dominate almost all other departments of life. Thus, within a religious movement, there may well be a need for the conscious maintenance of a balance in combining new techniques and rational planning as effective means for the promotion of devotion to the unique, arbitrary and transcendent values that are its ultimate goals.

IKEDA: Flexibility in one's approach is the key. People of religious conviction, like all others, are children of their times. It is only natural that, when seeking organizational models for their activities, they should choose ones ready to hand and familiar in the way that the early Christians patterned their church on the Roman Empire. If the teachings of a religion oppose the contemporary social structure, the followers of that religion will react in a revolutionary way and choose new and different forms as their organizational models. But, when its goals far transcend considerations of revolution and social structure, a religion can compromise on minor organizational points to give the people an arrangement with which they are familiar and comfortable as long, of course, as no major doctrines are violated. In other words, a religion can follow existing traditions without losing sight of its ultimate goals.

In Soka Gakkai, we have until recently adopted the traditional pyramid pattern. Nevertheless, in keeping with fundamental Buddhist egalitarianism and in harmony with prevailing social trends in Japan – especially among the younger people – we are in the process of shifting to a basic circle system of organization, ensuring total equality and solidarity. We by no means insist, however, that other related groups in other countries follow our lead in this matter. All peoples and nations have their own individual traditions and backgrounds, which ought to find a reflection in local religious organizations. In the matter of adapting systems to suit local needs, I also believe flexibility to be the most efficient approach, as long as basic doctrines are correctly interpreted and explained and as long as the maximum number of members is allowed to participate in organizational control.

WILSON: The opportunity for extensive lay participation, for some expression of the individual's own unique contribution to the movement and its goals, must be matched by mechanisms of co-ordination, mobilization and deployment of all those individual efforts. Purely devotional activities may be sustained by individuals, either at home or in local congregations. The dissemination of teaching, missionary work and publicity, and the various other activities that a modern religion must undertake if, among the abundant competing claims for the attention of individuals, it is to be heard, all need more systematic organization and effective leadership. Somewhere between the two poles of congregational quietism and bureaucratic efficiency a modern religion must balance the allocation of its dispositions and concerns.

IKEDA: I see what you mean. The elements of inner personal assimilation and of outer missionary-type work – which are found in most religions – are essential to both the individual and the group as a whole. Making sure that both goals are effectively achieved frequently means not only adaptability, but also a degree of compromise. This is why I believe that you quite justly point out the need for modern religion to balance its allocation of dispositions and concerns between what you call "congregational quietism and bureaucratic efficiency".

Put in slightly different terms, this means that an organization must allow every member to participate in all phases of its work with complete independence, while at the same time assuring a nucleus of authority capable of presenting doctrines of faith in an undistorted form which the membership will readily accept. Of course, this authority must derive neither from mere power nor formality, but from the ability to convince and to dispel religious doubt.

I return again to the need for flexibility. For it to function effectively under the widest possible range of circumstances, a religious organization must be able to combine the authoritarian pyramid structure with the egalitarian circle structure in just the right proportions to suit the instance in hand.

The Limits of Organizational Growth

IKEDA: No matter how energetically a sect may grow, it ultimately reaches its limits. How can we explain this phenomenon? What are the elements that constitute the apparently insuperable limits to the growth of religious organizations or movements?

WILSON: Our theories of the growth and decline of religious movements are far from adequate, but the phenomenon that you observe, the limitations of growth, has commanded the attention of a number of sociologists. Perhaps our best model for understanding the process is one that deals in relative growth and magnitudes. This theory suggests that once a movement reaches a certain size it begins to exhaust its potential clientele, since it has recruited a given proportion of the people whose social circumstances render them the most likely converts. Thus, a movement that finds most of its adherents among, shall we say, the lower middle class, mainly urban white-collar workers, might have difficulty in attracting significant numbers from among other social groups, such as from among those living in rural communities or from among blue-collar workers. Once a movement has acquired a certain public image with respect to the sort of people who are likely to belong, this may in itself act as an impediment to the recruitment of people of different social strata, education or social circumstances. A movement may acquire a style reflecting that of the social constituency from which it initially recruited, and this style may be uncongenial to other sections of society. The highly-charged emotional services, the spontaneity of expression, the relatively indecorous enthusiasm, and the jazzy tunes which characterized the style that many early twentieth-century Pentecostal movements adopted were a distinct disadvantage when those movements sought to recruit clerical workers, whose life-style was more sedate and whose training demanded that they control both spontaneity and any strong feelings which they might have. Other movements came up against other social barriers, including differences in ethnicity, status, education and even the off-putting effect of a relative preponderance of one sex in their ranks (as in the case of Christian Science, which has always had a highly disproportionate number of women members).

IKEDA: There can be no doubt that initial impression plays a prominent part in public reception and consequent growth of a religious movement. Soka Gakkai began its work in keeping with the Buddhist teaching of compassion and salvation for the poor. Later, when our mission extended to people who were comparatively better off than the very poor, we encountered an enlightening phenomenon. Some people who were interested in the faith we profess hesitated to make their interest known because, convinced that Soka Gakkai was an organization solely for the impoverished and the sick, they were afraid that association with us might cause friends and relatives to despise them. Fortunately, today, while we still believe in the importance of saving the poor, many people from other strata of society participate in our activities and the old image of our group is fading. Now the majority of our new members are students or young people seeking a faith that can serve as a foundation on which to build the rest of their lives.

Instead of being associated exclusively with any one single aspect of society we hope to conduct our missionary work in a balanced way that will reach the poor and suffering as well as those in more fortunate circumstances.

WILSON: The theory that a movement's first public image sets limits on its future expansion presupposes that society itself is considerably differentiated and that these differences, which arise from the basic economic and technical structure of society, affect not only the kind of world-view men find congenial, but also such matters as their patterns of sociation, the range of their sentiments, their relative capacity to control or express their emotions, and so on. Certainly, in the industrialized world these differences have been evident in the past. They may, of course, diminish in societies that become more technological in character, in which there is more radical economic and social equality and in which educational and cultural differences are eliminated. In such circumstances, the theory would, of course, need considerable modification, if it were to survive at all. For the present, we may simply note these assumptions and see how far the theory takes us.

If we can define the social constituency that serves as the potential recruiting ground for a movement, we can say that, up to a certain point, each new convert a movement gains improves its prospects of gaining others. Eventually, however, a point is reached at which it has already drawn in a sizeable proportion of the potential public; thereafter each additional adherent will be secured only with increasing difficulty. The exact point at which this occurs must depend on a wide variety of factors, relating to such things as the racial, cultural, class, status, educational and other social characteristics of the population at large. The general social climate (for example, the extent of religious toleration and the incidence of secularity); the range of effectiveness of competing organizations, both religious and secular; the character of a movement's teachings in their specificity to a given culture or historic period; these are also determinants.

Even within a well-defined constituency, no movement will capture everyone or, perhaps, even a majority. Many individuals may be non-joiners. Others may already be involved in other religious movements and may be held there by kinship ties or other extra-religious loyalties. Some people, despite their own social circumstances, may be inclined to embrace the ideas or religions of other sections of society. Some may be committed to secularism. There will also be the inert, the over-extended, the feckless and the indifferent. Given all these considerations, which we must take as normal, a movement may, even if it commands a not very large minority of its designated constituency, count itself a success.

In the case of most movements that have links to the prevailing cultural tradition, it is kinsfolk of existing members who – in Western society as well as in Japan – are most likely to be recruited. Even movements that publicize their activities widely and deploy their members to take the message to relative strangers (by calling at doors, visiting workplaces or stopping strangers in the street) still depend to a very considerable degree on the recruitment of members' kinsfolk for the gains that they make. Within such a potential constituency, other loyalties are called upon to reinforce the appeal of the religious teaching. Obviously, this area of growth has its own limitations. The individual member soon canvasses his kinsfolk, and those most susceptible – his children – mature only slowly. Without some outside recruitment, the rate of growth would fall steadily once all the kinsfolk had been contacted. There is another tendency affecting the process. Those who belong to a religious movement are increasingly likely to choose their friends and perhaps their marriage partners from those already within the movement, thus consolidating religious solidarity but reducing the range of outsiders and thus potential converts. Outsiders may know about the movement and may join in building a wall of insulation between themselves and its members. The lines of social influence weaken, and the edges of the movement begin to set.

Any such model of the limitations on religious growth must allow for contingent factors. The contours of this loosely stated pattern may suddenly be broken, for example, by an unexplained wave of revival, by deliberate changes in policy or strategy or by the recognition of a newly discovered relevance by some previously uninterested section of the public. Such adventitious, episodic developments can be explained, not by a general theory, of course, but only by a detailed historical analysis of each case. After a period of growth, or of renewed growth, a movement may settle down to dependence largely on internal recruitment (from the children of members), as has been a typical development for many religions, at least in their "home territory". Internal growth and recruitment account for the normal expectation of development of most religions for most of their life-span, not taking into account any rise in numbers as a result of deliberate external missionary work. (Christian mission enjoyed, for most of its success, the advantage of being the religion of the technically more advanced people and of association with imperial power.) This consideration apart, the sudden outbursts of energy that usually mark the beginning or some early stage of a religion's history are difficult to sustain for periods of long duration.

IKEDA: I believe that the story of Soka Gakkai's growth in Japan is one of those developments – perhaps adventitious, perhaps not – that fall outside your general theory because it includes at least two different kinds of development at different social levels.

For more than a decade after the end of World War II, under the leadership of our second president, Josei Toda, Soka Gakkai grew explosively. Thereafter the pace, while remaining steady, slowed down. I sponsored the slowdown for two reasons. First, it seemed desirable to avoid the public friction that might arise from overly vigorous missionary activities. Second, the time had come for us to accompany our growth campaigns with attempts to fulfil and enrich the lives of individual members and the functioning of our entire organization.

During the following period of structural and theoretical ordering, our membership seemed to have stopped growing. Actually, however, growth continued at a regular, moderate rate.

When we later entered a new phase of development, members of a class of society different from the one that had been the major source of our original membership began taking part. Although, this time, the pace of growth was slower, the circle of people endorsing our movement steadily widened. In our first growth phase, we had frequently encountered antagonism from outsiders. In our second growth phase, however, many people who are not part of our membership none the less understand the ideals and appeal of our movement. Indeed, the number of such people is many times larger than our actual membership. As the years pass, many of them will come to take an active part in our work, and many others will support us from the sidelines. The old antagonism has not completely vanished; but we are greatly encouraged to see that, as the people who oppose us grow fewer, our supporters grow more numerous.

Social and Cultural Activities

IKEDA: In the past, Buddhist temples used to occupy an important place in the social life of the community in Japan, as churches apparently do today in the United States. Often, nowadays, such is not the case, although those religious organizations which offer a wide range of social and cultural activities are warmly regarded by the people. What is your opinion of the optimum relationship between cultural activities and guidance in religious faith?

WILSON: In time past, the local congregations of the major religions were often the dominant agencies of communal activities. They organized or superintended a wide range of social work, providing education for children, alms for the poor, hospitality for travellers, solace for the bereaved, care for the sick, and cultural and social participation for the community at large. Problems have arisen for all such religiously sponsored endeavours, however. There is a tendency for all long-sustained activities promoted by religious bodies to become sacralized, to acquire a certain intrinsic sanctity by dint of the association. The very methods and styles that religious agencies employ tend to become credited with intrinsic merit. This often comes to mean that the communal, personal and even amateur character of such ancillary activities and commitments are prized both for their affectivity and as establishing a sacred norm for all such endeavours, even when they are not particularly efficient. Yet, as other, secular agencies arise in the fields of social work, culture and recreation – sometimes as government responsibilities – so the contrast of the affective amateurism, on the one hand, and of clinical, impersonal professionalism, on the other, becomes pronounced. Amiability and personally felt concern are measured against rational use of resources and impressive records of achievement. Affectivity is contrasted with effectiveness.

Religious bodies which maintain local or sometimes antiquated forms of social, cultural or recreative activity find it increasingly difficult to compete with governmental and commercial agencies, which in the welfare states of the West, at least, often operate with lavish budgets and up-to-date technology. In welfare work, religious bodies often operate on the fringes in areas in which state action is neglected or where it presents peculiar problems: such is the welfare activity of the Salvation Army, with its cheap hostels and help for those who do not fully qualify for state assistance. In cultural pursuits, religious bodies face the commercialism of the entertainment industry, which is uninhibited in exploiting man's baser instincts and in satisfying primitive appetites of lust, aggression or greed. Even in less noxious pursuits, religious bodies which lack resources or professional advice cannot easily compete. In a pervasive climate of hedonism, in which novelty, sensationalism and sensuality are much vaunted, what they offer may often seem tame and unexciting. Religious bodies may also suffer from being suspected by some of promoting cultural and recreative activities as ways of winning new converts.

In their wider charitable endeavours, the larger, better-organized religious movements tend to concentrate on relatively impersonal endeavours through specialized agencies. Their propaganda emphasizes the element of personal responsibility and the fellowship of man, but there is little real communal involvement in the rational, impersonal and sometimes bureaucratic operations. In the West, at least, the major religious denominations do not feel much continuing responsibility for the cultural and recreational opportunities of their members; and even in the field of education, denominational schools are steadily giving place to the provisions of the state. Not only do these denominations not provide much in the way of distinctive events and facilities of a cultural or recreational kind, but they also rarely see the need to offer specific guidance to their members about the extent to which they should participate in secular culture. Most religious movements disapprove of pornography and of entertainments that cater to the baser appetites, but there is rarely unanimity, even among leaders, on such matters as blood sports, the martial arts or even gambling. Abstract guidance, such as the counsel of "moderation in all things", is perhaps as near as many religions now come to providing counsel about how their members should negotiate the secular culture.

Sectarian movements often, but by no means always, adopt a much more restrictive moral stance, disapproving of many manifestations of secular culture and recreation, and sometimes even of education. In some cases, there is disapproval of any activities which might compete with religious allegiance; in others, there is an embargo on activities which, although considered to be intrinsically unharmful, would involve the sectarian in undesirable association with outsiders. For these last-mentioned groups, making one's own entertainment is acceptable whilst similar activities with non-members is not. Such groups sometimes also reject state welfare provisions in their preference for self-help and complete dissociation from the world.

The reaction to non-religious activities of a cultural or recreational kind varies greatly between religious bodies. The major churches offer only very general guidance on such matters, and whilst many sects adopt a restrictive posture, others utilize just such secular pursuits almost in the spirit of public relations. Thus, the Mormons receive extensive publicity from the tours organized by the Salt Lake City Tabernacle Choir and from its recordings, as well as from the promotion of sports, including ballroom dancing. Christian Science earns considerable prestige from its publication of a secular daily newspaper in the United States. No one becomes an adherent of such a movement because of its cultural enterprises, of course, but such activities bring public acclaim, and reinforce the organizational loyalty of existing members by giving them "something to cheer about".

Authoritarianism

IKEDA: The exercise of authoritarianism in religious organizations can stifle free debate and creative thinking and thus lead to debility of faith and total devitalization. All mankind loses when a religious faith of outstanding quality and vitality is marred in this way. What is your interpretation of the origin of religious authoritarianism and how do you think we can combat it?

WILSON: The implicit tendency to become authoritarian probably derives from the typical claim made for a religion that it has transcendent authority for the truth of its teachings. In Christianity, the purported authority of God or of his Holy Word has often been invoked to justify the demand for complete obedience to whomever proclaimed himself to be invested by that authority. The claim to possess absolute truth easily became the claim to command absolute obedience. Religious leaders have often invoked the teachings they proclaimed, or the God in whose name they spoke, as the source of their own authority. In some cases, for example in that of Roman Catholicism, the Church is built on authoritarian lines: absolute obedience is assumed. Nor, despite their commitment to some measure of democracy, have Protestant groups escaped authoritarianism. What has sometimes been called "working-class authoritarianism", the demand by the lower classes for strong leadership, was a marked characteristic of early Methodism under the autocratic rule of Wesley and of his successor, Bunting. In that movement a democratic soteriology, according to which anyone might be saved and have an assurance of going to heaven, was conjoined with an autocratic polity within the Methodist Church itself. Even at the local level, band-leaders exercised considerable power, and perhaps only the division of functions and interests between trustees who governed local chapels and the relatively temporary ministry of those who preached in them saved Methodism from ossification into a thoroughly authoritarian movement. Even among the supposedly highly democratic Quakers, where no formal ministry existed, a pattern of strong informal leadership evolved, and the same phenomenon occurred in some branches of the Brethren movement. These cases, and others, could be documented, but perhaps their lesson is fairly readily seen.

Authoritarianism appears to arise because people demand certainty about ultimate religious truth. Therefore, they see contradictory or deviant teachings as misleading and even threatening, since these teachings might lead men to perdition; hence, there is a demand for the suppression of heresy and false doctrine. To be certain about what is properly prescribed, people demand that religious authority be fully legitimated and it must brook no rival. Supernatural authority purports to transcend all other claims to authority. Because of their profession of such authority, religious movements, more effectively than any other type of social organization, derive justification for authoritarianism in matters that go far beyond the strictly spiritual sphere. Authoritarianism should not, however, be seen merely as the exertion of power by leaders. Within wide sections of the population, there is undoubtedly a demand for certainty and clarity, and a desire to have issues set out in an authoritative way. Reverence for learning, for organizational ability, for competence, and above all for the capacity to induce awe leads people not only to accept, but also to expect and even to welcome firm regulation, even if at times self-interest and external control come into conflict. Since, in religion, the individual is indeed learning to reject many of the promptings that arise from selfish concerns, willingness to accept guidance and even control from leaders may be represented as appropriate self-denial and discipline.

IKEDA: I agree that authoritarianism is not solely imposed from above, but also supported and perhaps even generated from below by what you call a demand for certainty and for an authoritative way of setting forth issues. However, although a segment of the group may welcome subjugation, there is almost certain to be another segment violently opposed to it. Forcing such people to bow to authority is tantamount to inhuman subjection, which must not be tolerated.

Consequently, I think we must teach members of such organizations to have a critical eye, to realize that pleasure in subjugation to the will of others is not conducive to one's own best interests. We must constantly be on the lookout to prevent the lapses into authoritarianism to which religious groups are, as you suggest, more prone than other kinds of organizations. Being aware of this and making the necessary alterations in our behaviour and in organizational structure, if necessary, is the key to the creation of religious groups with lasting vitality.

WILSON: The elimination of authoritarian tendencies is more difficult in religious movements than in others. Clearly, the cultivation of a critical spirit, which might be encouraged in, say, a purely intellectual context, might, in a religious movement, militate against harmony, and in such movements like-mindedness and shared commitment are features that are seen as precious in themselves. Perhaps authoritarianism can be discouraged in religion only if leaders at every echelon realize that they must encourage participation and responsive interplay from those immediately below them in the movement. The diffusion of responsibility is in itself a way of hindering the development of authoritarian tendencies. The idea that each individual has a unique contribution to make, not merely in directed service, but also perhaps in ways that call for more positive initiative, promotes differentiation of activities, and this in itself impedes the formation of the characteristic pattern of authoritarianism – unified control and prefabricated mass response. Leaders may, at times, refuse to lead: they may demand discussions, suggestions, alternatives and participation. They may indicate to their followers the issues that remain open as matters for personal choice and discretion, simply invoking the enlargement of the spirit that the faith supplies as the context within which such choices are made. There are dangers in such a policy, of course. Formerly hidden divisions may be brought to the surface. Only if there is already a basic confidence and a deep-seated understanding of shared responsibilities can such a risk be run. When such a profound commitment is common, however, and when members already have a strong sense of mutual reinforcement, to use individual experience and personal competencies as complementary talents for the good of all is perhaps a technique for preventing a purely one-way flow of information and instruction that so easily feeds authoritarian responses.

IKEDA: You hit the mark accurately when you say that we can discourage authoritarianism in religion if leaders encourage participation and responsive interplay from the people immediately below them and allow each individual to make his own unique contribution. Moreover, I agree that employing individual experience and personal competence as complementary talents promoting the good of all is a useful technique in countering authoritarian tendencies.

None the less, I suspect that characteristic elements within a religion exert a strong influence on whether its followers will be more or less prone to desire, and therefore have, authoritarian control systems. Furthermore, it seems to me that the Judaeo-Christian religions are more likely to favour authoritarianism than Buddhism. Relying on the Word of God as unalterable and divinely inspired, followers of these religions, and especially the Christians, have indeed demanded certainty in matters of the spirit and have often vigorously, even cruelly, suppressed what they considered heresy and false doctrine.

The teachings of the Buddha are much more voluminous than the Bible or the teachings of Christ. However they are considered, not prophetical revelations of the will of a divinity, but the extremely wise counselling of a human being who himself attained ultimate enlightenment. The vastness of the teachings has prompted immense diversity of interpretation, which has most often been carried out in the spirit of the wisdom of Shakyamuni Buddha himself.

Buddhists believe that the teachings contain either direct or indirect guidance on all major matters of faith and that matters not contained in the teachings are, from the strictly religious standpoint, insignificant. In connection with them, diverse interpretations are as natural and as easy to accept as diversity in human appearance and personality.

Buddhists have often actively stimulated debate and polemic among sects who interpret the teachings in different lights. Interestingly enough, in Japan and China the loser in such debates agreed to accept the interpretation of the winner; representatives of secular authority attended the discussions to make certain proceedings were carried out in a just fashion – a very different role from that played by secular authority in Western church councils, if my understanding of them is correct.

I am not trying to give the impression that authoritarianism has never found a place in organized Buddhism. It has. However Buddhists have, I think, given greater priority to the teachings and to wisdom and morality derived from them than to individual interpreters who might tend to become authoritarian. The few instances in which traditions of reverence have attached to individuals are exceptions to the rule.

Missionary Work

IKEDA: Missionary work is an indispensable part of religion: a person who believes that his religion teaches a good way of life feels that keeping this way to himself is selfish, therefore wrong. Ways in which religions are propagated vary from authoritarian enforcement to humble missionary teaching. The missionary work conducted by the organization to which I belong depends on person-to-person contacts and dialogues for the sake of a revolution in the awareness of the prospective member. We employ very small discussion groups at which people share common experiences. Though our method may seem roundabout, it preserves the flame of enthusiasm, since it depends on the strong self-awareness and spirit of faith of each individual. What are your opinions of these three ways of engaging in missionary activity?

WILSON: As you say, mission is implicit in religion, even if there are religions that are selective about prospective recruits (as in the case of ethnically-based religions such as Hinduism and, for many centuries, Judaism, as well as some of the contemporary movements among black peoples). To convert eligible outsiders is a strong religious disposition, and, indeed, the function of conversion is not merely to bring in new members, but also to reinforce the faith and commitment of the man who engages in missionary work.

In the modern world, the possibilities of authoritarian religious coercion have considerably diminished. Modern states no longer regard religion as an important adjunct to political power and are becoming increasingly indifferent to the religious predilections of their peoples. Although there is, at times, suppression of particular sects, the enforcement of religion from above has generally diminished even in trenchantly Catholic or (with one or two exceptions) Islamic countries. Many rulers have, no doubt, realized that although outward conformity might be induced by coercive means, the effective operation of religion depends upon the voluntary commitment of its votaries. Compulsory indoctrination can at best have only very limited and partial results in the dissemination of religious belief and practice.

My own studies have convinced me that the most effective techniques of missioning in the modern world are not by mass rallies. Some organizations in the West still follow this pattern of disseminating their teachings. For them, rallies are occasions on which considerable emotion is expended and converts are encouraged to express their feeling spontaneously and unreservedly whilst under the influence of the evangelist's words. The result is often dramatic, and the occasions are often highly memorable for those who attend. Yet the effects of this kind of missionary activity are generally short-lived. The stimulus to proclaim oneself to be convinced is disproportionately easy compared to the effort required to maintain conviction and to lead the life that conviction is supposed to entail. There is too little socialization before the initial change of heart and mind is accomplished, and too little awareness at that time of just what such a commitment would demand were it to be taken seriously. Even given elaborate after-care of the converted, the vast majority of those who declare their decisions in such missionary campaigns slip back into their old attitudes and abandon their newly endorsed beliefs. The life in the churches they join is, of necessity, more settled and less exhilarating than the original missionary meeting at which they were supposedly converted, and disappointment at this lack of exhilaration leads many to eventual disaffection.

Nor do impersonal appeals through the press or the mass media appear to be successful in really effecting profound processes of religious change. In the United States, many television evangelists have considerable success in gaining audiences and in persuading them to donate money to sustain their programmes. Yet, it is difficult to say how much of this activity, undertaken in the name of religion is, in the last analysis, of much religious significance or whether it is at all effective as missionary activity. We do not know whether such programmes often, or ever, convince the previously unreligious or convert people from other religious persuasions. Indeed, there is reason to think that these television preachers reach only those people who already share at least their general convictions, and who are gladdened to hear views like their own put forth through the media. The contribution of a donation may be less an earnest of religious faith than a way of buying off a bad conscience for having done little either to spread religion or even to lead a particularly moral life. We may even question whether this form of activity is to be regarded as missionary work.

Personal contact certainly appears to be the most effective technique of mission, whether it occurs between acquaintances or total strangers. At this level, the richness of individual experience, the talents of the missionary and the personal qualities and resources he commands may all be deployed to aid the process of communication. For some people, the mere fact that a stranger approaches them, appears to care, takes time to talk and seeks to share something is enough to stimulate an initial, positive response. Subsequent induction into a group of potential friends through personal introduction reinforces the effect. In a world in which everyone learns to grow cynical, for example, about advertising, the fact of personal genuineness may in itself be so refreshing that the message is more adequately communicated even by a relatively ignorant missionary than by a technically adroit media advertisement with absolutely authoritative information. When lay members are given responsibility for missionary endeavour, their own dedication is likely to be sustained at a higher level. The missionary activity functions to strengthen the integration of the movement and to induce like-mindedness among those who belong to it.

Studies that I have conducted in European and African countries indicate that movements which emphasize personal contact in their missionary work and which regard active missioning as an obligation for all members have a much higher rate of growth than those that rely on the activities merely of paid evangelists, mass meetings, rallies and advertising. Obviously, such work, which begins with the intimation of friendliness, prospers best when further personal contact with members confirms these early impressions of helpfulness, warmth and love in the newcomer's experience of the movement. Small groups, whether for discussion, study, prayer or even for social activities, clearly reinforce the possibilities of stimulating wider personal relationships. Religious loyalties are then strengthened by personal and social ties, and this augurs well for the wider success of the religious organization.

IKEDA: The Buddha relied on the small group for discussion, study and other activities. It is true that he sometimes addressed vast assemblies, but these were always gatherings of already-converted believers who wanted to learn more. In carrying out missionary work, he relied on the person-to-person discussion method because, since each person thinks and reacts in a different way, each requires a distinctive, individual approach. Talking directly to an individual can stimulate the intellectual and emotional change that slowly, through steady application, revolutionizes the person from within. Mass religious rallies cannot do this.

Notably emotional creatures, human beings may be swept away by the mood of the rally and inspired to profess devotion or adopt a new faith. Professions of this kind are superficial, like cosmetic make-up, and reveal no profound underlying spiritual change. When the paint has been washed away, the old blemishes remain. Realizing that this is true, we of Soka Gakkai follow the precedent set by the Buddha and his disciples, by Nichiren Daishonin and by Tsunesaburo Makiguchi and Josei Toda, the first and second presidents of our group, by conducting missionary discussion meetings of no more than ten or so individuals and which we consider among our most important activities.

Where Reason Fails

IKEDA: Although the spiritual appeal of religions depends on inherent elements defying rational explanation, in missionary activity, it is important to make doctrines as clear as possible so that the uninitiated can grasp their meaning. There comes a point in these matters, however, beyond which reason cannot go and where doctrines and belief must be accepted on faith. My own conviction is that, at this point, new converts must be shown the limitations of reasoning and the necessity of allowing faith to take over where reason fails. How do you interpret the relation between reason and faith?

WILSON: It is clearly necessary for the missionary to take prospective converts as far as he can by virtue of common reason and the fruits of experience. In the modern world in particular, people are used to having things explained to them, and there is a widespread general expectation that rational explanation, empirical evidence and pragmatic testing will be forthcoming as the basis of knowledge in all departments of life. Religion, as you say, transcends these desiderata, and in all religions there is a point beyond which people can be convinced only by making what is often called "the leap of faith". It remains something of a sociological and psychological – as well as spiritual – mystery that some individuals successfully make that leap, while others can go only as far as empirical proofs will take them, finding the step beyond too difficult or the prospect beyond it insufficiently compelling. Despite the tendency for modern society to be increasingly rational in its organization, ultimately the values that prevail among men are arbitrary preferences. Our traditions and our cultures are justified only by their previous and continuing existence; the artistic forms we admire are approved almost entirely because they are already familiar. These things, and much else in our way of life, cannot be defended on rational premises. We confer meanings on many of these arbitrary items and endow them with sentiments. In turn, our further meanings are moulded from them. At best, our preferences can be defended by saying that it would be irrational to abandon them and that any alternatives would be equally non-rational and would represent arbitrary choices without even the advantage and legitimation of tradition.

If society cannot be totally rationalized, it is even less possible for the individual human life. Human dispositions; the search for bodily gratifications; human sexuality; our long-term dependence as infants; our need for affection as children and association as adults; our awareness of decay, the passage of time and death are all biological data that must be accepted and accommodated as arbitrary, given aspects of the human condition. I call these things arbitrary because they are substantive items that do not arise as the product of deliberation and reasoning. Around them, men must build their philosophical or religious theories. In consequence, these theories cannot be entirely rational either. Of course, many people may live life relatively blindly, never accepting or understanding any general world view. However, for most intelligent people, at some time in life, and for some people for most of their lives, these issues and others pertaining to such matters as suffering, human inequalities, ethical action, the source of human virtue, spirituality, inspiration and epistemology demand interpretation within a wider framework.

Not everyone who remains actively conscious of life's contradictions, tensions and uncertainties will feel impelled to accept a religious solution. Some men will remain seekers, and some will seek while young and idealistic, only to abandon that search, or a once acceptable solution, as everyday problems crowd out wider-ranging speculations and longer-term perspectives. For others, there will be the compelling or comforting leap of faith which, once made, provides a re-orientation and a new perspective, not only on those things that were the erstwhile imponderables of life, but also on the place and significance of the rational order itself. The empirical world, which bears down on practically everyone with its demands and restrictions, will acquire meaning from what has been perceived through making the leap of faith.

Although today many people recognize the limitations of human reason and perceive the anomalies and contradictions that sometimes arise from its application, none the less rational structures are increasingly imposed on modern man. It is now our normal assumption that the means to be employed for almost any purpose will be rationally justified (often by reference to the principle of cost-efficiency). Furthermore, we all acknowledge that the proximate *ends* of one rational procedure are regularly transformed into the *means* towards some further purpose. There is an infinite regress, and the final ends of the system disappear from view. In fact, of course, those final ends cannot be specified in the terms of a purely rational system, which is essentially a system of means. The final ends, were they ever to be designated, would have to be specified in some supra-rational – possibly religious – terms. This circumstance is one in which many people find themselves profoundly dissatisfied. The values of the system cease to have any substance: the only values the economic and technological order comprehends are merely procedural values. We come to know how to do things without knowing why we do them or what ultimate purpose they serve. As Max Weber perceived, total rationalization, the application of reason to everything, leads in itself to a transcendent irrationality.

There is another important contribution to man's dissatisfaction in the technological and bureaucratic rationality of modern society. Each individual is called upon to perform a specific role in such a system. Each role is a well-defined set of tasks integrated with other roles. Together, role performances contribute in a predictable and calculated way to a specific end: they are rationally co-ordinated. Role-performers thus contribute, like parts in a machine, towards the building of a rational structure of action. Whenever possible, these human functions are transferred to machines, since machines are more controllable and can be even more rationally deployed than human role-performers. Thus, human beings are induced to contribute a rational input to an increasingly rational system, the purposes of which far transcend those of the individual role-performer. Yet, the human beings who are pressed into behaving rationally are themselves men with non-rational requirements and goals. The system to which they contribute becomes cumulatively immensely and immeasurably more rational than they themselves. The end result is that man, with his arbitrary human dispositions, becomes alienated in the face of the increasingly rational order of his own making. Our modern Frankenstein sometimes terrifies us all.

Not only are there things human reasoning cannot encompass, but there are also consequences of the use of human reason from which men may understandably feel they need salvation. In our day-to-day affairs, we may frequently glimpse not merely the irrationality of a system in which all means tend to be rationally justified and which has no final ends, but also the terrible and alienating "other-ness" of such a system in comparison with the personal human dispositions and strivings of man himself. Man's need for religion may indeed arise from the limitations of his reasoning abilities, and from his need to reassert both the primacy and the ultimacy of arbitrary, given values as a way of protecting himself from the aridity of total rationality. This, I believe, might be the point at which religion can communicate with modern man – the point where reason ceases to be sufficient.

IKEDA: I certainly concur with your analysis but feel that one point deserves cautious treatment. I agree that religion can communicate with modern man at the point where reason ceases to be sufficient, but insist that maximum moral and ethical scrutiny must be exercised in relation to the irrational applications of religion. The so-called primitive religions employ ritual, prayer and magic to satisfy human desires for food, shelter, comfort, and so on. The higher religions attempt to come to grips with and control human desires and to guide man in the direction of worthwhile goals, transcending both individual irrational human goals and the goals of the immense irrationality of our totally rationally organized system.

The important thing is never to allow the inevitably irrational elements of religious goals to become licence for such totally unspiritual ends as military victory over enemies, self-aggrandizement or even sexual conquest, as has been the case on countless occasions.

Buddhism divides human existence into Ten States, six of which – hell, ravenous demons, beasts, wrathful creatures, human beings and heavenly beings – might be called the proper sphere of reason. The other four – direct auditors of the teachings, persons enlighted solely on their own and for themselves, bodhisattva and Buddha – are the realm of religion oriented towards the inward perfection of the essential being. The enlightenments and truths discovered in these four realms must be applied in dealing with all aspects of the six states in which reason can appropriately be exercised. In short, wisdom arrived at by non-rational, religious means provides goals that should be guidelines in actions suitably controlled by the reasoning faculty.

Charisma

IKEDA: Those special qualities that enable some men to be leaders of others are extremely difficult to pin down and vary, no doubt, according to the social setting and needs of the people in question. The Buddha was a human being, not a god, but he attained enlightenment to the nature of the Law behind the universe. This and his own outstanding characteristics made him a great leader and teacher to whom millions of people over the ages have paid homage as the *Bhagavat*, or World-honoured One. He undeniably possessed those traits often referred to today as charismatic.

Yet charisma is not necessarily related to the moral worth of the person possessing traits striking and attractive enough to win allegiance. Adolf Hitler, for instance, had a personality powerful enough to mesmerize the

Germans into a calamitous course of action. Human beings tend to long for powerful leaders in whom they can put their trust; but the leaders, as Hitler's case proves, are not always worthy, in spite of their charisma. I should very much like to hear your opinions on the nature and origins of charismatic powers in special relation to leadership, and the kinds of leaders human beings ought to choose for themselves.

WILSON: In the strong sense in which the word is used (rather than in the somewhat debased form in which it is applied by journalists to almost any one with a shining personality) charisma implies that an individual claims (or has claimed for him) a unique endowment with supernatural qualities. The attribution of charisma is, of course, social, in the sense that only when a man of striking personality actually commands allegiance may we properly speak of his having charisma – a man claiming supernatural powers who is accepted by no one is regarded as deranged. Charisma is an attribute conferred upon a leader by his followers: their willingness to believe in his divinity or supernatural inspiration justifies the term, "charismatic leader". At times, a public has come into being which has credited such powers to a man or a woman who, from an external point of view, appears to have nothing remarkable about him. There are cases of children, half-wits and mountebanks who have been credited with such power and who have won the allegiance of a devoted following.

Such faith in a human being reflects a level of mentality at which men find it difficult to see how their problems can be resolved except by some very exceptional person. The severity of conditions and the experience of deprivation, disaster, or trauma may induce whole populations to clutch at the idea that only an act of will on the part of a powerful man is capable of putting their world to rights. Such desperation is the birthpoint of charisma. A condition of charismatic demand arises because people see no other solution to their problem. They believe that things happen because they are "willed" and only a man, or a god, of stronger will can restore normality. Clearly, these conceptions are primitive, but I believe that in them lies the origin of charismatic leadership.

Today, most people in advanced societies distrust the idea of charisma, which is out of temper with the times. In a social system in which there is increasing dependence on rational techniques and technological devices (and technology is itself the very encapsulation of rationality), the idea of depending on the chance gifts of some inspired individual is altogether alien. Yet, at the same time, it is not uncommon for men – perhaps even for the same men who voice their distrust of charismatic leadership – to complain about bureaucratic authority, and bureaucracy (the term is used quite neutrally) is today the principal form in which legitimate authority is exercised. When people say, as they often do, "Where are the great leaders like those we had when I was a child?", they reveal the deep-seated human demand for an infallible father-figure. It is often said, too, that our contemporary politicians are pygmies compared to the giants who once peopled the political scene. What this shows is that men lust for the charismatic but find they can no longer believe in it: they can no longer confer that idea of superordinate quality on their leaders. They have come to rely on rational procedures, and they know that, compared to the complexity of our technical system, no man is remotely as capable, as knowing or as omni-competent as our computers, our data retrieval systems or our electronic devices. The message of the times is, virtually, "When so much is known, no one man can know much", and so our technological systems diminish the stature of us all.

IKEDA: No doubt what you say about the way sophisticated technological systems diminish both us and our leaders is true. However it seems to me that other factors need to be considered. Great leaders are usually called forth by circumstances. In some instances, threats from without demand leaders who can ensure the security of people at home. In other cases, internal disorder makes it essential for leaders to harmonize contending elements within. Although the world has not known total peace since the end of World War II, there has been no open conflict among the major powers of the kind that created the stage on which the great leaders of the past acted. In other words, there has been no need to guarantee safety from external threats. Moreover, with some exceptions, the major powers have already established such firm social and economic systems that internal disorders are insufficiently grave to evoke leaders of powerful will. Circumstances of these kinds partly explain why, as we rely more on rational systems and structures, we consider depending on the fortuitous characteristics of inspired, charismatic leaders totally alien.

WILSON: Yes, but this quite comprehensible distrust of the charismatic seems to offer no reason why those who do attain eminence in a given sphere should not be accorded special dignities. One may not need to assert charisma to recognize that rare qualities, great virtues, exceptional wisdom and skill may all be attained by individuals, and it seems to me to be virtually a requirement for human relationships that differences of status, acknowledgment of worth, and the differential dignity of office and attainment should be recognized and sustained. Democracy becomes a travesty trading on hypotheses that ill accord with the real world when radical equality is demanded regardless of individual differences. Were such an acknowledgment of achievement and distinction not made, were status differences not sustained, then the ennobling and civilizing efforts of mankind would go unsupported, stimulation would be diminished and an important source of support of human values would be destroyed.

Men, I believe, like to accord honour to those who lead. Recognition of guidance induces a sense of gratitude and respect. Obviously, the process can go too far, and the tendency for Shakyamuni to be deified by his later followers may be a case in point. Much the same thing happened in other religions. In Christianity and in Islam, a notion of sainthood, by no means supported by the founders of these faiths, virtually institutionalized the endowment of supernatural powers to individuals. Since differences persist in human ability, application, emotional stability and pertinacity, among many other attributes, perhaps we must accept not only that leadership is inevitable in human affairs, but also that there will always be emulation of the more successful and more advanced by those who lack the same resources or who begin their spiritual journeys at a later point in time. Emulation, esteem and the search for exemplars are surely appropriate in those who wish to learn. On the other hand, leaders should always make sure that the goals they have attained are recognizable as attainable by others. In that way, leadership remains human, accessible and inspiring, and avoids the element of the magical contained within the notion of charisma, while the respect of followers for their leaders is then appropriate and functional for their own advancement in their pursuits.

Inspiration and Organization

IKEDA: Somewhere in your writings you say that new religions have some or all of the following characteristics: stress on acquaintance with special, mystical knowledge; belief in salvation as liberation of powers within the self; belief in salvation as attainable through membership in a sacred community. Although these traits may be present in, or may be stressed by, the founders of religious organizations, they seem to become less apparent or less important in later generations of leaders whose major roles are generally administrative or connected with what might be called public-relations tasks – devising appealing slogans and so on. What does change of this kind say about the growth process of religion?

WILSON: At different stages in its development, a religion necessarily emphasizes different facets of its message. Sometimes, the message actually undergoes a process of change, but in any event, the issues that are most salient in the early days, when a following is being called into being, differ from those that need to be asserted when a movement has acquired a settled and stable body of adherents. At its beginnings, a movement is often characterized by urgency. Hopes are high, and expectations are entertained either that the movement will itself radically change the nature of society or that its emergence is itself a sign that such changes are imminent. Later, when such expectations have been accommodated to reality, the benefits of belonging to the faith are presented in a different way.

Once a movement has developed a *modus vivendi*, the administrative tasks grow in importance. There are recurrent needs, and periodic, weekly, monthly, seasonal and annual events which come to constitute a regular pattern of activities, and which, although routinized, are now stage-managed as occasions of stimulated excitement. The spontaneity of the early days disappears, and the regulated and measured commitment of officials and laymen is required to sustain a planned programme. Intensity, fervour and even excessive enthusiasm – all of which marked the early days – become less acceptable unless they can be carefully controlled. The emphasis is now on systematic, standardized and routine performances. Even access to mystical knowledge ceases to depend on the inspired but spasmodic utterances of leaders, and depends increasingly on regulated courses of study. Although faith and subjective commitment continue to be doctrinally affirmed as the *sine qua non* for salvation, objective performances, obligatory rituals and creeds, formal qualifications for membership (and hence for grace) come to be required. In the course of time, these may sometimes even become routinized and perfunctory.

Perhaps more than other social institutions, religion is always threatened by processes of attrition and atrophy. Because the product of religious activity is intangible, and because religions must supply their own objective reference points (in contrast with economic, judicial, political and, in considerable measure, educational activities, which have objective products), the renewal of commitment is a recurrent requirement if ossification is not to occur. There is a tendency in religion for all of the accoutrements, apparatus, procedures and even the rhythms of religious activity to become sacralized. In extreme cases, such as that of the Amish Mennonites, a Christian sect that has chosen to live in isolation, even the trivia of everyday life came to be seen as sacred. They came to regard even their mode of dress as of religious import, making any departure from their traditional seventeenth-century peasant costume (and customs) an act of sacrilege: thus to replace the old-fashioned hooks-and-eyes by buttons was seen as heretical. This is an extreme instance, but it illustrates a general tendency for the mundane incidentals of religious activity to become encrusted with a sanctified lustre. Functional gestures become ritualized, and objects and procedures acquire sacred symbolic significance even though their origins were purely functional. Sacralization is part of the goal of religion, of course, but it is also simultaneously a threat to the capacity of religion to inspire men to new commitment and to those processes by which their lives are infused with higher ideals.

Routinization and sacralization are sometimes associated processes. Each indicates the shift of leadership from that of the prophet to that of the men who are more concerned with system and order, whether that order be that of the priest or of the administrator. In contemporary religious movements, the phenomenon of sacralization is little in evidence. Such movements show a considerable capacity for rapid internal change, and this militates against sacralization. As they grow, contemporary religious bodies often come to reflect the patterns of organization prevailing in the wider society, which increasingly depend on the extensive division of labour. The specialized needs of fund-raising, control of property, the production of literature, the promotion of mission, public relations, and so on, force the abandonment of amateur control and its replacement by specialized technical experts. Such men tend to prefer safety, set rhythms and procedures, consistency in action and systematic planning to the impulse of sudden and radical inspiration. They make a religious organization efficient and they create a safe image, but they sometimes do so at the cost of the vibrant and vigorous spiritual expression that marks a religion's early days.

PART IV

Some Historical Perspective

Love and Conflict

IKEDA: The struggles to establish orthodoxy in the minds of as many people as possible that characterize much of the history of the world's religions have resulted in schism, faction, internal strife and mutual alienation of disagreeing parties. Buddhism too has had its share of schism. A century after the death of Guatama Buddha, the Order split into the conservative Elders (*Theravada*) and the more progressive Order of the Majority (*Mahasangha*). Later, in the Christian era, Buddhism split further into what has come to be called Hinayana and Mahayana, which have remained the two main currents of the Buddhist faith. Yet at no time have Buddhist believers attempted to use force to compel others to see their point of view. In general, Buddhism is marked by a permissiveness so great that some scholars have described its history as a triumph of heresy. Perhaps it is possible to trace this lenient attitude to characteristics inherent in India, where, as has often failed to be the case elsewhere, religion and secular power have usually seen eye to eye.

Though it advocates love as its main spiritual element, Christianity, on the other hand, has experienced repeated violent conflicts, often interwoven with disputes over secular power. Why has this religion of love been unable to promote mutual harmony and understanding among its factions? Does its failure point to the limitations of the spirit of love itself? Are there examples of sects that, after coming to the verge of schism, have reached amity as an outcome of love, dialogue and mutual understanding?

WILSON: The history of Christianity has certainly been far from peaceful despite the explicit commands of its founder to "turn the other cheek". The Church has been regularly and repeatedly recruited to legitimize warfare, sometimes explicitly in the interests of Christianity, as in the Crusades, but more often to bolster the claims of secular authorities who were eager to have spiritual, or at least churchly, endorsement of their cause. The widespread invocation of the Church to legitimize secular princes, the accumulation of secular power by the Church, and the operation at times of the Roman Church as a secular principality in its own right, all go some way to explain the extent of its involvement in warfare and in the secular quarrels of Christians. Of course, the Church might claim ancient precedents for its military activities stemming from the role of God Jehovah who, in the Old Testament, was regularly depicted as a partisan of the Jews, aiding their efforts in battle. Christians engaged in warfare have frequently invoked God throughout Christian history, and in World War I He was the object of supplication by both sides. The buckles of the belts of German soldiers bore the slogan *Gott mit uns*, while many British troops – and some priests – believed that a heavenly host of angels had appeared in the sky at the Battle of Mons to encourage the Allied armies. These are instances of secular wars in which Christianity became involved, but some wars – such as the Thirty Years War in Germany – have been fought out explicitly in the name of religion, whatever other preoccupations religion may have served to conceal. In all, such a history is a strong indictment of the failure of a gospel of love to bridle and discipline men's other concerns effectively, much less persuade them to desist from violence.

Within the confines of their own community, disputes have repeatedly arisen among Christians over explicitly religious matters. At such times, the advocacy of love has certainly failed. In part, the steady accumulation by the Roman Church of elaborate hierarchy, perquisites of office, patterns of protocol and a distinctly feudal articulation of status differences has eclipsed the simplicity of the original Christian message and created an artificial air of worldliness, pomp and antique privilege, which had little relevance to the simple counsels of brotherly love. Recurrent attempts to return to simplicity have met successive failure, and the process of institutionalism has, like a process of the hardening of the arteries, been an incurable ailment in Christian religious life. Each attempt to reassert pristine values has, of course, been fraught with tension, often leading to conflict and almost always to acrimony – even when reformist movements, such as those represented by the early Benedictines and the first followers of St Francis, have remained within the Church. There is no doubt that generations of officials of the Roman Church have been deeply preoccupied, and at times obsessed, with power. The break in the authority structure of the Church represented by the Reformation was the first significant inroad into the strength of the Roman Church, and it heralded both the gradual decline of religious power as such and the diminution of the influence of religious agencies over secular authorities. Fear of the loss of both religious and political power had inspired the repressive measures that occurred under the Inquisition, and Catholic casuists were not beyond representing their activities as acts motivated by pure love and concern for the souls of those who opposed the Church and its doctrines.

Christianity is, of course, an exclusivistic religion. From its very early days, it has been unprepared to tolerate mere equality of treatment among different faiths. It claims to have the complete, absolute and unique monopoly of truth and even though, today, it is not always as stridently asserted as in the past, this claim remains implicit in the whole *raison d'être* of the Church. In consequence, schism and heresy have been regarded as particularly baleful phenomena, impugning the sanctity of the Church and the validity of its claim to absolute truth, and consequently as representing some form of distinctly devilish treachery. The intolerance to which this position has given rise has justified the most extreme measures, including torture, imprisonment and death, for those who dared to dispute the authority of the Church or to proclaim any other than the official version of its truth – or even to proclaim the official version under auspices other than those that it approved. So great was the claim to sacerdotal monopoly that sacrilege could occur simply when unauthorized people took upon themselves tasks reserved to the priesthood, even those acts that were not intrinsically unlawful when performed by laymen. Practical intolerance is difficult to reconcile with universal charity of mind, and the Church has frequently been prompted more by its insistence on its own privileges and monopoly of function than by the counsels of love embodied in its received doctrines. One historian has described the development of Christianity as a steady development from love to law: the legalism of Canon Law eventually precluded the operation of love.

Although the Protestant reformers proclaimed a greater tolerance in religious affairs and broke the authority and the legalism of the Roman Church, they inherited the same tendency to claim a monopoly of truth; and, at times they, too, were capable, albeit in far fewer instances, of perpetrating vengeful acts imitating those of the Catholics. In fairness, it must be said of both Catholics and Protestants that it was usually the secular authorities who inflicted penalties for heresy, so-called sacrilege and schism. At the same time, both churches regarded penalties exacted by the

State against those whom they saw as their religious enemies as fully in accord with God's will, whether those enemies were Cathars or Marranos, for the Catholics; Quakers or Jesuits, for the Protestants; or merely those accused of practising witchcraft. In general, however, Protestants were less disposed to seek the utter suppression of schismatics, and the concept of heresy was less rigorously interpreted. Some Protestant states became noted in the late seventeenth century for their relative leniency in religious matters. Sects which demanded the elimination of all sacerdotal elements from Christianity and which proclaimed that laymen were no less eligible than priests to perform the sacred acts of religion tended to suffer the greatest opprobrium.

As to instances in which schisms have been avoided, some certainly exist. The Franciscans might easily have broken away from the Roman Church at an early point in their history had not counsels of forbearance prevailed. In more recent times, divergent sects have sometimes recognized that they had different and limited missions, which might at least operate in symbiosis if not in complete union, and there are instances of such recognition, at least in the missionary field, between groups as divergent as Mennonites and Pentecostals. The separation of the Methodists from the Anglican Church was scarcely amicable, but it was affected with only incidental violence and without the encouragement of hostility by the higher church authorities. The Salvation Army, which might once have become a part of the Church of England, went its own way as a separate movement after earnest conversations with the officials of the Anglican Church. These talks certainly represented a process of dialogue. Within the Anglican Church there remain fairly distinct parties that have managed to remain in communion with each other despite persistent, and in some ways far-reaching, differences in doctrine and liturgical practice, but perhaps they are held together more by commitment to a national institution than by specifically religious bonds of amity. The record of Christian divisions, however, is, as you suggest, not one in which love can be said generally to have triumphed.

IKEDA: No, it cannot be called a triumph of love. However an interesting case comes to mind in which Christian theologians and philosophers propounded a universalist theory of the nature of divinity and, in doing so, opened the door for a less exclusivist course of development. In the second and third centuries of the Christian era, Clement and Origen of Alexandria advanced the idea that the care proffered by the divine Logos was not limited to Christians but extended to Greeks, Indians and others who did not profess the Christian faith. Unfortunately, however, their idea was branded and forbidden as heresy and never enjoyed great currency in Western thought.

To a Buddhist like me, this seems a pity since the Logos, as Clement and Origen interpreted it, resembles the totally impartial Dharma, or Law, which we believe to be the truth permeating all things. In other words, I cannot help thinking that a faith based on an ideal law at work in all phenomena everywhere is likely to be more conducive to peace and harmony than an exclusivist faith based on an anthropomorphic vision of divinity.

WILSON: Of course, Christians are hoist with their own petard in such matters. Since, in the hands of philosophers, Christianity came to stake everything on its intellectual truth, propositions held to be true could not be abandoned for ideas that were more attractive, nor even for ideas that might be, as you put it, more conducive to peace and harmony. Although Christians believe (in a way which I do not) that the good and the true must ultimately converge, they have also been cautious of apparently attractive, practical, humane and beneficial proposals lest these turn out to be no more than the seductive wiles of the Devil.

Schism and Hatred

IKEDA: Religious sects newborn as outcomes of schism often strive vigorously to overcome opponent sects. Indeed, the malice entertained by two differing sects of the same religion is often more bitter than the emotions felt for each other by two entirely different religions. Why is this?

WILSON: Religious schism is indeed usually marked by intense bitterness. As you say, the hatred engendered by schism is more intense than that felt by two completely different religions with nothing in common, even though, ostensibly, the warring schismatics may agree about almost everything except one of two specific items, which are sometimes trivial in the extreme – for instance, whether it is legitimate to use musical instruments in religious worship; whether the cup used by Christians in their communion should be one cup for all or separate cups for each; whether the beverage drunk as a symbol of Christ's blood should be fermented wine or non-alcoholic. Such hatred is apparently intense because the parties among whom division occurs continue to regard each other as a significant reference group. Whereas what Muslims do has never been of much consequence for specific Christian sects since they are too far "outside the pale" to be paid much attention, what other groups of Christians do touches them more nearly. Most of all, what is done by those who until recently were among one's own religious fellowship becomes a matter of the greatest moment: it is their conduct and practice to which reference is most immediately made. That they who so recently shared the intimacy of religious ritual should now have gone a separate way stirs the passions and provokes the feeling of betrayal.

To this must be added the more general fact that it appears easy for human beings to transmute strong positive affect into negative affect. The emotions of love, warmth and fellowship are more easily transformed into negative emotions of hostility, hatred, and loathing than into merely neutral feelings. Love and hate seem to be difficult to engender in connection with persons towards whom one has been no more than neutral. For objects of love, however, sudden alienation readily induces intense feeling of an opposite kind. When tensions within a sect come to occupy the profound attention of all concerned, the ultimate outcome is certain to engender profound emotion – of renewed and intensified love when division is fully avoided or of intense hostility when division occurs. In the abundant Christian examples, charges of doctrinal error have been quite commonly compounded by subsequent condemnation of the life-styles, frivolity, and even the profligacy of persons who, till the split occurred, were embraced as "beloved brethren".

Renaissance and Reformation

IKEDA: I regard the Renaissance not as a break with Christianity, but as a time when Western civilization finally assimilated the Christian spirit of equality of all peoples in the eyes of God. During the Renaissance, the medieval Church's hierarchical monopoly of Christianity was broken, and the teachings of Christ became available to all classes. Perhaps symbolic of this wider basis of Renaissance Christianity is Dante's choice of Virgil, a pagan Roman, as a guide to lead him through a Christian-style world-beyond-the-grave in the form of Hell and Purgatory. Still another symbolic indication of the broadening of the religious basis was the liberation of Satan from a fixed location in Hell and the realization that, as the angel of evil, he dwells ubiquitously in the minds of all men. (This particular development had unfortunate consequences. Believing that Satan can be found anywhere, the overzealous sought him with too much cruel vigour in heretic trials, the Inquisition and witch hunts.)

Do you agree that the Renaissance can be interpreted as a time when direct contacts between Christianity and a segment of the population wider than ever before contributed – of course, together with revived interest in the classical culture of Greece and Rome – to the blossoming of a splendid and vigorous culture?

WILSON: The Renaissance was the first and perhaps most vital of the currents influencing the formation of modern European culture and society. Its contours are not easy to define, and our evidence is largely from the writings of a particular literate class, and, understandably, many of them were within the Church. We unify under the term *Renaissance* a process of re-discovery of classical knowledge and its dissemination. The content of that knowledge was itself diverse and included, as well as the broad humane perspectives, the scepticism and the philosophical epicureanism of Greek thought, all kinds of occultic and astrological speculation. It gave impetus to theism and to new art and scientific enquiry. It would be easy to commend the rationalism of the humanist perspective as represented in some Renaissance writers and to account this the dominant influence of the period, but we know, from their own accounts, that many Renaissance intellectuals were men whose consciousness was profoundly divided between their belief in ancient superstitions and a mixture of theism and humanism that led them to doubt medieval Christian dogma and to challenge the narrowness of the intellectual basis of the medieval Church.

Although occultism and astrology flourished widely, the intellectuals' search for a new integration of classical philosophy and Christian thought and a more open form of scholarly enquiry triumphed in the end. If various pagan survivals acquired new impetus from a better acquaintance provided by classical texts, it was eventually a spirit of scepticism and detachment that prevailed. Perhaps this is why some regard the period as one in which the medieval façade of Christianity became irreparably breached. Yet, in other respects, and you may have this in mind in your own comment, the powerful theistic orientation in the Renaissance was a continuation of the general secularizing thrust that Christianity had inherited from Judaism. That many learned men still dabbled in astrology and believed in ghosts and witches was no more than should be expected for men at the time. That was the prevailing mode of consciousness, the very terms in which men thought, and centuries of superstition were not to be discarded with the first awakening of a new rationalism. For a long time, men went on believing in different and even incompatible things. In the long run, such predilections gave way to more sceptical intellects and more detached attitudes. The scepticism of the classical world may eventually have fortified the men of the Renaissance in their disposition to disbelieve in local or occult magic, but, perhaps of greater significance, the appreciation of a more integrated theoretical structure as the basis for scientific investigation rendered pagan folk-lore and myth at first irrelevant and finally untenable. And all of this, as the more enlightened saw, could go, at least for a time, hand in hand with a Christianity that was shorn of medieval accretions and enjoyed a restoration of the theistic and transcendentalist orientations of its origins in prophetic Judaism.

The elimination of immanentist elements from religion was paralleled by gradual preoccupation with ethical concerns and with the re-discovery of more universalistic ethical principles. Ethics displaced magic. Men increasingly saw the world as working according to general, perhaps universal, principles, rather than as manipulated by particularistic dispensations from such principles, with which magic was concerned. The confused ideas of free will and determinism, which were so tortuously entwined in both magic and astrology, were recognized and disentangled with increasing philosophical sophistication. Christianity itself was liberated from the influence of the accretion of pagan superstitions by the bold contours of the new theism which, for the intellectuals, provided it with new respectability. The Christianity of preceding centuries was transformed by the Renaissance, and this new style of religion steadily influenced a wider public, whilst, among the intellectual elites of European society, it gave impetus to intellectual and artistic endeavour within the framework (but at times transcending the framework) of Christian religion. Dante's choice of Virgil is indeed a symbol of enlarged humanism, even though Dante shrank, as other Renaissance writers sometimes did not, from actually admitting an unbeliever to the Christians' heaven. The Renaissance represented a belated claim to a wider cultural inheritance than the Church had previously transmitted, and in many respects the Church became, at least for a time, the vehicle for that enlarged and enlightened culture.

IKEDA: Yes, I see what you mean. Certainly the inclusion in culture and art of the pagan gods of Greece and Rome demanded a certain amount of inventive thought on the part of Renaissance Christians; but they did, as you say, succeed in enlarging the humanism of their times.

Including pagan elements as respectable parts of the Christian tradition seems to have made it equally respectable to re-evaluate both that tradition and the Christianity that was its basis. Furthermore, the right to make such re-evaluations was no longer confined to Church theologians, but was entrusted to artists and poets, who were able to influence ordinary people directly through creative work. If it was a breakaway from the medieval Church, stimulated by the rediscovery and dissemination of classical learning, the Renaissance was also an incarnation of Christian elements – flavoured and decorated with a classical garnish – by a wider public. As this apparent contradiction between a break with the Church and expanded assimilation of Christian teachings suggests, the Renaissance is a highly complicated phenomenon.

WILSON: Yes, and its effect was, of course, many-sided, and the historical scene is complicated by what I take to have been an even more significant development for European Christianity and for the evolution of European civilization: the Reformation. The Renaissance revitalized learning and provided the intelligentsia with an intellectually more compelling basis than medieval Christianity had possessed for re-ordering their perspectives on the world and for the incorporation of a new ethical humanism. The Reformation also wrought other transformations, and in particular it carried forward the need for inner conviction at the cost of outward forms, which a sacerdotal Catholicism has so much treasured. Of course, at many points the influence of the Renaissance runs into the Reformation, and later figures of the new learning, such as Erasmus, pre-echoed significant elements in what was to follow. Perhaps the most significant contribution of the Reformation was to shift the balance of control in society from the community to the individual, as is very clearly manifested in the elimination by Protestants of auricular confession. Henceforth, for Protestants, the voice of individual conscience was given a larger place in man's judgement of how he should conduct himself, and the institutions of the Church were relied upon less. My own feeling is that the Reformation and the currents that subsequently ran through Roman Catholicism had a profound effect on the integration of religious ideas and ethical conduct throughout Europe, leading men away from the magical expectation of instant and particular results towards a situation in which their faith reposed in objective and universal standards of morality. Of course, in the Puritan phase, in some places and for some periods, the process of internalization became so intense that there was a profound reaction against cultural artefacts in any way tainted by Romanism or worldliness. Those aspects of Puritanism would now be judged negatively by most men. Even so, I wonder if you agree with me that we cannot overlook the elevation of individual conscience, the stimulation to take a more rational and detached view of things, and the assimilation of religious values into daily life which the Reformation heralded.

IKEDA: You significantly clarify the discussion by expanding it from the Renaissance to the Reformation. Although superficially the Reformation looks like a rejection of the pagan classical elements introduced by the Renaissance to the Christian tradition, it was certainly humanistic in that it elevated the individual conscience to a position of great importance. The unification of religious values and everyday life constituted a reformation that might be called internal, in comparison with the more external one characterizing the Renaissance.

The Withering of the Church

IKEDA: As I have already said, I consider the Renaissance to stand for a flowering of the true egalitarian spirit of Christianity. Although, in a real sense they opposed the ecclesiasticism and authoritarianism of the Roman Catholic Church, the Reformation, the growth of scientific learning and the rise of nationalism drew sustenance from this same spirit. Ironically, however, in later times, elements in all these movements undermined Christianity by leading to sceptical attitudes towards things beyond rational explanation – rightfully the province of religion – and by sundering the body of the Church and thus drastically reducing its hold over the minds of many men. The result has been a marked decline in the power of Christianity to influence non-religious matters. What do you think are the factors that have brought about this state of affairs? Do you think vitality remains in Christianity?

WILSON: Christians are often prone to regard the beginning of the thirteenth century as the great age of faith, pointing to the success of Pope Innocent III in enforcing and enlarging the *plenitudo potestatis* of the Roman Church. He asserted his will over secular princes and saw it as the pope's duty to pronounce on their moral comportment, and to have the final right to legitimize them in their exercise of secular authority. However, the successful assertion of the power of the institutional church in this period is by no means evidence of the uniformity or ubiquity of the faith. At that time there were rampant Christian heresies and even more widespread, persisting pre-Christian paganism, which flourished throughout Europe. Indeed, one might say that the Christianization of Europe was far from complete at the level of popular religion when, three centuries later, the Reformation broke the unified authority of the Church.

Certainly, the Reformation drew on vital strands within the spirit of the Christian faith; at its best, setting the simplicity of Jesus' teachings over and against the cumbersome hierarchic authoritarianism of the Church. All the specifically ecclesiastical aspects of Christianity had been invented only after the death of the founder of the faith, and many of them are difficult to trace even to what is known of the churches of the apostolic or early post-apostolic period. The authority of Romanism relied on later accretions to the basic rudiments of simple Gospel Christianity, and in part this is what Luther, and, even more powerfully, some of his contemporaries, sought to demonstrate. If the mainstream of Reformation Christianity eventually found it difficult to dispense with many aspects of church structure, none the less, a radical thrust towards a less centralized and less politicized system of authority was evident in the currents of the churches and sects of the Reformation. The cost, of course, was to reduce the role of the Church in society. The pre-eminence of religion and its presidency over other departments of life disappeared and, with the emerging power of the secular state, the Church became subordinate to the state.

The Reformation drew vigorously on a different aspect of the Christian tradition in contesting the practices of the Roman Church. Whatever may have been the beliefs of Jesus and Paul with respect to the operation and potency of evil spirits (and there is scriptural evidence that both of them believed literally in such things), Christianity acquired from its Judaic origins the dispositions of a secularizing agency. Judaism had powerfully rejected the idea of ubiquitous magic, necromancy, and the power of local gods and spirits and had asserted the total and transcendent power of one god. Christianity inherited this orientation despite the various points at which it temporized with polytheism (eventually in such teachings as that of the Trinity; the gradual elevation in the hierarchy of the mother of God; and the accretion of innumerable local saints, some of whom were old pagan gods, thinly veiled in Christian trappings). Christianity, too, was a secularizing religion. It sought to define, and hence in a sense to confine and circumscribe, the operation of the sacred. Like Judaism, it drew a distinction between the profane and the sacred and rejected pagan notions that the world and all its phenomena were full of vibrant and potent mystical force. The Roman Church sought to destroy pagan magic even if, at times, it did so by absorbing local pre-Christian religious lore.

Undoubtedly, the Reformation drew on the pristine Christian spirit in re-envigorating the process by which magic was eliminated (and, in so doing, continued and consummated the criticisms to which some earlier Roman Catholic theologians had already given voice). It sought the elimination of persisting magical elements within Catholicism – most explicitly by the rejection of the power of relics, but also in the eradication of the sacerdotalism of the Roman Church. Priests performing rites were no longer to be regarded as working mysteries. The Reformation was a great demystifying force. Nationalism, which the Reformation facilitated, led to the assertion of the primacy of political power and the total overturn of the conception of the relation of religious to secular authority for which Innocent III and successive popes had striven. From this time, one can see the steady, if at times very slow, subordination of church and religion to the state. At times, religion continued to be invoked to support national or regional politics, to give credibility to the demands of cultural minorities, or even to legitimize political parties, but the general course of the subordination of Christianity to worldly concerns in both civic and popular life was always evident.

IKEDA: And remains in evidence today. Explaining the generation of such subjugation is too complex a subject to deal with here, but it seems to me that one of the major causes was preference on the part of the populace for the material security offered by the national state over the spiritual security held out by the Church. Moreover, as time passed, national states took over some of the authority formerly allocated to God himself; this too accounted for a shift in popular allegiance from the sacred to the secular.

Certainly the state cannot be said to have relied totally on the charity and grace of Christ in ruling subjects – for that matter, the Church frequently resorted to more authoritarian than loving means to keep the faithful in line. None the less, I do see an element of Christian grace and charity in some of the operations of the Western national-state system and, for this reason, have said that it derived sustenance from the Christian spirit, which was, however, gradually subordinated to worldly concerns, especially as scientific inquiry grew increasingly vigorous.

WILSON: The influence of scientific enquiry may have worked more slowly to undermine Christian belief, even though the Roman Church saw the potential danger early enough and remained consistently hostile to empirical enquiry into such matters as human anatomy and astronomy, where they threatened to challenge the cosmology written into the creation myth of the Judaeo-Christian tradition. Certainly, as you suggest, the scientists of the post-Reformation period drew on their own Christian doctrines, and particularly on ideals of this-wordly asceticism and the demand for mastery of worldly things, as a justification for scientific investigation. Undoubtedly, many seventeenth-century scientists were committed Puritans, and there is reason to believe that some of them saw their scientific work virtually as work in a religious cause. Eventually, of course, the fears of the old Roman Church were proved correct: scientific knowledge acted as a solvent of Christian belief. Even though, today, it is fashionable for many theologians (and a few scientists) to argue that there is no conflict, they can do so largely because the war is over and science has won. In one area after another, the Christian religion has been obliged to abandon its assumptions and assertions about creation, the nature of man, and the entire physical, chemical and biological character of phenomena. In more recent times, modern psychology and sociology have effectively challenged basic Christian premises on moral and social matters. Were he able to see its teachings and practices, the medieval Christian would find it hard to recognize in modern Christianity much that belonged to the Christianity of his times. For example, what might be called its cosmological, terrestrial, biological, sociological and psychological assumptions are now discredited almost everywhere.

Most of all, as we have discussed elsewhere in this volume, I believe that changes in social structure have been responsible for the decline of religion in the West and for its relegation to the sphere principally of private life. In relation to the operation of society, Christianity has become insignificant in most Western countries. Its declining political presence is matched both by the diminution in the economic resources the churches themselves control and by the churches' loss of influence over the economic order. The clergy of all churches have lost social status, as well as having suffered severe relative deprivation in respect to financial rewards. All of this makes plain the changed condition of Christianity. We may then ask what remains vital in Christianity? It still has a considerable institutional presence in many Western countries, even though, little by little, its properties and buildings are being sold off and put to other uses and the number of its clergy is diminishing, certainly in Europe. It no longer greatly influences the operation of law as moral matters cease to command legal enforcement. In education, it retains a lingering presence, in some countries in a specifically religious school system; but even in such cases the significance of "a Christian education" is much diluted in an age that puts technical skills at a premium and religious knowledge at a discount. In Britain, religious instruction in schools, although demanded by the law, has become a dead letter. In the United States, of course, religious instruction, even of the most minimal kind, is forbidden within the system of public education.

The churches still sponsor a wide variety of social and welfare activities and agencies. In comparison with other religions, Christianity has always been strong in its organizational structure, and since they are distributed almost like public facilities, churches become – especially in the United States, but also still in Europe, even in such countries as Sweden, which have low figures of attendance at church services – obvious foci for the life of the local community. In an increasingly urban, industrialized and highly mobile society, community life is in itself much diminished, since many people no longer sleep in the districts in which they work. Only for certain groups, and particularly for the elderly and the very young, is the local community, what remains of it, the context in which life is lived. And even for these groups, the near-housebound, the wider world impinges into the household and the thought-structure of everyday life through the medium of television. Yet the churches still manage to cater to them and, perhaps also, as a token or a recollection of what community life is supposed to have been, to a wider, commuting, suburban public. Intellectually, despite the continuance of vigorous debate among theologians, neither the general public nor the more specifically intellectual strata of society appear much concerned about what churches have to say. Christianity is, at best, only ineffectually represented in the mass media, and the whole world of mass marketing, consumerism, productive enterprise, finance, and civic and social administration operates with, at best, only scant recognition of the existence of churches. In private life, Christianity retains some vitality; used most for the rites of passage and in the assuaging of grief and distribution of comfort, the churches continue to function, albeit in a situation of increasing and more efficient competition from both counselling services and other agencies. It is a limited role: yet one cannot say that Christian influence has disappeared, even though the extent of its outreach has conspicuously withered at all points of national, public and social life.

IKEDA: The war between science and Christianity started with the Christians' own efforts to provide rational substantiation for the truth of the teachings of the Bible. Ironically, however, their efforts have relentlessly proved quite the opposite. Still, to my view, this ought to cause much less concern than it does in the West.

As I am certain you will agree, the proper field of religion is dealing with those things that are admittedly beyond rational explanation. If this is true, there is no need for hostility between science and religion as long as religion stays in its own realm and as long as science is willing to admit that not all phenomena are – at our present state of development at any rate – liable to rational verification.

In Buddhism, as in Christianity, some doctrinal elements have turned out to be inconsistent with scientific truth; this in no way invalidates the fundamental teachings of Buddhism, or of Christianity. Such truths as the teaching that persistent anger and greed lead to unhappiness deal with the profundities of the human mind and spiritual state and therefore transcend historical period, social structure and degree of scientific knowledge. Obviously, the Judaeo-Christian insistence on an omniscient, omnipotent, infallible, anthropomorphic god makes conceding error, even on matters that are insignificant from the standpoint of faith, highly embarrassing.

The Decline of Western Christianity

IKEDA: To continue the line of thought we started in the preceding section, I should like to pursue in greater detail the question of the decline of the power of Christianity to exert definitive influences on private and public life in the West. Although reasons for this loss of appeal probably vary from region to region, one factor that seems prevalent everywhere is intensified concern with the material life and a lessening interest in spiritual matters – part of what you mean by the process of secularization.

I do not intend to minimize the importance of material well-being. (In Japan we have a saying to the effect that courtesies – and presumably other spiritual matters as well – are to be dealt with only after sufficient food and shelter have been ensured.) However, when a religion becomes excessively abstract and rarified and fails to compete successfully with undeniably important secular concerns, it loses its hold on the popular mind. And this is why I think the cause of its decline must be sought in the very nature – the basic teachings and doctrines – of Christianity itself. What are your thoughts on this subject?

WILSON: It is widely held that Christianity – and not only Christianity among the world religions – maintained its appeal among the masses of the people largely by offering spiritual rewards (and particularly values pertaining to the after-life) as a compensation for the material deprivations and hardships of life on earth. The poor were persuaded to behave morally, to be contented with their lot and to cultivate spiritual attitudes, by promises that in the hereafter they would reap their just desserts. The theodicy of Christianity was an explicit promise that the injustices of this world would be balanced by the due rewards of the next. The eschatological scheme represented an elaborate compensatory system, in which contemplation of benefits to come assuaged the anguish of hardships presently experienced.

IKEDA: Hope and reward and a better condition in the world beyond the grave is common to other religions. Even some forms of Buddhism, which generally takes a more here-and-now view of the human situation, hold out hopes for rebirth in paradise for those who profess faith. This represents a lower level of development than religions which, while taking into consideration the important needs of present life, strive to assist their followers in controlling desires and improving themselves from within for the sake of true spiritual fulfilment and happiness. This seems to me to be both a more realistic and a more satisfying approach than a grin-and-bear-it regime, which urges people to hope for better things in another world.

WILSON: Yes, and if such hope of compensation was a major source of the appeal of Christianity, then certainly the development of a more affluent condition of society such as the West has experienced in recent generations, with the elimination of material want for the vast majority of people, may have done much to militate against the diffusion of spiritual values. The emphasis on present benefit may have induced people to suppose that their best experiences were to be here and now, and all our public-opinion poll surveys show that there has been a rapid and extensive decline in belief in the after-life among Western peoples – even among those who specifically proclaim themselves to be Christians and who believe in most of the other central tenets of the Christian faith.

Although I think it may reflect a rather different and independent development, the Christian churches also do appear to have become more preoccupied with abstract ideas. The literal truth of many of the basic doctrines of the faith, as they were expressed in the past, are not canvassed by nearly so many priests as once was the case. Even the principal doctrines of the faith, as formulated in the various creeds, are now openly repudiated by theologians and go unmentioned by many clergy. Matters that would have been open heresy a century ago are now accepted as common sense, and these include some of the basic elements in traditional Christianity. In this, many of the practising laity undoubtedly have a much simpler and more literal faith than the clergy who serve them, and many are undoubtedly puzzled by the rejection of numerous items that, quite rightly, I believe, they regard as indispensable elements without which Christian faith is either confused or nonsensical. Since they have often abandoned their traditional liturgical functions and since they display increasing indifference to church traditions to which many of the laity are themselves still very much attached, these clergy become – usually against their will and even in contradition to what they think they are doing – somewhat remote from their parishioners.

The general decline of Christianity arises, I believe, from the apparent irrelevance of Christian beliefs and practices to the technological age. Fundamentally, modern society has become increasingly rationally organized, and that rationality is evidenced in the development of both technology and bureaucracy. Men are increasingly deployed as if they were parts of a well co-ordinated machine. They are also enmeshed, in most of their concerns, in institutions that are *societally* organized, at least at the level of the nation state, and sometimes in institutions and economic concerns that are in fact international. Such structures operate according to a logic that transcends the particularities of the Christian religion and according to norms that make the moral code of Christianity appear merely personal, parochial in its preoccupations and inconsequential for the impersonal character of modern institutions. The specific beliefs of Christianity increasingly appear to be peculiar to the age in which they first gained expression, or appropriate to the much more communally-based social order that persisted throughout subsequent centuries and until relatively recent times. Since the modern social system operates without regard to the supernatural, religion is becoming relegated to the interstices of social space, to the leisure time of individuals in their private lives, and so becomes inconsequential to the system as such. All the major areas of public life – economy, politics, judicial proceedings, education, welfare and recreation – operate without reference to the Christian shibboleths that once formed the main guidelines for activity in all of these departments of life.

What follows is that even in the private sphere, where Western man still has the opportunity to maintain his religion, the specific elements of Christian teaching have less congruity with individual experience, and Christian morality appears increasingly to be a morality limited to the now diminished sphere of personal relationships. The concrete, personalized and localized particularity of the Christian myth makes it less applicable than once it was, since the relationships it epitomizes are now by no means the exclusive, and perhaps not even the dominant, social experience of most people. Given the uncertainty about these myths among contemporary theologians and churchmen, whatever remains of the appeal they might have as models for private life is further diminished by this professional scepticism. The process of secularization in the West appears to have various causes, but I would myself attribute much to the incongruity of the Christian religion and the rational technological social order that has come into operation in Western nations in recent decades.

Religious and Ideological Totalitarianism

IKEDA: In your book, *Contemporary Transformations of Religion*, you describe the age of faith (the age of Innocent III) as one in which "the church controlled not only the moral fabric of society (perhaps that least of all) but the formal processes of political, juridical, commercial and social intercourse – the institutional operation of society". Do you see a resemblance between this situation and the one prevailing in modern totalitarian states? In what essential way does a world in which the social order is "religiously prescribed" differ from one in which it is ideologically prescribed?

WILSON: It had not occurred to me to compare the dominance of the Church under Innocent III to that of the modern totalitarian state, but now that you point it out, I see that there are some clear similarities. The intention is certainly similar, namely to regulate as fully as possible every facet of social life, and to impose a pattern of order. The means do differ: to exert its authority, the Church had to work through secular powers which alone commanded the means of coercive force. Its sanctions differed, too: threats (of hell) and blandishments (respecting heaven) being among its principal weapons, even though the Church also powerfully influenced the criminal and political codes of secular society. In practice, the Church was also less effective: its means of communication were limited, even though it had a virtual monopoly (of the arts of reading and writing). When not relying on secular powers, the Church's control depended on its normative authority over its local agents, and their moral integrity, despite their religious commitment, was by no means always to be counted upon. The modern ideological system relies less on the moral character of its personnel than on the exaction of compliance by organizational sanctions, coercive power and intimidation. There is, of course, a notorious bureaucratic inefficiency in all totalitarian systems, but with modern means of communication, and technical rather than moral manipulation, local variation in the implementation of policy can be more effectively controlled from the centre.

The principal difference between a religiously prescribed social order and an ideologically prescribed order, then, lies in the nature of religious socialization. All religions rely on the internalization of an ethic, no matter what additional measures they resort to in order to enforce external social compliance. The coercion to which the Roman Church made frequent recourse in medieval times was ultimately ill-accommodated to the spirit of the Christian ethic, in which there is an emphasis on the special merit of free will. Political ideologies do not encounter even this measure of constraint, and whilst it is not possible even for the state to command total and overt assent to the dominant ideology, it can take action to suppress dissent. Open coercion is a feature of both left-wing and right-wing totalitarian regimes. Religion, in contrast, purveys values to which men are expected to become voluntarily committed, even though, in Innocent III's time, the Church sought to deny men any real choice. Totalitarian states espouse systems of politics and ethics that are purportedly derived from the objective facts of history and society. In itself, this is little different from the claims made for Christianity in the period of its dominance in Western society, except that secular ideologies do not depend on any deep internalization of their values – outward conformity is all that is demanded. Thus, whereas religion depends on the creation of a psychological orientation (which may have to do in some measure with the supernaturalist character of religious inducements and constraints), ideology requires only that the individual comply, not that he necessarily subscribe. Ideology represents itself as factually true, whereas religion may be primarily offered as being symbolically true. Ideologies represent the interests and values of a particular nation, race or class, whereas religion represents a cluster of values to which – at least in the cases of Christianity, Buddhism and Islam – the individual may voluntarily subscribe, hence the need for heightened self-consciousness with respect to commitment. In a situation in which religion is as socially dominant as it was in the time of Innocent III, coercion may indeed augment, and in some instances actually supplant, the voluntary, internalized commitment that we should regard as being more characteristic of religion in most parts of the modern world.

State Religions

IKEDA: In many nations today, a specific religion, or non-religion, serves as a national conscience on which are based all political and educational policies and which determines the directions art and other fields of human endeavour must follow. I am opposed to the approach adopted by many Islamic and some predominantly Roman Catholic nations because, although a religion can more easily influence culture if it borrows support from political authority, in the very act of doing so it loses something much more important: the chance to verify its own values and attain a higher, purer level of truth through objective observation and criticism. No matter how large its membership, a religion that chooses to rely on the power of political authority has chosen the path of decadence. Even religions that gain the trust and faith of large numbers of people must never allow themselves to become so-called state religions but should strive to transcend the national framework. What are your opinions of state religions?

WILSON: Religion claims to bring men into contact with supernatural law or power, and it is perhaps implicit in such claims that religious leaders should regard true religion as transcending the level at which state or political authorities operate. The great religions of the world had all become widespread and more or less socially institutionalized before the *modern* state emerged and before the concept of the distinct, separate and integrated state system was well articulated either in theory or practice. Thus, state religions as such emerged at a particular phase of social and political development, as nascent states began to form. A state is established when, within a given terrain, there is an effective claim to a monopoly of political power and, ultimately, of coercive force. The new state societies naturally took cognizance of the religion of the people, as they did of other pre-existing social phenomena (for example, of language). The state necessarily endorsed religion, particularly since princes needed the legitimation of those who could claim to speak for transcendent spiritual powers. In Europe, it became usual for the state to protect the places sacred to the Church, to accept its ministry, and to confer privilege upon its officers.

Christianity was, of course, effectively organized in the time of the old Roman Empire and claimed to sustain a higher form of civic order on the ruins of that dispensation. It claimed ideological monopoly and thus could neatly divide responsibilities in a partnership of temporal and spiritual power with the princes of medieval Europe. The Church claimed pre-eminence, even though Church authorities were only occasionally able to assert their will effectively over competing princes. In contrast, where pre-existing religion was deeply indigenized, local, intricately bound into the fabric of everyday social life and lacking organizational hierarchy and coordination, it was scarcely in a position to become an effective state religion. Such was the case with Hinduism which, partly in consequence of these same factors, was syncretistic, eclectic and tolerant of religious diversity. For reasons similar to those which affected the development of religion, in India the state did not take on the form it acquired in Europe.

Christianity and Islam were already identified with rulers before the modern state was properly formed, and those rulers were often deeply influenced by religion. Such was the case with Louis IX of France or Edward the Confessor of England, both of whose lives and whose statecraft bore the evidence of religion, no less so than those of Ashoka. Christian and Muslim influences, however, worked for the expurgation of multifarious indigenous religious traditions, which were seen as making competing claims to spiritual competence. To this end religious leaders in these traditions induced secular princes to exert their coercive powers. It became a religious duty for secular rulers to protect the faith, and this often meant the persecution of religious minorities and even involvement in war at the behest of religious authorities. So the idea of religion giving its imprimatur to secular culture developed. Religion served the social elite and provided them with a culture. The protected religion claimed the spiritual allegiance of all those who owed the prince obedience as subjects. In Europe, the Church claimed an objective existence transcending that of political powers and even, when it was fully formed, of the state, since it claimed to be the one source of grace and salvation for all princes and for all mankind.

The identity of interests that was forged between spiritual and secular power was such in countries like France and England that the highest religious dignitaries occupied great offices of state, sometimes ceasing to be particularly active in the practice of religion. In Islam, in which political and religious institutions were much less differentiated, the law itself was religiously prescribed, and the political involvement of religious leaders was inevitable. State formation was, however, so retarded among Islamic nations that, until the twentieth century, specific association of religion and state in any way comparable to that found in Christian Europe was only to be seen in the Ottoman Empire, although one should not overlook the powerful thrust Islamic revitalization movements later gave to state formation, most recently in the cases of Libya and Algeria.

Perhaps we ought to acknowledge a distinction between states that adopted a religion and created its institutions and states that inherited one. From early times, Roman Catholicism was able to claim spiritual superintendence of temporal monarchs, and although the Church always demanded secular protection, its leaders were aware of the fact that the Church had a presence in many states. The Protestant churches were, in some cases, much more explicitly state religions. They, and we may count the Church of England among them, were churches instituted by the state, and their leaders acknowledged the state as an agency apart from the church, over which the state justifiably exercised temporal control. The position was admirably rationalized by the Anglican theologian, Richard Hooker, who provided state religion with its most cogent apologia.

Puritanism gave rise to the creation of states implicitly (if not always actually) committed to the ideal of a republican commonwealth under God, in Calvin's Geneva, in Cromwell's England and in the states of New England. The Christian scriptures became the source, and almost the model, for civil government. Despite this coming together, in Protestantism and Puritanism, of the religious and political spheres, the long-term consequence was indeed the secularization of society and the loss by religion of its claim to special sanctity. State religions became increasingly moribund, sometimes corrupted by political intrigue, as religious offices were utilized as rewards for political activity, and at other times reduced to near bureaucratic servitude. Such religions became unlikely contexts for spiritual initiative, and it might be true to say that, when religious revitalization occurred, it usually challenged the leadership of state churches and sometimes could develop only outside their structures. Certainly in the case of Christianity, there are many examples to confirm your conclusion that, when religious movements depend on political power, the risk of decadence is considerable. We have seen not only the revolt of dissenters within officially Protestant countries, but also the disruption of the church in Roman Catholic countries when the association of the state and its political leaders with religious authorities has given rise to mistrust and dissent among the rank and file, as is the case in so many Latin American countries.

The association of religion and the state is perhaps today no longer regarded as useful by politicians, whilst some churchmen have become aware that close identification with the state may sometimes stimulate opposition that in other circumstances they might have escaped. With a few lingering exceptions in Roman Catholic and Islamic countries, religious freedom today is less threatened by the influence of state religion than it is by secularist ideologies (in communist countries) and, less explicitly, perhaps by the extension of the essentially secular powers of the state itself. The tendency of the modern state to intervene in ever wider areas of public life, and to integrate services and facilities according to rational criteria of public planning, may affect the practice of particular religious groups in more serious ways than anything that might arise through the instigation of official state religion.

What Will the Communists Do?

IKEDA: Although in the Soviet Union, China and other communist nations freedom of religion is constitutionally guaranteed, citizens are not free to engage in missionary activities or other work to spread religious faith, because religion itself is considered to be a remnant of the old, class-ridden society against which communists struggle. In other words, communists pretend that religion is no more than what they call an opiate, something to take the minds of the oppressed off their troubles, thus making them amenable to further oppression. It is true that many religions turn their eyes from the suffering of the actual world and incline people to accept temporal affliction and oppression in the hope of a better after-life. However not all religions adopt this kind of illusory approach, and it seems to me that communism alone is incapable of filling human spiritual needs, which demand a religion that gives a likely forecast of the future and provisions for present spiritual fulfilment. I predict that, to satisfy this need, in the years to come, communist nations will become more liberal in relation to religion. What is your interpretation of the role religion can play in communist societies?

WILSON: Communism has often been represented by sociologists as being in itself a religion, or at least a surrogate religion. Like a religion, it has been argued, communism has a creed. Communists eulogize their founder, revere a set of sacred scriptures, subscribe to an interpretation of history and its ultimate culmination, and organize in cells and manifest missionary zeal; the movement itself fulfils the functions of religion in providing occasions of reunion for its votaries and the promotion of social cohesion for the group. All other ideologies are proscribed and, almost as if borrowing from the worst excesses of medieval Christian intolerance, believers in these other ideologies are persecuted. In spite of all this, however, it is apparent that communism has not been able to fulfil all the functions of religion. It provides little if any support for individuals at the traumatic moments of the life cycle. It offers people no comfort when they face death themselves or when they see their kinsfolk do so. It affords no means of consummating or enhancing emotional life, for example in joy at times of birth, adulthood or marriage. Demands on the individual by the Party (and hence by the State) to sustain collective goals that transcend the individual's own life purposes are all too nakedly asserted. There are no subtle mechanisms to persuade, to motivate or to convince: communism lacks the techniques of socialization. Only in a narrow, sometimes arid, intellectual sense can it present itself as a way of salvation. It has only weak agencies with which to persuade the population to self-sacrificial acts, either for others or for the much-vaunted collective good. It depends on coercion or on other agencies to create this effect. The type of almost heroic self-denial, altruism and detached goodwill that is found in all genuine religious traditions has inspired very few communists. In the last war, it was the ethnic-nationalist idea of Russia, rather than the dogmas of the official political Soviet creed, that was consciously exploited by the Party to stiffen the morale of the Russian people. Given all this, one sees the inadequacies of communism even for a mass public that has known no remotely effective alternative ideology and among whom the remnants of traditional religion are archaic in style, unscholarly in character and ineffective in operation.

IKEDA: As Christianity has declined, in Russia and in Western Europe, too, several different surrogate religions have assumed prominence: faith in ethnic groups, faith in social structures, faith in the national state, faith in capitalism, and so on. Ironically, communism, which loudly propounds atheism and anti-religious themes, is being forced to try to play the part that religion once played but, as you say, without notable success.

WILSON: There is evidence to suggest that, at least in Russia, the most advanced of the communist countries, the process of secularization characteristic of other advanced industrialized nations has been occurring. In general, scholars believe that the development occurs not because of the effectiveness of official Soviet propaganda and its advocacy of secularism as an ideology, but for very much the same sort of reasons which have occasioned secularization in Western countries – namely, because religion becomes increasingly irrelevant to the operation of a modern social system. They attribute the process to social-structural, not to ideological, causes. If this is so and, if they were to come to recognize it, Soviet leaders might eventually break out of the paralysis of fear and dogmatic conservatism in which they appear to be gripped. If they were really sophisticated about the way in which societies change, they might see that they had little to fear from religion or from the extension of tolerance to the followers of different religious beliefs. At the level of individuals' private lives, they might acknowledge that religion had something to offer by way of comfort and reassurance and that this in itself, far from challenging the communist regime, might even provide it with a useful cushion. As an explanatory thesis, Marxism itself lacks an effective social psychology, and communism as practised in Russia lacks the dimension of human understanding. Freedom of religion might reduce the oppressiveness of communist society without undermining, and without even much affecting, political stability. I wonder if you concur with this interpretation?

IKEDA: I do in part. My sole reservation is related to the nature of religion itself. I can easily see that, if the communist leaders did relax their oppressive conservative stand in connection with religious freedom, sincere followers of religious teachings might well be compelled in all good conscience to live in ways that would pose a threat to the communist social system, although I suspect that such threats would be of much less significance than continued religious oppression.

Religion: a Stimulus or a Stumbling Block?

IKEDA: Whether religion is a forward-oriented leader in civilization or an anachronism inhibiting advances in other fields is a question of great importance. Throughout human history, religion has exerted a strong, not always progressive, influence on culture. The relation between the Church and natural sciences in the medieval period is a vivid illustration of the kinds of stumbling blocks religion can put in the path to progress. It is therefore easy to sympathize with people who are wary of allowing religion to play a role of great leadership. None the less, I believe that religions which sincerely examine the profound aspects of the human situation can provide essential guiding ideals for mankind. Do you agree?

WILSON: The inextricable association of religion and culture in all traditional societies, including those that have evolved into advanced industrial nations, suggests that civilizations have been powerfully influenced, although not entirely shaped, by religion. Certainly in the West, one might point to various examples of the determining effect of religion in stimulating and sustaining particular attitudes and dispositions and even on the very languages of different countries. However, with the impact of modern science, which is, in its own way, trans-cultural but which has its own impact on culture and civilization, the influence of religion has considerably diminished. Not only has the role of religion declined in shaping human civilization, but certain religious leaders – for example, most significantly in the Roman and Anglican churches – have almost abandoned their most explicit claims to exert an influence on culture, virtually to the point of discrediting their own past. From circumstances in which religion sometimes acted as a brake on a variety of cultural developments, we have now come to a point where many religious leaders are content to accept the intimations of science, the mass media and politics and to relinquish the claims that religion once made to contribute a distinctive style and a more solemn content to everyday life and to the civilizing agencies that worked upon it.

In the past, Western religion sought to moderate the excesses of human emotion, to regulate greed, to induce attitudes of responsibility and mutual concern, to soften manners and habits, and to persuade men to be contented with their lot and merciful to their fellow creatures. Much the same counsels prevailed in the religious teachings of Buddhism. These civilizing influences, however, have been cumulatively offset by the measured and systematic acquisitiveness that pervades all levels of modern economic systems, by the indifferentism that characterizes bureaucratic operations, and by the relentless impersonality of technology (to leave unmentioned the hedonism, cynicism and frivolity which, in the relentless presentations of the mass media, so effectively trivialize human life). Much has been done in the name of progress that has carelessly overridden the interests, feelings and even the lives of human beings. It is not certain that, even had religion remained vigorous in advanced countries, its influence would have been exercised towards halting these consequences of scientific and economic development, but there appears to be no other source from which humane dispositions might have been marshalled. The contemporary processes of technological development gain momentum without regard to human susceptibility, even though they always brandish the slogans of progress and the good of mankind. There are signs of concern in movements for the preservation of the environment, the protection of endangered species, the conservation of scarce resources, and the control of potentially dangerous technical and industrial processes. As yet, we do not know just how much we are endangered by some of our technical advances, but one can safely say that we are likely to notice the purely physical effects on the environment first – physical pollution, for example. No one has yet even begun to assess the character of what we might call psychological pollution, although that is just as assuredly happening and may indeed pose an even more serious risk to what we might loosely call civilized values and human culture.

I am not in general optimistic about man's ability to control the noxious forces at work in the contemporary world. Perhaps, if anything can be done at all, it can be done only through some new diffusion of deeply felt and seriously considered values to which millions of men will subscribe. The difficulty in anticipating such a development is that, to be effective, such a movement must be international and must operate in many different cultures. To do that, the values it espouses and the attitudes it disseminates must be expressed at a very high level of generality, since they must have application in many different cultural contexts and among widely divergent conditions of men. Yet, it is also clear that the more general and abstract the values that are pronounced, the more difficult it is to summon strong and intensely felt concern for them. People busy themselves with their own lives and take up their problems in language that has local and specific application. It is not easy for men to see how their personal wants and their families' concerns are related to the wider, perhaps global, issues that confront mankind, and it is difficult to recruit men to support what they may regard as "lofty" ideals. If the link were ever to be made and the gulf ever bridged between, on the one hand, numerous diverse local concerns and, on the other, general, over-arching goals of global civilization and the culture(s) of all humanity, perhaps only religion would be capable of doing it.

IKEDA: I suspect that modern civilization and life styles contribute greatly to the reduction of what you call humane dispositions. Furthermore, I believe that it is the role of religion to strengthen, enrich and deepen those dispositions. The necessary improvements cannot be made through social, scientific or economic measures alone but, as you suggest, require reformation of awareness on the level of the individual – what Josei Toda, second president of Soka Gakkai, called the human revolution. Because I view the situation in this light, I am in complete agreement with you when you say that religion is the only source from which humane dispositions can be marshalled. Certainly, it is the duty of people of religious faith to bridge the gulf between numerous diverse local concerns and the general goals of global human civilization.

Cultural Relativity

IKEDA: You have suggested in your writings that contemporary society is less legitimized than any previous social system, partly because of the collapse of a shared conception of transcendental order. Such a shared conception unifies and gives confidence to society. The mass-media society offers a flood of information that is, as you say, chaotic and confusing. Still, it makes possible honest comparisons. I cannot believe that the opportunity to compare one's own ostensibly transcendental standards with the ostensibly transcendental standards of other cultures is bad. A person can retain confidence in those aspects of his culture that are shown by comparison to be superior. If all aspects of his culture are shown to be inferior, why should he retain confidence in them?

WILSON: Cultural relativism was heartily endorsed by anthropologists and sociologists in the 1940s and 50s. They found particular merit in exposing students to the details of other cultures and other systems of religion and morality, as a way of making them reflect about their own. Their examples were taken principally from tribal societies. Once the element of "shock" was overcome, students were likely to ask themselves whether it was any worse to live in, say, a society in which competition was inhibited; or where women worked and men spent their days at leisure, dancing and dressing up; or in cultures in which younger people deferred to the elderly, even to the point of having their marriage partners chosen for them. The intention was to shake students free from the assumption which, in those ethno-centric days, was so readily made, that their own society enjoyed a

"natural" moral order, and that all other peoples were more or less be-
nighted. This type of instruction made students aware that there were
diverse possibilities of social organization, and that human personality and
psychology were highly malleable, adapting to the social and moral
patterns prevailing in the society in which the individual was born and
reared.

Cultural relativism made apparent the variety and diversity of cultures,
but it lacked a basis on which evaluative assessments might be made. The
social scientists of that time either felt no need for such judgements or
rejected the idea that there were any criteria by which they could be established. The questions persisted, of course: why could not social science
produce grounds for, for example, "proving" that Nazi social and cultural
orientations were less desirable than those of other societies? Cultural
relativism was not enough. Somewhere, there had to be recourse to other,
perhaps transcendental, values if people were to find terms in which to
appraise cultures. Social science has difficulty in adopting any value
position of its own: factual study does not give rise to the endorsement of
specific values. The social scientist endorses ethical neutrality. Were it not
so, then there might be a Nazi sociology of psychology, a Soviet social
science or a capitalist anthropology – attributions that are not acceptable
for academic disciplines that purport to be scientific, and which eschew all
ideological orientations.

The situation is made still more complex because the sociologist might
seek to undertake a comparison of the transcendent value systems of
different societies. Others' values become the sociologist's facts, the data for
his analysis. Yet his study is not expected to lead to judgements of relative
merit. He leaves it to others to decide about the inferiority or superiority
of their own and alien cultures. Generally, men have a strong, conscious or
unconscious, bias in favour of the familiar, and this prevails even about
trivial things such as tastes in food, tolerance of climatic conditions, and
such things as the incapacity to make (or even accurately to hear) unfamiliar speech sounds. To the Greeks, the Chinese and the Japanese, all
other peoples were traditionally regarded as "barbarians". The British used
to say, "Wogs begin at Calais". Such examples of xenophobia could be
multiplied and found in every society. It is difficult for people to come to
the conclusion that their own culture is inferior, since this makes them feel
inferior themselves, and such an appraisal might be deeply felt and produce
untoward consequences. We know from the reaction of Melanesian
tribesmen faced by the apparent superiority of Western culture that some

of them simply abandon their own cultural values and, since they cannot effectively espouse the values and artefacts of Western society, they come to describe themselves as "rubbish men", and often lose heart and courage for living. In contemporary Western societies, the relatively coherent value-systems of the past have collapsed in the face of both the new cultural pluralism (multi-racialism and multi-religiosity) and the impact of technologization. One consequence has been the loss of a sense of cultural identity among some of the young who now call themselves "punks" (a term of total derision implying worthlessness, which, none the less, they apply to themselves). The idea is reinforced by the conscious adoption of clothes and accoutrements which signify absurdity and absence of purpose, while tattoos and freak hair-styles and colours imply total abandonment of respect for their own bodies. Like the Melanesian "rubbish men" who have lost all confidence in themselves, their culture and their compatriots, punks proclaim their loss of pride in human dignity and effectively declare themselves to be rubbish. Such is perhaps the consequence of coming to a negative judgement about one's own society and culture.

The question thrown up by both cultural relativism and cultural collapse is by what objective criteria cultures might be judged, and this presents a problem since we are all, to a greater or lesser degree, "culture-bound" in our language, thought-processes and habits. Serious comparison of cultures is important for all of us, but the methods of social enquiry provide no certainties about the basis for ultimate value judgements, whilst the loss of a sense of cultural identity appears to presage serious social problems.

Contributions to Peace

IKEDA: Although everyone wants peace, the fear of being unable to retaliate in case an enemy should initiate aggression leads to self-defence measures, military preparedness and consequently the arms race. When nations exist in a constant state of armed readiness, the smallest thing can trigger a war. For this reason, I feel that total, global disarmament must be one of modern man's prime objectives. Humanity must necessarily resist madmen of Hitler's kind; but no nation should attempt to subdue another through force. If all nations are to disarm and thus to abandon dreams of military conquest, what contributions can religion make to the process?

WILSON: In the past, as we have already observed, religion has often been invoked as an excuse for war, as an agency that has helped nations to legitimize their warlike policies. Among the world religions, this has been particularly true of Christianity and Islam. One may safely say that, with the possible exception of a few Islamic countries, the idea of "holy war" is now generally dead. We recognize that the term is not merely a paradox but indeed an obscenity.

Although we may rejoice that religion is now much less likely than heretofore to be a cause of war, it does not necessarily follow that religion is likely to be a particularly powerful agent in helping to secure peace. Nations nowadays need no religious justification for the conflicts in which they become embroiled. In consequence, religion may appear less relevant to the discussion of the issues about which potential international conflict is likely to arise. This in itself may make it difficult for religious leaders to influence the policies of nations with respect to disarmament. Apart from this, politicians today have recourse to other types of advisers and rarely believe that religious leaders comprehend the issues with which they – the politicians, employing the full benefit of technological advice and secret intelligence – must grapple. For example, a couple of years ago, the head of the Anglican Church, the Archbishop of Canterbury, publicly expressed his wish to speak to the British prime minister of the day on some matter of general social and moral concern. The prime minister publicly announced that he was too busy to see the archbishop, and kept him waiting for two weeks. If that could happen in a country like Britain, in which there has never been anything remotely resembling a significant anti-clerical movement and in which the monarch remains temporal head of the Church (and spiritual head of the state), then the influence of religious leaders in such countries as France and Germany (to say nothing of the world's two great officially secular powers, the United States and the Soviet Union) must be counted as limited indeed.

If religion is to have any influence in the affairs of nations ever again, it appears that there are two possible ways in which this might occur – both, of course, remain quite hypothetical. A precondition for the re-acquisition of such influence appears to be some large-scale and rapid process of religious conversion that would bring to religious organizations a widespread and deeply committed following, which might, indeed, be recruited with the express aim of demanding disarmament. Given such a situation, the new religious community might seek, by spontaneous demonstrations, passive resistance or even strikes, to influence political decisions. Alternatively, such a religious body might bring into being a political party devoted to the one specific goal of peace, and such a party might, in a more orderly and conventional way, seek to exert its influence through normal political channels.

The background hindrance is that religion is very differentially represented in the different power blocks of the world. No one would oppose multilateral, or perhaps even bilateral, disarmament of the major powers; doubt arises over unilateral policy. It would take a great change of heart, I think, for the majority of people in the West to become convinced that unilateral disarmament was a viable policy. To be effective, I suspect that religious influence would have to operate both in Russia and the West, but the social circumstances for religious development remain, while divergent, equally unfavourable in both regions. Were religious feeling for peace to grow simultaneously in both contexts then, I believe, politicians might be persuaded, but do you think that that is a realistic prospect?

IKEDA: Given the state of world politics at the present time, the outlook for such a development is, I must admit, dim. Still, something has to be done. Politicians have tied their own hands by creating a situation in which the powerful dare not wield their might for fear of global destruction. As we said in the preceding section, it is the duty of people of religious faith to strengthen, enrich and deepen humane dispositions – one of which is assuredly the disposition towards peace. We must strive to disseminate, by means of personal contact, dialogue and all other means at our disposal, those elements of wisdom found in many religious teachings and in humane philosophies that, although not strictly speaking religious, have as a goal the betterment, not the annihilation, of humanity. As a Buddhist, I find much of this kind of wisdom in the teachings of the Buddha and intend to go on doing my best to introduce it to peoples all over the world.

Religion and a New World Order?

IKEDA: You have said in one of your books that at no time in history have religious cults been as rife as they are today. Perhaps. But your comment – "They seek mystification rather than rationalization" – sounds so much like a remark that a cultivated Roman citizen of the second century might have made that I should like to ask whether you feel yourself part of a civilization on the brink – or in the process – of decline and fall. If Western – specifically Western Christian – civilization is in its last throes, what kind of world order do you predict – or hope – will emerge to take its place?

WILSON: The profusion of new religious and quasi-religious movements in recent decades certainly exceeds anything previously seen in history. In part, this proliferation results from the ease and speed of international communication; in part, it represents spiritual and social uncertainty in response to the accelerated processes of cultural disruption and attrition which are certainly evident in Western Christian culture. Many of the new movements offer people new ways for succeeding in, or escaping from, the demands of everyday life in the modern, highly rationalized world. Yet, even when new movements promise better ways to get on in life, they usually do so by advocating techniques which we might describe as mystical, or which are legitimized by reference to mystical ideas. Even the most conspicuously "scientific" of the new religions, and even those which seek to routinize the processes of learning and religious experience, necessarily embrace some ultimate commitment to super-empirical propositions and arbitrary, non-rational elements. One might, of course, recognize these as implicit in all religious commitment.

It is, however, far from my conception of things to suggest that the inroads being made into traditional Christian culture arise from the new religious movements: they are not the cause of the contemporary malaise, but are to be regarded rather as responses to it. It seems highly unlikely that a distinctively Christian culture will be restored despite the emergence in the United States of the "electronic church" and the "Moral Majority", or the spasmodic campaigns in Britain that arise to express a persisting disquiet about the erosion of so-called Christian values. These movements are ephemeral; they lack co-ordinated policies; their constituencies are amorphous and incapable of being mobilized except briefly and erratically. Their concerns, serious as they are as manifestations of social discontent, become no more than rearguard gestures in defence of temporary positions that, one after another, are overrun by the tide of technical change and hedonistic values.

Nor can Christians hope for much from that other relatively widespread reaction of contemporary Christians – the Charismatic Renewal Movement. That movement, which encourages believers to spontaneous utterance "in unknown tongues" in praise of God, has won the approval of some eminent clergy in various denominations, Catholic and Protestant. Yet, it is no less amorphous and inchoate in its membership, which constitutes an indeterminate and perhaps only transiently involved section of the Church. Worse, the implications of the doctrine that justifies "speaking in unknown tongues", namely that the Holy Spirit may infuse men directly with his power and impart to them puissant spiritual gifts, clearly implies that there is no need for either church hierarchies or ministerial counsel. If the Holy Spirit directly inspires men, Church organizations becomes an otiose remnant of an antiquated Christian culture. The implication of Charismatic Renewal is that the Church and its traditional pattern of faith and order may now be de-structured. Such an implicit assault on the established organizations that have carried Christian culture for centuries can scarcely be regarded as auguring well for that culture.

The new world order, I believe, will be dominated by essentially rational and technical arrangements. That order will lack substantive values, and it will operate in accordance with procedural, that is to say, instrumental values. The emergent social system will not function in response to any set of specifically religious conceptions of human or social purpose. Religious organizations will surely continue, and some of their representatives may well be publicly conspicuous, but it is difficult to envisage the social system accepting the primacy of spiritual values or being significantly influenced by religious concerns. The strength of the emerging rational and technical social order will lie in its transcendence of national, cultural and religious differences, and in the objectivity of the criteria that will be established for a wide range of international, social and political activities. Such a new order will have its weaknesses, however: because of its lack of salient psychological supports for man's emotional awareness, it will have only a limited capacity to motivate men; it will lack means of diffusing the sentiments of social cohesion; and it will have very little ability to stimulate spontaneous and voluntary commitment to the maintenance of social order.

Religion as a Basis for Social Revolution

IKEDA: There is something to be said for the view that social revolution based on religion is desirable. There is also something to be said for the opinion that such revolution restricts freedom of discussion and faith and tends to over-regulate public morality. It is therefore necessary to ascertain the extent to which the dogmas that are embraced by those who advocate such a religion-based revolution might influence popular daily life. Different religions look at this situation from various viewpoints, but Buddhism involves no infringements of human freedoms. A violation of its teachings, on the basis of the law of cause and effect, brings about its own appropriate retribution without the intervention of political authority. What is your opinion of religion-inspired social revolutions and of the Buddhist standpoint in connection with them?

WILSON: Religious revolution is often what has been called "revolution by tradition", the call for men to return to religious prescriptions that have fallen into desuetude. The religiously inspired revolution in contemporary Iran is perhaps of this order. In practice, the past is never restored. The very attempt to retrieve the past is compromised by the false representations that invariably prevail. External circumstances cannot, in any case, be so amended that restoration falls within the bounds of possibility. What religious revolutions or revivals produce is something that is new, no matter how much they invoke tradition.

Within the Judaic and Islamic traditions, any programme for a restorative revolution would have to reassert a whole corpus of specific regulations for the conduct of everyday life: the religious tradition admits of no other interpretation. Hinduism offers more diversified prospects, according to the specific traditions and scriptures to which appeal is made. In Christianity, fundamentalist revival movements tend to seek the reinstitution of literal creeds, dogmas and moral prescripts, and these would certainly require the close regulation of public authorities. To many people in the contemporary West, such a programme would be seen as constituting an infringement of human freedom. Christian movements sometimes invoke the idea of a theocracy as a form of government that God might institute at some future time, and such a prospect implies that social life would then be regulated by the enforcement of God-given moral teachings. Such a revolution remains speculative, awaiting the time when, some Christians believe, God will intervene in human affairs. The idea of Christian social revolution occasionally receives more practical expression – most recently by the Moral Majority in the United States. Yet, even when such groups support victorious political parties, their ideas appear to have no real effect on government.

In its reluctance to enforce a common code of morals, and in the absence of hierarchic organization, the nature of a Buddhist revolution would be different. Its approach might be paralleled by that of some would-be Christian reformers: revolutionary goals would be achieved by the re-dedication of the faithful to an intensified ethical commitment. Can such a programme work, however? Will men choose to behave morally because of what they learn about karma and the law of cause and effect? The premium is small (although it is not small enough to prevent some groups, perhaps the Marxists, from suggesting that even this degree of suasion is a subtle form of coercion instituted by regimes too cunning to resort to open, outright, oppressive action). Is the premium sufficient to elicit widespread, well-adjusted, moral response? This seems to be an open question. There is great pressure on modern men to behave *a*morally, to do only what is required by their roles, and to shelter behind the anonymity that contemporary urban life confers. Can any religion counteract these influences?

Modern society is faced with a deep crisis of control, more evident in the West than in the East. Our technological order induces us to suppose that we can rely entirely on external agencies of control, as if men were only the "automatic pilots" of their own lives. Such controls would, however, be impersonal, abrasive, coercive and eventually perhaps relentless, and men might eventually rebel against them. Already, we see the growing tide of complaint in Western countries against police action, police files, telephone-tappings, data-retrieval systems, tacographs and electronic eyes. The alternative is a moralized society in which individuals exercise self-control, and in which a humane body of established social custom tempers and cushions the direct operation of impersonal legal and technical regulation. It may not be too late for man to recover the benefits of a self-sustained moral order in spite of the increased reliance on technical devices and constraints. Slender as the prospect appears, such a re-moralization of man may be our last chance to mitigate the worst excesses of the over-rationalization of our entire social order, but there appears to be no source for a revolution of this kind – unless it be religion.

PART V

Matters of Mind and Body

The Medical Art: Curing or Calculating?

IKEDA: In the past, we Japanese called medical practice the "humane art", by which we meant a compassionate craft of curing. Today, unfortunately, doctors' interpretations of their profession have changed – with a resultant loss in public trust. The foundations of human, personal exchange between doctor and patient have crumbled; people sarcastically refer to medicine as the calculating art, since doctors are interested in little other than calculating profits.

Of course, individual personalities are partly responsible for this change, but the nature of modern medicine too plays a part. Modern medical science is based on sophisticated technology, and the doctor has come to regard the patient as an objective case to be analysed and treated coolly. Nevertheless warm, human concern is essential to sound therapy, and a man who lacks it cannot be called a doctor in the best sense of the word. Two apparently contradictory things – cool professionalism and warm involvement – are demanded of doctors, many of whom, while living up to the former, sometimes fall down in the latter and become mere medical technicians.

I suspect that only religious faith can enable a doctor to combine humane concern with technical proficiency. Obviously, a great deal depends on the nature of the religion, but faith breeding deep love for mankind is vitally important to the cultivation of the kind of compassionate personality associated with a true healer. What is your interpretation of the spiritual qualifications for a good doctor?

WILSON: The rapid growth of specialization, both within medicine and in the preliminary and ancillary sciences pertinent to it, has induced a remarkable corresponding change in the nature of the curing art. The doctor who once was something of the all-round man, treating his patient as an individual who was reasonably well known to him, is now often a narrow technician dealing not with a person but only with, at best, an "interesting" case. The case is that bit of the body or the psyche in which the specialist deals, and not the whole person. Modern technology has increasingly taken the doctor into the hospital, where he has access to the resources that he now needs for his practice: the practitioner working in his own or in the patient's home becomes a less and less familiar spectacle.

IKEDA: Yes, treatment and diagnosis, too, have been taken into the hospital with the result that, employing the latest technical equipment and data, the doctor sometimes passes judgement on a patient solely on the basis of test results, without ever meeting the ailing person himself. This procedure conditions the doctor to think of the patient, not as a human being, but as a thing or, at best, a pathological example. Lack of contact between them destroys all hope of a sense of trust between patient and physician.

Traditionally, oriental medical practice has insisted that the doctor stay in constant contact with the patient because the symptoms of the same disease vary according to the individual. Furthermore, since the condition of the patient changes day by day, unless therapy is gauged to suit altering symptoms, no cure can be effected.

This approach seems to come closer to setting forth the fundamental relationship that should exist between patient and doctor. In other words, from the philosophy of the doctors of old – especially in the Orient – we ought to learn the importance of trust in treating both the mind and the body.

WILSON: At one time, the principal characteristics of those occupations that, in the West, acquired the name of profession (most conspicuously, medicine, law, the military, teaching and perhaps the Church) were that their practitioners had a particular expertise, which in itself was relatively rare and properly accredited; that they espoused an ethic ensuring a certain standard of performance; that they enjoyed autonomy in the performance of their professional role; that they controlled the situations and institutions in which they practised; that they regulated training, certification and admission to and expulsion from their own ranks; and, above all, that they maintained a fiduciary relationship with their clients. They were people in whom the client reposed his confidence not merely because of their expertise, but also because they were men of character who elicited a much more generalized trust. Humane concern was an expected part of their demeanour and virtually a part of their professional qualification. One trusted not the expert, but the whole man who was the expert and whose total person, and not merely whose technical skills, would be exercised on one's behalf.

The very traditional organization of the professions in Britain may have enabled many of them to retain a certain human warmth and personalized style, which, in countries that have undergone more rapid processes of social change or in which, as in America, tradition is less highly regarded and less deeply rooted, have become things largely of the past. In Britain, too, the development of group practices, the increasing location of doctors within hospitals, and the subdivision of labour among experts whose skills are increasingly refined, all push the profession in the direction you so graphically indicate. Even strong religious faith may not eliminate the effects of these technically dictated divisions of labour and competence. As long as the general practitioner remains, however, there must be a place for some agency of socialization that gives the professional man a humane understanding of his clientele quite outside the specific competencies of his profession.

IKEDA: I think I see what you mean by the humanizing influence of tradition on the British professions, including medicine. In the past, Japanese medicine was swayed by a similar tradition and took into consideration the financial standing of client families and participated in many of their major and minor domestic activities. Before World War II, medical fees in Japan were not standardized; private practitioners often asked larger fees from the rich than they did, for the same care, from the poor. House calls were common, and doctors often joined their clients in a game of *go* after the day's treatment had been concluded. They served as go-betweens in their clients' children's weddings, knew a great deal about the people they cared for, and offered them daily health counsel and advice on private affairs. I have heard that their education included instruction on the healing mission, on the joy of healing and on a general philosophy of life as well as on medical philosophy. Today, however, medical-school education apparently concentrates solely on technical skill and knowledge.

After World War II, the private practitioner underwent a transformation. With the institution of a nationwide health-insurance programme, medical fees were set, and doctors found themselves forced to live within them. Their only way of augmenting their income became seeing as many patients as possible and distributing maximum amounts of medicine. A doctor who conscientiously gave patients as much time as he thought was needed and who engaged in ordinary human intercourse with them would have had to satisfy himself with very modest means. The health-insurance system has been examined and criticized for various reasons, but this flaw remains to the present day.

In my opinion, the modern Japanese medical profession has ethically degenerated for two reasons, related to the outline I have just given. First, today doctors consider patients not as living human beings so much as things or cases, as you have already mentioned. In spite of its great technical sophistication, by taking a purely objective view of human life, modern medicine dampens doctors' innate emotional warmth. The second reason, which may be peculiarly Japanese, is doctors' tendency to think of their work as no more than a way to make money. The physician who uses the national health-insurance programme skilfully can live very well. And many of them have this as their specific, primary goal.

I am sure that you will agree with me when I say that restoring the medical profession to a higher ethical plane and re-establishing profound humane trust between practitioner and patient is a very difficult task. To preserve its humanity, over and beyond techno-scientific expertise, medicine must have deep ethical roots. I think that to achieve the desired aim, medical education itself must be broadened to enable doctors to better understand the meaning of human life and the nature of suffering, and to inspire them to reflect on the ways human beings ought to cope with illness and death. In other words, reawakening them to an awareness of the lofty mission that is theirs may rehumanize the general practitioners' viewpoint.

WILSON: In the past, in Britain, we relied to a considerable extent on the humane tradition of education (so well maintained by our now politically extinguished grammar schools) to furnish prospective professional men with a background knowledge of and sympathy for human culture. Today, education is also becoming increasingly specialized, and the more diffused humane disciplines are just the ones that are most easily crowded out of the curriculum by the ever-expanding demands for increasingly technical instruction.

IKEDA: Japanese medical education has followed a similar course. For instance, when technological advances make it necessary to study fields like anesthesiology, cerebral surgery, neurology, and so on, the humanities are the first things to be sacrificed. Very few Japanese universities offer courses in medical philosophy or medical ethics or teach broad theories of medicine in general. Doctors, today, are convinced that they cannot make a living unless they concentrate on the accumulation of essential medical knowledge and refine their own skills as much as possible. They may be right. I still cannot help doubting whether a man with no interest in or familiarity with ethics, philosophy, history, religion and everything we call the humanities, can have an understanding of human life or can become a friend and partner in patients' battles with illness. To put it bluntly, I do not think a person who is incapable of making loving care for patients the greatest joy in his life is qualified to be a good doctor.

In addition to medical skill and knowledge, a broad background in the humanities, and a spirit of altruistic devotion to his task, the doctor must have a profound respect for the mysteries of nature that can only grow as a result of experience with and awe before the mystery of life itself. The attitude a doctor feels when he grasps the wonder of a single human life can only be called religious.

Respect and love for life in all forms must manifest itself in a caring disposition towards patients. And such caring strikes me as being both one of the essential elements of religion and the ultimate goal of medicine.

WILSON: Without a broad infusion of liberal values, a knowledge of the human past, and an awareness of the diversity of culture, what can supply the medical man (or indeed the lawyer, the teacher and even the clergyman) with the breadth of sympathy that augments and enlivens his professional role? In the West, religion would once have been a part of the content of that socialization. Today, it is less and less likely that a religious perspective will have a part in the professional's self-interpretation of his role. Even in Catholic countries, in which medicine has been closely associated with religion, particularly through the role of nursing sisters, it is recognized (and we have good studies from Belguim – a country with an interesting mixture of religious and civil medicine) that there is little difference between a Catholic hospital and one established by the state. Even Catholic doctors adhere to the technical norms of their profession and are scarcely different from their more secular colleagues in their attitude to patients or to the issues that are at stake in medical ethics. Where religious commitment of a more intense kind is associated with the medical profession, there is indeed some evidence for your views. Thus, doctors who are brought up in the faith of the Seventh-Day Adventists (a Christian denomination in which there has been a strong preoccupation with medicine and bodily health from its beginnings) are well known in the United States for their caring dispositions. In contrast to many other doctors, who are seeking more profit and a more comfortable life-style, Adventist doctors often accept practices in remote rural districts where there is great need, little profit and far fewer of the facilities and comforts of modern life. Dedication of this kind is found in other Christian denominations among those doctors who go into the mission field, often working in conditions that are not only personally discomforting, but that also render their professional practice difficult.

Organ Transplants

IKEDA: Although the difficulties of accurately determining death and of preventing rejection reactions have meant that heart transplants are currently less a topic of general conversation than they were a few years ago, research in transplanting other organs and in devising artificial organs is continuing with some success. Artificial lungs and kidneys have been successfully installed, with the result that life has been prolonged, and continuing study is gradually improving the functioning efficiency of artificial hearts and livers. Indeed, research is considering the production of artificial brains and may soon challenge the problems of brain transplants. At the present stage, such an operation is impossible, but medical technology has not stopped advancing. Do you think medical reconstruction of the body ought to go as far as to attempt to deal with the brain, or should a halt be called before this point is reached?

WILSON: I suppose that we are all somewhat daunted by the prospect that part of our brain – which modern man has come to regard (in contrast to the views of man in so many eras of the past) as the principal locus of his unique being – might be replaced by the brain of another individual. Perhaps we regard the kidneys, and even the heart, as merely functioning entities, and we might fairly easily accept the idea that, if need arose, an organ from someone else might replace our own. It is, I think, still natural that we should all be more hesitant to take the same attitude towards the brain. I wonder if what I take to be universal hesitation is stronger in some cultures than in others – for example, stronger in the West, with its more vigorous and emphatic individualism, than in the Orient, where religion and tradition allow men to assimilate their own lives and feelings to those of a wider humanity more readily?

Perhaps, too, many of us might feel that when the brain itself is at issue, the uniqueness of the personality might be radically affected by the receipt of the living tissue of another person. Which of us would care to be fused so intimately with an unknown other, and what sort of awareness of ourselves would we have thereafter? What moral questions might arise if, subsequent to a successful operation of that kind, a profound change occurred in the individual's behaviour or in his attitudes and dispositions? Such speculation might be entirely misplaced, of course, and one awaits the verdict of medical science about such possibilities. Clearly, the less precise the information and the less it could be stressed that the organs concerned are purely functional, motor-control parts of the brain, the more anxiety an individual might show. Might such anxiety in itself have a consequence for the effectiveness of such an operation?

IKEDA: Perhaps, as you suggest, the whole thing is still very speculative. Some experiments are, however, currently being carried out on brains. For instance, a monkey brain has been removed from the animal's skull and kept alive on artificial circulation. It would seem that the next step after such support of a brain in isolation would be transplantation. Connecting the brain with the central nervous system is still beyond the skills of the most dexterous surgeon.

On the other hand, attempts are now being made to extend neuron processes. If entire-brain transplants are unfeasible, partial ones may be possible in the future. In such cases, doctors may become capable of curing anencephalic newborn infants by transplanting cerebral tissue from other human beings into their bodies. In even more extreme research, entire heads have been transferred from one monkey to another. In connection with human beings, operations of this kind conjure up images which are too grotesque and revolting to entertain.

More in line with your comments, brain transplants, partial or entire, and the whole field of cerebral surgery make us uneasy because they seem to threaten the independence of the human individual. You are right to point out the greater Oriental sense of the communality of all things in the universe, including human beings, and our consequent under-emphasized individuality. Nevertheless, we Oriental peoples prize our identities; and the idea of tampering with and possibly upsetting or destroying our individuality by means of brain surgery is as unwelcome to us as it is to the Westerner. This is true in the case of partial as well as total brain transplants. Like you, however, I have no objection to brain surgery affecting purely motor-control parts, the tampering with which in no way alters the individual personality.

WILSON: Perhaps, most of all, one feels that brain transplants might render the patient even more of a mere "case" than any other, the victim of the medical profession's desire to see if they could actually get so far into the natural realm as to make this, perhaps the most complex, and certainly potentially the most intimate, form of transfer of organs, actually work.

IKEDA: We must be very cautious about future developments in medical science because, in addition to brain transplants, a number of techniques could, if put into practice, have irreversible and not necessarily beneficial consequences. Among them are the cloning of living beings, including human beings; crosses between human beings and other animals; and attempts to control the brain by means of chemicals. The path which physicians have followed in the past leads us to suspect that their future attention will be concentrated almost entirely on technology. As you have pointed out, devotion to technical skill and improvement, when this is put before everything else, can make the patient a sacrificial victim instead of a living human being in need of understanding and help. This can have perilous consequences for all mankind. In other words, I believe that there is a line that must not be crossed thoughtlessly between the desire to verify the possibility of a certain medical technique and the actual implementation of that technique. Some of the things that are possible from the medico-technological viewpoint are harmful to individuals and perhaps to all humanity. Consequently, representatives not only of the medical-science field, but also of society at large ought to examine scientific advances and proposals and, when it is deemed necessary, call a halt to developments in patently dangerous directions. Medicine exists, not for the sake of its own advancement, but for the sake of mankind. The patient is there to be helped and cured, not to serve as experimental material. The time has come for all of us to re-examine medicine from this standpoint.

Tampering with Genetic Structures

IKEDA: Experiments in genetic reorganization, in spite of their therapeutic value, involve ethical and moral issues since they may result in the production of potentially dangerous genes. Two opinions are current on the subject. One group of scientists insists that all such experimentation should cease at once. Another group insists that experiments conducted in accordance with NIH (National Institute of Health) guidelines are perfectly safe. Where do you stand on this issue? Although I am in favour of continued study in this field for the sake of the good it may do in curing hereditary illnesses, I believe that not only members of the medical profession, but also philosophers, men of religion and representatives of the general populace must be fully aware of the great dangers involved. Study of genetic reoganization ought to continue but must be accompanied by serious, constant surveillance and examination from many viewpoints, especially when actual application of experimentally obtained results is contemplated. What is your evaluation of the limitations that should be applied to this kind of research?

WILSON: One is tempted to respond to an issue of this kind with an adaptation of the old cliche, and say that health is much too serious a matter to be left to the doctors. Obviously, in every technical respect, one must respect the judgement and rely on the ethical standards of the medical profession and of those branches of science which serve it. To that end, we must try to ensure that we maintain the highest standards – ethical and cultural, as well as purely medical and technical – for admission into the ranks of these professions. We need men who are themselves exceptional in the strength of their ethical sensitivity and whose standards of personal integrity match their standards of technical expertise. Even given this desideratum, the questions at stake transcend the narrow interests of both the medical profession and scientific research.

IKEDA: Indeed. After all, genetic engineering reaches to the very fundamental basis of human existence. And you are quite right in quoting the cliche: the situation is much too serious to entrust to doctors. All society must participate in judgements related to it. Furthermore, I agree entirely that in these fields we require men of great ethical sensitivity and personal integrity. Perhaps this is less important when genetic engineering is being used solely to improve plants and micro-organisms. When it is applied to human beings, scientists must not be permitted to be lax in connection with safety policies or to avoid responsibility for accidents. Furthermore, doctors and scientists must not be allowed to experiment in secret, where no effective social restraints can be imposed on their actions. In addition, their work should be submitted for examination by specialists from other fields and must be evaluated in the light of philosophical, ethical and religious considerations.

WILSON: I agree. It is a good thing for a body of medical specialists to keep issues of this kind under review, but it would be better if a lay body of eminent and established men of affairs drawn together from diverse fields of public life acted as an independent commission to which such questions might be referred. I do not mean a committee of politicians, of course, because, since (in free countries) they must be re-elected, their interests tend to be narrow, often limited in time perspectives and calculated with regard to their own careers.

Ideally, such a commission would be recruited from public-spirited citizens who were established in their own professions and whose concern could be guaranteed to be disinterested. As laymen, they would need to have the issues set before them in a form no more technical than was necessary, and they might need the service of an independently recruited staff of technically qualified men, behaving as the best form of civil service and recognizing it as their duty to prepare objectively and neutrally the information on the basis of which others should make decisions. All these considerations indicate the difficulty of creating and servicing such a review body, but I would myself much rather trust such a body, properly and carefully appointed, than a committee of technical experts standing too close to the specific professionalism of the field, and perhaps insufficiently involved in the wider life of society or unaware of its values and concerns.

There is a background problem for a solution of this kind, however, and I wonder if it obtains in Japan as fully as it does in Britain? The growth in professionalism is such that, today, few people can stand back as disinterested amateurs, as men of detached goodwill who can afford the time to devote themselves to public service of this kind. Formerly, there was, within the British class system, a section of society with the means, the education, and a strong ethic of public conscience and civic goodwill, all of which prompted them, often at a financial cost to themselves, to undertake this sort of voluntary work. Today, this class has disappeared. One of the incidental malfunctions of an increasingly egalitarian system is the reduction of everything to a level of professionalism. People work for money and increasingly only for money. The ethos of such a society is that everyone is "worthy of his hire". There are, however, tasks for which no hire is appropriate and which, if they are to be done well, are best done by people who expect no pecuniary reward. It would be a pity to establish a so-called committee of lay persons and to find that it was itself becoming a new profession, acquiring expertise not in the technicalities of medicine, but in committeemanship. There are signs of just such a development at various levels of local and national government in Britain. I wonder if the same phenomenon occurs in Japan?

I concur with your views about the importance of surveillance, and I like to think that modern society could produce well-educated people with the right disinterested sympathy to man the type of review body that you have in mind, and that such a body could keep its sights above those of the medical profession or its ancillary experimental research officers. I fear that the professional society is one in which these sorts of ethical concerns are increasingly difficult to sustain, partly because we are all at the mercy of some other profession's expertise and partly because we lack an independent class, sufficiently educated but sufficiently unprofessional, to take on the tasks that you and I should like to assign to them.

IKEDA: The citizens of Cambridge, Massachusetts, formed a committee made up of case workers, nurses, city planners, architects, epidemiologists and even a dealer in heating equipment, to study and make judgements on the techniques of genetic alterations when they felt this issue was reaching the crisis stage. Meeting practically weekly, with specialists in the field, they made a careful study of the situation. And, although it is true that steps should be taken to prevent them from deteriorating into professionals in committeemanship, groups of this kind partly fulfil the requirements you set forth. In Japan, public awareness is beginning to take genetic engineering into account. The field itself is developing rapidly, and not long ago, when a research institute decided to build facilities for viral and bacteriological experiments, citizens from the surrounding region organized protests. Civic groups have also been organized to study the DNA problem.

In general, in Japan today, where most doctors work only for money, there are very few people with the leisure and the public conscience and goodwill to undertake this kind of activity. Particularly over the past three decades of rapid economic growth, the Japanese have become greater professionalists. We hear that, before World War II, this was not the case and that doctors took an active part in public endeavours unrelated to their own field of special study. This rarely happens now.

I believe that religion can help cultivate people who, even if they are short of leisure time, none the less suppress their own ego and professionalism and have a sense of mission towards humanity and society. Given the cooperation of people with specialist knowledge, amateur committees made up of such people can evolve the strength to pass sound judgements on issues of major public interest.

Biological Evolution

IKEDA: Criticisms of the Darwinian interpretation of evolution fall into two general categories: those which question the very theory of biological evolution and those which, while recognizing biological evolution, question the idea of change within a species through sudden mutation. (Among Japanese scholars, this is the major point of contention.) Although fossil remains put the truth of biological evolution beyond doubt, fundamentalist Christians – especially in the United States – continue to reject it because it runs counter to the Judaeo-Christian story of the Creation. A long course of biological evolution is manifestly beside the point if the Creator God created all things as they are now in six days. (Some people in California complain that teaching human evolution from lower animals while not teaching the story of the Creation as told in the Old Testament violates the right of freedom of religion.) I should be interested to hear your views on the ways Christians and Muslims – who believe in the Creator God – deal with this contradiction.

WILSON: The Old Testament creation story is common to both Judaism and Christianity. The Koran too declares that man and the universe were created by a special act of the deity. Certainly, until the end of the nineteenth century, orthodox Christians, whether Catholics or Protestants, were expected to believe the story of the creation literally. Man was regarded as a special creation of God. Darwinism, however, indicated that man, as a species, had emerged by a process of natural selection after a long course of the evolution of lesser species. The idea of evolution had been steadily growing for more than a hundred years before Charles Darwin published his work; indeed, his own grandfather, Erasmus Darwin, had been an evolutionist.

It was the thesis of natural selection, with its stronger implication that the biblical story of special creation was a fiction, that shocked the ecclesiastical dignitaries of the Christian community. It took time for some of them to come to terms with Darwinian ideas; but, as the theory came to command the general assent of intellectuals, only a minority of Christians remained unconvinced and continued to press for the literal interpretation of the scriptures. Even some fundamentalists, most of whom are, today, members of separated sects, have developed ingenious theories to attempt to reconcile the geological and archaeological evidence with the biblical account of the origins of the universe and the special creation of man.

Although they are not acknowledged, either openly or tacitly, by most Christians, there are serious implications in evolutionary theory for Christian theology, a basic tenet of which is that each man is possessed of a soul. Orthodox Christians have always denied that any other living creature possesses a soul: man is held to be a unique form of life. The theory of evolution, however, leaves no place for the specific development of the soul, so Christians who accept it have an unresolved intellectual problem that goes to the heart of Christian philosophy and anthropology.

Because they present the account of creation in concrete terms and depict it as occurring at a specific point at the beginning of historical time, the three Middle Eastern religions have all been embarrassed by the findings and the theories of empirical science. The weight of the scientific evidence gradually caused most educated Christians, including clergy, to relinquish their belief in the scriptural account of creation, although there has been an attempt to re-evaluate it by emphasizing its allegorical, poetic or symbolic importance. Christian and Jewish laymen, today, even though they might otherwise remain religiously committed, usually accept contemporary scientific theories of evolution and genetic transmission. The problem for Muslims has, in practice, been less acute than it was for Christians. There is no doubt about the teachings, of course. The Koran declares "He [Allah] created you from a single being, then from that being He created its mate . . . He moulded you in your mothers' wombs by stages in threefold darkness'. Of course, intellectual assent to a coherently formulated body of doctrine has been less emphasized in Islam than in Christianity. Islam is a religion in which practice, as governed by law, matters more than purely intellectual commitment; there has been less need to make formal acknowledgment of obvious contradictions by modern science of the thesis of special creation. It was among intellectuals in Christian countries that theories of evolution developed, and in Christian societies that the evidence was presented. Since, for a long time, the theories had little practical import and since they did not immediately impinge on Muslim intellectual life, acquaintance with the ideas of evolutionism occurred only very gradually and was only a small part of the much wider confrontation of Islam with the modernizing thrust of Western science and technology.

As such, it was not itself a prominent element in that confrontation and had no particularly direct or dramatic implications for Muslim thought and practice. Despite the totalitarianism of Islamic law, Muslims manifest extraordinary pragmatism in dealing with actual issues: wherever incentive has been present, the law has been more easily reinterpreted than might be supposed from a literal acceptance of the basic principle on which it operates – namely, that law should determine society and not the reverse. Clearly, in a largely intellectual matter (which does, however, increasingly come to have possible practical implications), the issue has not had to be firmly grasped. In a variety of cognate issues, for example such matters as family planning, Islamic countries have been much more accommodating than might be expected of a religion in which conservative ethics are so strongly underwritten.

IKEDA: Because Buddhism includes no creation myth similar to those of the Judaeo-Christian and Islamic traditions, Japanese Buddhists had practically no difficulty with Darwinian evolution.

As you know, the Buddhist teaching is that a life entity goes through repeated births and deaths and that not all of those births need be in any specific form; that is, the life that is human this time may be non-human the next time round. As a result of karma, a life is reborn – not always in the same species as in preceding existences – with the traits suited to its karmic background. In other words, all kinds of changes, evolutionary and otherwise, are possible. Characteristics may be passed from parent to offspring, as is compatible with the Buddhist theory of consistent continuity of life from past, to present, to future.

Although from the Buddhist standpoint the idea of biological evolution itself presents no difficulty, two important points remain to be resolved. First, within the overall evolution of all life on earth, each individual living being can be shown to alter and evolve within the continuum composed of past, present and future. Buddhist philosophy explains these changes as the result of karma and cause-and-effect relations. Our problem is to determine the relationship between karmic influences and biological evolution. Second, Buddhist thought must come to grips with the still unresolved issue of relations between karma and sudden mutation and accommodation.

Should Incurables Be Told?

IKEDA: Since, in all but a limited number of varieties, cancer is incurable, telling a dying patient the truth of his condition can inflict the fear of death in him. Today many doctors debate the advisability of revealing the nature of the illness to a cancer patient. Sometimes the shock of the announcement is so great that people whose lives might have been prolonged die prematurely. Do you agree that, for this very reason, the nature of the sickness should be kept a secret practically until the end?

Some people insist that telling a patient he has cancer allows him to make the fullest use of his remaining time. Still others argue that telling the truth in such instances is the duty of all sincere human beings.

Although, in many cases, I advocate keeping the truth from patients, I realize that people who have firm faith and a sound philosophy can prepare themselves better if they know what is happening to them.

WILSON: What you say on this point seems to me to be the best counsel, and I feel that one must be guided by knowledge of the patient himself. Some people are resilient and spiritually strong enough to withstand the worst news and quickly find a way of coping with the immense initial anguish induced by the knowledge of the nearness of death and the fearful complications and pain that cancer causes. Others may be much more frail and may need handling with care, so that the shock is cushioned. Obviously, if they learn of their diagnosis early, such people may live for months in a hopeless condition, whereas concealment might at least give them moments of comfort, hope and even joy during the last months of life. We need to recognize, however, that we are not always able to tell just which individuals are frail and which resilient from our past observations. Men who have appeared strong and resourceful in health may became spiritually feeble in sickness, and sometimes the apparently broken reeds of the everyday world discover and display hitherto unsuspected inner strength.

Thus, while I do not believe that the naked truth is always to be demanded in every situation, I acknowledge the difficulty of deciding how to proceed in individual cases. Human life is civilized by the cultivation of subtle skills of caring and loving; at times discretion, postponement and gentle self-restraint may be of more ultimate value than a bold commitment to absolute truth, whatever the circumstances and whoever the recipient. Such advice can obviously be represented as deceitful cowardice and the abandonment of absolute values. My own feeling is that it is impossible to justify this kind of judgement *tout court*. Circumstances must alter cases, and whilst we may maintain that absolute truth-telling is a high ideal that, other things being equal, is an obligation upon us, none the less, we need to recognize that other values may at times modify one's supreme commitments to absolute truth. In practice, none of us tells all that we know all the time; it might even be dangerous, sometimes imprudent and often unkind to do so. There is some point, I think, in the old English saying that one should "temper the wind to the shorn lamb".

IKEDA: The saying is very much to the point. A number of things must be taken into consideration in determining whether to reveal to a patient that his illness is cancer. First, is it in an early stage amenable to therapy or a terminal, ultimately fatal stage? Second, is it one of the kinds of cancer that contemporary medical skill finds relatively easy to cure? If the disease has not developed quickly or is susceptible to therapy, the patient should be told, the announcement should be accompanied by a thorough explanation, and all co-operation should be afforded to the patient in his struggle against the illness. If the situation is past help, however, deciding whether or not to tell the truth depends on the psychological strength and resilience of the patient. If the person is strong and wishes to make the best of his remaining time and to die well, he should be told.

At any rate, today, knowledge of cancer is fairly widespread, so patients, even without being told directly, sense the nature of their illness, especially in the late stages or when therapy such as radiation treatment is employed. The important thing is for the patient to make mental and spiritual preparations to combat the fear of death. And, in this, doctors, nurses and men of religion can be of immense assistance. Indeed, teaching people, not only how to live, but also how to die may be one of religion's most important functions. Conceivably, through the help of medical and religious advisors, the patient could develop attitudes towards life and death that would be a source of great psychological strength, which might in turn generate physical energy to help overcome the disease.

Cancer and the Mind

IKEDA: Many people recognize the importance of psychosomatic elements in illness, and in recent years the possible mental aspects and influences involved in cancer have been a topic of consideration. For instance, the subject was discussed at the Fourth International Council of Psychosomatic Medicine, held in Tokyo in 1977; and an article on it was published in the June 1978 issue of the American journal *Science*. Study has shown that psychological changes for the better in an individual's mental state or a revolution in his philosophy of life have been known to cause a natural reduction of tumours. The patient's mental state is important in foretelling the amount of time he may have left to live. Worsening in mental outlook is thought to have a more deleterious effect than worsening in the actual physical condition. If these things are true, religion, which helps human beings evolve a philosophy of life, can play an important part. For instance, if it can be shown that religion assists in revolutionizing the individual's philosophy or in improving his psychological state, and thus influences the course of development of cancerous tumours, its importance for medical therapy will become undeniable. What role do you think religion has to play in medical therapy, especially in the treatment of illnesses such as cancer?

WILSON: The intimate association of religion and curing has sometimes been represented as evidence of man's recourse to the supernatural realm at those points at which his reliable empirical knowledge ends. In the face of uncertainty and lack of knowledge, men have turned to magic, prayer, charms and exercises justified purely by spiritual or metaphysical theories. In consequence, it became commonplace for orthodox medicine to disparage religiously prescribed methods of curing. Obviously, in social situations in which there was ignorance of medical science and empirical testing, much was done that was at best useless and at worst harmful. Yet it is true that the evidence is not all of one kind. Just as the old herbal remedies prescribed by folklore have sometimes been found to be effective, and at times have even proved the starting-point for medical pharmacology, so the possibility of beneficial therapeutic effects of religious practice have increasingly been acknowledged, even when the precise mechanisms of religious cause and somatic effect are not precisely understood.

IKEDA: No, the mechanisms are not always clearly understood, but the importance of mental attitude in all psychosomatic conditions is beyond question. Since religion and faith often have a calming, balancing effect on the mind, it is easy to see that they have somatic effects. Indeed, Western medical science is increasingly taking this kind of effect into consideration, as the whole nature of sickness, at least in the industrialized nations, has changed drastically.

In many parts of the world, epidemics, which formerly took high tolls in human life, are now rarities. In their place have come such illnesses as cancer, circulatory diseases and all kinds of stress-related troubles. Finding that the classical methods of anatomy, cytology, physiology and all the other purely physical aspects of their science no longer effect perfect cures, doctors are paying attention to psychological effects, including stress, and are evolving a new field of psychosomatic medicine.

It is known that the mental condition of the patient is related to his ability to combat cancer, since stress greatly lowers the body's powers of immunization, whereas a bright, resolute attitude towards illness raises them. Religions that help believers to cultivate such attitudes clearly have direct therapeutic effects.

WILSON: There are, I think, a number of problems, in this obviously highly complex area. First, sometimes the therapeutic benefits claimed for specific religious practice are difficult to substantiate, because the religious authorities either object to medical diagnosis or see no need to refer such cases for medical diagnosis. Thus the claims for their specific religious techniques remain unsubstantiated by empirical medical tests. Second, religious therapists sometimes explain the results they achieve in terms, and with the support, of theories that are unacceptable to the medical profession and perhaps at odds with the assumptions and ideas that are generally current within wider society. Third, particularly in the case of faith healing and metaphysical healing, part of the technique of religious therapies may be to deny the existence or the reality of the disease that is to be cured. In consequence, it becomes difficult to assess just which cases are – from a medical perspective – real cases and cases which are, from the beginning, illusory both in the matter of the ailment and the matter of its cure.

The fourth difficulty applies more generally to religious therapies and less specifically to those religions that canvass particular therapeutic techniques or have distinctive metaphysical theories of healing. It lies essentially in the difficulty of reconciling the highly personalized influence of religion with the highly routinized and impersonal effect of medical science. Thus, one sees that whereas in one particular case, the influence of religious faith or practice apparently works an effect on a patient, in the case of another individual who is no less devoted to his religion no such gain is achieved. Medical science would hope to discover standard effects from identical therapies, and in general its treatments work equally well with comparable cases. We know that, in the matter of religious influences, effects are highly variable. Of course, this may arise from differences in religious commitment which are impossible for the outsider to perceive. Two apparently equally devout men may, in their heart of hearts, be differently committed, differ in the measure of their faith, and have different records of private religious practice and devotion. Unfortunately, since these interpersonal differences are not available for objective tests, we do not know with certainty that deeper commitment in itself leads to better therapeutic results. The paradox is one that religious leaders have not failed to observe. Jesus said to those whom he healed, "Thy faith hath made thee whole"; but the Judaeo-Christian tradition recognizes that sometimes the wicked "flourish like the green bay tree", and the psalmist virtually asks God for an explanation of this apparent injustice.

There seems to me to be no doubt that men who have acquired positive dispositions, who can maintain mental equilibrium, affirmative orientations to their fellow men and an open, receptive attitude to others and to the world, may receive enormous benefits in life, including a capacity to withstand or to overcome illness in ways that we do not yet wholly understand. The problem lies, I think, in learning – if it can be learned – how such positive power may be mobilized and harnessed and wherein the differences in capacity of various individuals actually resides.

IKEDA: You may have mentioned religions that reject diagnoses and therapy by medical science. I find their attitude highly suspect. If it is to be convincing, a religion must explain whatever therapeutic powers it claims in terms acceptable to medical science and society. Beyond matters of this kind, it seems to me that, today, doctors – both men of faith and men with no religious interests at all – are beginning to recognize the importance of faith and religion in combination with scientific diagnostics and treatment. For instance, many of them – notably specialists in psychosomatic medicine – continue to employ such standard practices as medication, surgery, immunization, radiation treatment, and so on while at the same time introducing psychiatric and psychological methods and even certain kinds of religious training. According to reports, the International College of Psychosomatic Medicine and the Japan College of Psychosomatic Medicine use meditation, various kinds of yoga and image therapy (based on Buddhist concepts) in treating cancer. In these instances, modern medical science is the therapeutic basis of all actions, which are explained in terms acceptable to medical scientists.

You are quite right to say that such highly personal elements as religious devotion and degree of commitment are not open to objective investigation, but is this not true of most of the other aspects of illness? Genetic background, life experience, personality and all the other elements that contribute to the formation of the individual psyche elude objective investigation. Changes in life style can often bring about drastic personality alterations.

Consequently, although a fundamental general theoretical basis may exist, therapy involving these personality-related inscrutables must, it seems to me, entail an intensely personal relationship between patient and doctor. The intertwining of two indefinites, like patient personality and attitude towards religious faith, so immensely complicates the situation that it is impossible to hope for easy objectivity. None the less, I feel confident that perseverance in the current attempts at psychosomatic treatment of illnesses like cancer can gradually elucidate the relations among sickness, the psyche and religion.

Euthanasia

IKEDA: The horrible agonies of sufferers from such illnesses as cancer lead many to consider euthanasia humane and even to advocate its legalization. In Japan, some people not only think this way, but are also taking concrete steps in the furtherance of legalization. They think that, when death is near and the patient is suffering intolerably, painless euthanasia should be allowed as long as more than two qualified physicians decide that the patient's condition is incurable. Most of its advocates insist that the decision to allow euthanasia should be based on the free choice of the patient. Do you feel that, if human beings have the right to live, they ought to have the right to die as well? My own opinion is that recognizing euthanasia, even on the basis of the free option of the patient, is extremely dangerous since, in the wrong hands, this drastic means could be converted into the kind of killings that were part of the Nazi policy of extermination of people they considered undesirable.

WILSON: It seems likely to me that an individual's personal experience of seeing the slow and agonizing death of loved ones may influence his reaction to the question of euthanasia, particularly in the modern world, in which — at least in the United States and to some extent in Europe — death has now come to be regarded almost as an obscenity. There has been an interesting reversal of attitudes in the last five or six decades. Whereas once it was the beginnings of life — by which I mean sex, birth and all that pertains to it – that was a taboo subject, now it is its termination, death. We see this in the very striking change in funeral practices: death was once an occasion for great social pomp, and the dead were buried with the trappings of the status that they had acquired in life (in spite of Christian prescriptions to the contrary). Today, the dead are hastily disposed of, and customs once associated with death have been abbreviated and sometimes eliminated. People are embarrassed by death, even about what to say to the bereaved. We now hate death in exactly the way in which a Victorian lady of proper refinement – whether English or American – was supposed to hate sex, or even the very mention of the word. When death was surrounded by a structure of social mores and customs, it was easier for people to face it.

The modern endorsement of euthanasia may, paradoxically, be less of an open and honest acceptance of the fact of death than just another facet of the embarrassment about it. Such embarrassment dictates that people say in effect, *Let those near to death die quickly, and let them die with their own full assent, so that the rest of us may feel, as little and as briefly as possible, any need to grieve.*

The contemporary campaign for euthanasia, which is vigorous in Europe as well as in Japan, seems to be in danger of becoming just another facet of the many-sided demand for permissiveness in modern society – as if individuals were entirely responsible for, and only to, themselves. No one can deny man's right to die, if that is the way in which the advocates of euthanasia care to put it. One might say, if one is to resort to rhetoric of this kind, that men also have an obligation to die: society depends on death and on the fulfilment of generalized expectations concerning it. Even though death may strike individuals unexpectedly and suddenly, our social systems have permanent contingency plans for a given statistical probability of deaths, and this not merely with regard to such matters as the disposal of remains, but also with respect to the reallocation of rights, property, roles and status. Succession and inheritance are well articulated institutions in all societies, and they are vital to every society's operation. We can see that even the occasional long postponement of death may, in certain cases, create difficulties with regard to social expectations about succession and inheritance. So much is this the case, that all advanced societies have introduced, for virtually all formally organized roles, an institution of *anticipatory death*. We call it retirement. However retirement is selective death: it does not encroach, or should not encroach, on the private, familial, spiritual or recreational facets of an individual's life – should not, in short, impinge too much on affective and primary life. In this area, the individual continues to carry social obligations and responsibilities to, and for, others.

In these various ways, then, death remains a social, not merely an individual, matter. And, even if we choose to concede that men "have a right to die", it does not follow that they necessarily have a right to decide on the time of their death. Their kinsfolk are involved, as are the medical and caring professions and, beyond them, other segments of the wider society. Life is not merely a personal thing, as I see it: rather, it is a complex of commitments and obligations to a society that includes others, past, contemporary and future. The individual's right over his own life and its extinction is far from being an absolute right, just as the way in which an individual comports himself in life is far from being a matter solely for his own personal discretion. He learns to live; how to live; and how to live with, and at times for, others. He must learn that this lesson extends to his departure from life as much as to his arrival in it, and to his passage through it. Thus, whilst I would not say that euthanasia was always and invariably wrong, I distrust the contemporary campaign and believe that the individual's life is far from being a matter solely for his own disposal.

IKEDA: Yes, family, relatives, friends, acquaintances and others are affected by an individual's death. And I think it runs counter to the respect which life deserves to say that the individual is free to dispose of his own life at will. None the less, at the verge of death, the individual human must suffer, and I feel it is a role of religion to help him understand his suffering so that he can cope with it.

For many an individual, the psychological worry about what will happen to one's survivors or how one will be remembered after death is more distressing than the physical pain of fatal illness. And no doubt, most dreadful of all is the awesome, lonely battle with the immense unknown that is death itself. (Buddhist philosophy has classified suffering into three kinds – suffering from torment, suffering from the prevention of pleasure and suffering at the knowledge of the impermanence of all phenomena – which correspond closely to the three kinds of suffering experienced by a human being on the brink of death.)

Modern pain clinics may some day be able to eliminate physical suffering altogether, but they can do nothing about the other two kinds. To deal with these, the patient must have the affectionate care of his family and of medical personnel, and must be able to draw on the compassion and love taught by religion. If medical science continues to make progress in the field of pain relief and if religion is allowed to co-operate with medicine to provide assistance in those fields in which science is impotent, the day may come when people will die well and content and when there will be no need to discuss euthanasia.

The Fear of Death

IKEDA: No matter the form in which death comes, all human beings must confront the fear of death. The book of conversations with people about to die written by an American psychologist, Elisabeth Kübler-Ross, caused a great sensation in Japan, and I consider her theory of the five stages to death to be correct. In other words, although her schema is formalized, I too believe that, upon learning of affliction with an incurable illness, people refuse to admit the danger; become angry about it; attempt to make some kind of bargain with fate; repress their sorrow; and finally accept it and confront the inevitable. I further believe, however, that the human being must face death, not in suffering, but independently, with an easy mind. Being able to do this depends on the person's philosophy of life and death; that is, on the philosophical foundation on which he has lived. The person who has lived a life of fulfilment in faith is able to die in the same way. In my opinion, it is religion that enables human beings to do both. Furthermore, it is the duty of religions to satisfy this need. Do you agree with me?

WILSON: The fact of death is something which practically all religions seek to interpret for their adherents. One or two unusual Christian sects, particularly in the United States, have taken a radical view and declared that the really true believer will not die and, in consequence, have regarded death as shameful for surviving kinsfolk. Rather more generally, the mention of death has been seen as indelicate, and dead people are referred to euphemistically as having "passed on", "passed over", "fallen asleep" or as being "on the other side". Such has been the modern fear of death.

Traditionally, death has been seen as a stark reality requiring religion to supply reassurance and courage for those who face it and resourcefulness and assuagement of grief for those who become bereaved. Obviously, to fortify men in the face of death entails the building of attitudes of self-discipline, seriousness of mind and purpose, and a sense of responsibility for one's life – and the cultivation of such dispositions is itself a life-time's work.

I think that some sincere and conscientious unbelievers have attained and maintained a high degree of integrity in their lives and have carried this nobility of spirit through to the end, facing death with composure and quiet resolution. Nineteenth-century Christians used to like to tell stories of opponents of the Church or agnostics who had defied the Christian religion all their lives but who, on their deathbeds, in facing the stark reality of extinction or damnation, had died either in terror or had become last-minute converts to Christianity. It is likely that most of these stories were told merely by way of religious propaganda and were all the more dramatic because of the Christian belief in hell-fire for those who died as unrepentant sinners or deniers of Christ. None the less, there can be no doubt that religious faith, Christian or otherwise, has been a great aid and comfort to many men facing death. In the Christian case, fears of an after-life of prolonged torment in hell and hopes for eternal bliss in heaven have sharpened the claims of religion to be of use to the dying, but all the great faiths see death as a time of reckoning, when men need to be able to come to terms with themselves. Dramatic deathbed conversions are a specifically Christian palliative for those terrified by death, but in the Christian case, too, a steady lifetime of conviction and faith must generally be counted as of more value than an eleventh-hour conversion (the parables of Jesus notwithstanding). The nineteenth-century Christian stories were told less to congratulate the dead or the dying, than to encourage a life of faith in the listeners.

From a more strictly psychological perspective, steady commitment and years of religious discipline are likely to allow men to encounter death with greater composure and equanimity than might be obtained from a sudden and dramatic change of heart in extremity.

IKEDA: I think so too. Interestingly enough, the Buddhist view is that to die a good death, one must have led a good life. Buddhist discipline and training are designed to help each believer to overcome suffering, develop the psychological strength to face crises like death, and steadily manifest from his own innermost depths his own Buddha nature. The knowledge that death represents the return of the individual life to the great universal life prior to another phenomenal manifestation is a source of splendid strength, rich with compassion and wisdom. As he strives to perfect himself by doing good for others, the Buddhist is constantly aware that death is a fulfilling and enriching part of life. For people who believe this, death is not defeat, but a wonderful stimulus to live more vigorously and more meaningfully.

WILSON: As you say, a life in the fulfilment of faith makes possible a death of the same kind. I would take it further and, without in the slightest wishing to diminish the benefit religious faith often confers upon men at the time of death (and, of no less importance, on their surviving kinsfolk), would say that a life of integrity and seriousness of purpose, whether informed by a particular religious faith or not, might also enable a man to die with dignity and contentment, even in circumstances of prolonged suffering.

Death and Consciousness

IKEDA: In recent years, in connection with what is called near-death experiences, doctors and psychologists have been viewing from the scientific standpoint some of those aspects of life after death that, in the past, have been the exclusive province of religion and a small number of people with paranormal powers. In his book *Life After Life*, Doctor Raymond A. Moody discusses points in common among the experiences of 150 people who came close to dying but who later recovered. After making a scientific critique of the work and conducting his own statistical investigation, Kenneth Ring endorsed Moody's findings. Karlis Osis and Erlendur Haraldsson found similarities in near-death experiences between Americans and Indians. Moody and people in sympathy with his research have reported that the majority of cases investigated described death as a tranquil experience. Working from the viewpoint of a specialist in cardiac diseases, however, Maurice Rawlings found that about half of the people he interviewed said dying was peaceful whereas the other half said it entailed hellish suffering. Elisabeth Kübler-Ross has suggested that references to heavenly tranquillity and hellish sufferings may both result from the influence of Christianity.

Of the ten common elements Moody and other researchers have extracted from their interviews, the one that is most characteristic and seems to come closest to holding a key to the mystery of post-mortem continuation of life is the sensation of separation from the physical body.

Rosalind Heywood of the Council of the Society for Psychical Research has reported on a number of cases in which individuals have experienced this sensation. For example, a certain doctor who was on the verge of dying later described his condition in the following way. He said that he became aware of two consciousnesses: A-consciousness, which was part of his non-physical self, and B-consciousness, which was associated with his physical body. As his illness grew progressively graver, B-consciousness lost cohesion and gradually faded out entirely; but A-consciousness became detached from the physical body, which it was able to observe. Both Moody and Kübler-Ross have reported that, at the instant of death, human awareness leaves the body and is capable of distinguishing various happenings taking place around it. As an interesting sidelight, I might mention the contention on the part of a certain Japanese author that in the distant past experiences of this kind were common in Japan, and that people often mentioned having gone to and come back from the post-mortem world. Some people claim that this kind of experience was elevated after the introduction of Buddhism into Japan to help generate interpretations of life after death. It is very interesting to notice the points of consistency between deep-rooted, Buddhist-influenced Japanese beliefs and current scientific research on near-death experiences. What are your opinions of the separation of the mental (spiritual) being from the body at death? How do you evaluate the various interpretations of a world after death that the religions of mankind have evolved?

WILSON: It is perfectly consonant with the manner in which, in our scientific age, we all tend to think, that the public at large is much more excited concerning the prospects of an after-life as revealed by an empirical enquiry into the experience of people who have come close to death than ever it would be by the centuries' old pronouncements of the great religions. We expect to be convinced by empirical evidence and not to have to make the leap of faith. The specific after-life schemes of the world's religions have ceased to command the credence that they once did. We know that there has been a steady decline of belief in heaven and hell among Christians; the fact that fewer believe in hell than in heaven reflects the hedonistic spirit of the age, but a large proportion of Westerners, at least a large minority, disbelieve in both. The alternative (and not very well reconciled) eschatological thesis contained in Christianity, which stems from Judaism and which avers that the bodies of the dead will be resurrected at a future time when this earthly dispensation ends, is part of the official creeds of Christendom but is, today, actively canvassed by only a minority of Christian sects.

When believers find their creeds difficult to take literally, then unbelievers like myself are unlikely to be persuaded by such notions. Christians themselves have no detailed idea of how such a post-mortem world would function. Once the questions are faced, it must be seen that the idea that millions would be restored to life after the resurrection entails tremendous problems. Would this population re-emerge at a particular age – perhaps at the age of their deaths? Would they then experience an aging process; would they breed, or would sexuality, the original sin of the Judaeo-Christian tradition, be terminated? If they procreated and if there was to be "no more death", then over-population would surely become a problem. In short, it is difficult to comprehend the Christian, Jewish and Muslim schemes for resurrection on earth. On the other hand, the ethereal Christian scheme of the continuance of souls (which is the more commonly emphasized Christian eschatology) raises problems about the location of the post-mortem worlds where the souls abide. No doubt, few Christians would regard Dante's imagined system as more than an elaborate fantasy, yet there is no easily described alternative vision.

Islamic belief deals with a paradise that most believers will not attain until after the resurrection and the judgement of the dead that forms so powerful an aspect of eschatology in Middle Eastern religions. As described in the Koran, such a paradise is no more than a realm of perfect bliss as envisaged by those whose lives were lived in desert conditions. The righteous will live in a place watered by streams and abundant with honey and wine; they will lead lives of indolence in sumptuous luxury, adorned with jewels and served by handsome slaves. In some respects, this expectation does not differ in voluptuousness from the ideal that, despite their personal earthly asceticism, some early Christian fathers entertained as the appropriate reward of virtue. For Muslims, as for Christians, the unrighteous will suffer in hell, the idea of which derives from Jewish sources.

We have no reliable knowledge about how many Muslims actually believe in the world after death which their faith depicts. The *hadith* and various Muslim writers are responsible for considerable modifications of the Koran's depiction of a post-mortem judgement and the states that the faithful and the wicked will inhabit thereafter. As in all the major traditions, accretions of folk religion, superstition and persisting paganism affect popular beliefs among Muslim populations. We may suppose that the sophisticated classes in Islamic countries are often as sceptical as their counterparts in Christian and Jewish populations.

The Eastern, one might say, originally Indian, conception of reincarnation is, certainly in its detailed delineation, quite alien to Western thought despite sundry evidences that, in a crude form, reincarnation is a concept that evokes some credibility at a popular level. (It is not uncommon to hear someone say, "When I come back again", referring to the expectation of another life, but it would be a mistake to attach too much importance to such folk beliefs.) Despite their diversity, Hindu systems of eschatology cope with death by positing a round of re-births, usually in association with a hierarchic scale of states of life. While some equivalent of the idea of karma, in the sense of reward (or punishment) hereafter for behaviour in this life, is not unfamiliar in the West, the implications of such a theory with respect to caste structure or to the ultimate universality of all forms of life, whether human, animal or insect, are not easy for Westerners to conceive. A still greater difficulty arises, however, when the very relative nature of this eschatological scheme is introduced: the concept of liberation from the cosmic process in the unity of the world, the soul and the Absolute, represents a level of metaphysical thinking that Westerners do not readily grasp. Occasional reference to reincarnation, in which a small minority of Westerners profess to believe, is rarely complemented by the more sophisticated belief that the world is illusory or that the true goal is to escape the unceasing cycle of incarnations by realization of one's identity with Brahman.

If those difficulties prevail for one brought up in the rational-empirical tradition of Western thought in appreciating Hindu eschatology, there is an added difficulty in the case of Buddhism, with its assertion that there is no continuing individual self to undergo this cycle of re-births (and re-deaths). Given the intensity of the process of individuation that has occurred in Western society, which was vigorously reinforced by Puritanism, and the subsequently evolved ideology of individualism, this aspect of Buddhism may be seen as standing in sharp contrast with fundamental assumptions of Western consciousness. For Christians (with Jews and Muslims), one life on earth determines life hereafter, and because this life is regarded as a unique, once-and-for-all experience, the sense of individual identity is powerfully reinforced. Whereas throughout an apparently unending cycle, in both Hinduism and Buddhism, the law of karma manifests an autonomy of operation, the post-mortem experience of the Christian is determined by the judgement of a deity. Western individualism draws further strength from the idea of a special, almost personal, relationship with that deity, or with an aspect of him.

All of this is, of course, a very long way from the rejection of the idea of a continuing human ego, as found in Buddhism. The difference is heightened by the metaphysical categories expressing the conceptions of life in Mahayana Buddhism, which are difficult to render in European languages.

IKEDA: Perhaps a difficulty in rendering the terms exists, but I think the content of the idea of transmigration can be made clear. Although it played a part in the thinking of Plato and Pythagoras, transmigration, as you indicate, found fullest expression in Indian religious thought. Its beginnings are in a relatively humble form found in the *Brihadaranyaka Upanishad* and the *Chandogya Upanishad*, where it is said that, according to the way a man lives his life, upon dying he will go either to the World of the Fathers or the World of Heaven (Brahma). Those who go to the World of Heaven need never be born again into this transient world of suffering, but will dwell forever in union with their own essential being (*atman*) and in contemplation of the great universal being (*Brahma*). Those who go to the World of the Fathers, after what is called the fire ritual, ascend first to the moon and then are born again to live on earth.

Whether the person goes to the World of the Fathers or the World of Heaven was explained as the consequence of karma. Similarly, karma was believed to determine the kind of rebirth a person underwent in the World of the Fathers. People who had done good in their lives were re-born as humans in fortunate circumstances; and those who had done evil were re-born as non-human animals.

Buddhism inherited the ancient Indian concept of transmigration but enriched and developed it in distinctive ways. The Buddhist interpretation is that individual life is determined by cause-and-effect relations and that – as you have pointed out – there is no such thing as a permanently persisting ego (soul). Other religions object that if there is no soul to persist from existence to existence there can be no transmigration. The apparent inconsistency is resolved if the Buddhist position is put this way: although denying the existence of an eternal, immutable soul, Buddhism recognizes a life entity that transmigrates while changing constantly when projected as a phenomenal existence. This is to say, what transmigrates is neither John Brown nor anything that can be identified as his soul and his soul only. What persists through time is a life entity that may have been manifested an infinity of times in an infinity of circumstances, all of which have left karmic effects for better or worse on the entity itself. John Brown is only one of those karma-determined manifestations, but he, too, has made his karmic contribution.

Primitive Buddhism explained life in terms of the six consciousnesses: the first five corresponding to the five sense faculties and the sixth roughly equivalent to the conscious mind. Mahayana Buddhism, however, expanded the categories to include a seventh consciousness, representing the sub-conscious mind, and an eighth (the *ālaya-vijñāna*), which has existed from the beginning of time and which is regarded as the most fundamental aspect of the life entity.

The *ālaya-vijñāna* is called the seed-storehouse because it is the source of all sub-conscious karma-energy. It contains the seeds of all the other seven consciousnesses and receives influences from them to produce good or bad causes resulting in good or bad effects.

In simpler terms, the *ālaya-vijñāna* is the fundamental life inseparably related to the seven other superficial consciousnesses. This relation persists throughout the duration of each life. After death, impressions made by the seven other consciousnesses survive in the *ālaya-vijñāna* consciousness, where they are stored to have karmic effects the next time the life entity is given phenomenal form through transmigration.

Mahayana Buddhism centred on the teachings of the Lotus Sutra posits a still greater, purer universal life entity, the operation of which can alter for the better the bad karmic seeds stored in the *ālaya-vijñāna*. Reaching the state where this universal consciousness is activated is what is meant by the attainment of Buddhahood.

Modern Western science attempts to delve into the previous existences of individuals by means of hypnotic trances, during which the subject's memory is extended farther and farther into the past. While under hypnosis the subjects describe past times of which they can have had no direct experience in their current lives. Examination of historical records and other data have proved their descriptions to be accurate. Professor Ian P. Stevenson of the University of Virginia has studied over two thousand children who have recall of previous existences, and their recollections have been shown to be accurate by comparison with known facts. Both kinds of study seem to support the idea of transmigration.

WILSON: Perhaps, but I still see several difficulties from the standpoint of the Western mind. The Theravada Buddhist idea of Nirvana as a void representing salvation is difficult, but the subsumption in Mahayana Buddhism of Nirvana into the idea of a transcendent metaphysical reality constituting all phenomena is no easier, despite some obvious similarities to the Western idealist tradition. Christianity made life the preparation for death; and, beyond death, for judgement; and, beyond judgement, for a heavenly or hellish eternity. In contrast, Mahayana Buddhism emphasizes the possibility of grasping, during earthly life — that is, within the cyclical process of change of all existence — an ultimate reality that can be taken as an affirmative principle for subsequent lives. Since life is to be regarded as the potential of even inanimate phenomena, death is thereby relativized. The ideal of becoming conscious of liberation whilst in the world replaces Nirvana as a way of transcending the cycle of change: and the possibility of this achievement is open to all men. Mahayana Buddhism, in consequence, is concerned less with a world after death than with the attainment of liberating life within this world. In certain respects, its "this-worldly" orientation, although more explicit, might bear comparison with the concern for mastery of the world of the seventeenth-century Puritans.

None of the eschatological schemes of the great religions is without logical or metaphysical difficulties. Christianity has in effect not one eschatology, but two, somewhat ill-conjoined. Hindu schemes present a wide diversity, with their contradictory philosophies, accretion of myth, and linkage with a very specific and now discredited social structure. Judaic conceptions of life after death are, in the biblical tradition, somewhat exiguous, but Judaism also experienced many accretions from folk religion, even though these are now almost entirely disregarded by all but a small minority of Jews. The Islamic tradition draws on contradictory texts and traditions, which are not always consistent with respect to the role of free will and determinism. And in all religions, at the practical level, there is often an accommodation of popular concepts (such as heaven and hell in Theravada Buddhism or of men becoming angels in Christianity), which do not belong to the more sophisticated exposition of each particular eschatology. In seeking to understand and come to terms with death, and thus with the meaning of life, men are unlikely to be satisfied with a single coherent scheme, even if one were available. The human condition is complex and ambivalent in itself, and this may explain the cumulative and syncretistic search for emotional support from palliatives and nostrums or for intellectually satisfying schemes and metaphysical speculations. Despite their internal contradictions and the strictures of their religious mentors, many people have managed to entertain several such schemes simultaneously. Perhaps, however, the subject does not readily lend itself to cut-and-dried empirical evidence and the elegant, but often arid, logic of Western scientific thinking.

When Human Life Becomes Vegetation

IKEDA: The famous trial concerning Karen Ann Quinlan in the United States has shown how complicated it is to decide how long to support life artificially when a patient is in a vegetable-like state, shows no improvement, and indicates no possibility of recovery and when the family insists that the life-support system be turned off. Do you believe that the vegetable-like person – who is after all still alive – should be kept on the support system? This issue clearly involves the dignity of human life.

Modern cerebral physiology has shown that even rectilinear tracings of brain waves indicate only that the cerebral cortex has ceased to emit waves. The human being is still alive as long as the brain trunk is active. This is the state of the vegetable-like human being who is desperately hanging on at the boundary between life and death. It seems to me that, in spite of their tragic plight, such people must be recognized as human beings with all the rights of the human condition. If they are not, the same rights might be denied to people with major psychosomatic handicaps, the mentally retarded and people who have been gravely damaged physically or mentally while still in the womb (like the victims of the Minamata disease in Japan). I believe that so-called human vegetables are human beings struggling with all their might to remain alive, and that all methods of dealing with and treating them must be based on this premise. Furthermore, we must strive to come to a general social consensus on ways to bear the economic burden of caring for them. Do you agree?

WILSON: As the techniques of medical science develop we must expect an increasing number of tragic cases like that of Karen Ann Quinlan. Paradoxically, the more we learn of how to sustain life at its extremity, the greater are likely to be our problems about the extent to which we should continue developing and using methods of maintaining lives that are on the very threshold of death. The Quinlan case is acutely poignant, since Karen Ann has remained alive during these eight years since the oxygen support was disconnected – validating your point that even humans in a "vegetable state struggle to remain alive". I find myself deeply divided on these issues. On the one hand, one welcomes every development that promises to extend and prolong the existence of any individual. On the other, one sees the anguish and agony for kinsfolk, when life is maintained only by elaborate techniques that, in themselves, may at times be regarded as severely impairing the individual's human dignity at the time of death.

There has, of course, been a persistent, if often muted, ethical dilemma for the religious conscience in the matter of curing. On the one hand, healing is an ancient religious art, and in Christianity in particular it played perhaps a vital role in the early fame of the founder of the faith and in its subsequent spread. Healing the sick, cleansing the lepers, casting out demons and even raising the dead were not only held to be basic features of early Christianity, but were also miracles that Christians were commanded to perform. In other religions, too, men have learned to pray for health and have looked to their religion for aid in the enhancement of physical and psychic well-being. On the other hand, the idea that men have an appointed time to die, that God or Allah wills such things according to his own inscrutable wisdom, has been common, and misgivings have sometimes been expressed, certainly in the religions of the Judaeo-Christian-Islamic tradition, as to whether man should seek to interfere unduly with what has been held to be divine providence. The growing efficacy of medical practice and the process of secularization have combined to quieten such doubts. The old religious assertions that life was a vale of tears and that God sent tribulations to put man to the test, which included an element of fatalism, have receded with the shift to social values in which fulfilment in this life has become a paramount concern. Once the promise of what might be achieved medically became, if not complete recovery, at least recovery to a point at which the patient might regain control of the majority of his or her bodily and mental functions, the ethical problem was less widely canvassed. Today, however, the problem arises again at a different point of balance. Now that medicine has advanced greatly as a technical science (if perhaps not always as a human art), we face the hidden conflict of the extent to which an individual human personality may appropriately be made to depend on purely scientific and technological devices that are, in themselves, only impersonally related to it.

One must, of course, always allow that the advance of knowledge (which may come much more from technical and genetic engineering than from directly therapeutic skills) may make possible the restoration of an apparent vegetable to a functioning human being. Would such a being, after a longish interval in a vegetable condition, resume what we might call a normal personality and a fulfilling life? If we suppose that such a possibility always exists, we have no right to interfere with the use of the best devices available to sustain life, and perhaps those of us fortunate enough not to be in such a condition must find means to meet the economic costs of such treatments.

There are, however, other costs for society besides economic ones, and these costs may be charged *against* life. Every social system, from the small community to the large-scale nation state, operates on the normative premises that the great majority of people will, throughout most of their lives, fulfil their social roles, discharging their obligations and exercising their rights. The sick, who are exempted from such expectations must, of course, be accommodated in the operation of such a system (just like the delinquent), but, no matter how humanitarian the principles that its ideology espouses, the system must always seek to minimize the social and human costs of caring for the sick (and of rehabilitating the criminal). It may seem almost offensive to put these two classes of people together, but from the viewpoint of social organization they represent two significant groups of people who (it is always assumed only temporarily) must be exempted from their normal role performances (even though to grant this exemption may require economic support that may often outmatch the contribution to wealth which they normally make when actually performing their roles).

IKEDA: Since about 1970, increasing numbers of cranial injuries and of cerebral circulatory damage and cerebral haemorrhage, coupled with the development of sophisticated brain-surgery techniques, have resulted in so many instances of patients reduced to vegetable-like human beings that the issue has become a problem on a wide social scale. In 1972, the Japan Neurosurgical Association established a system whereby any patient persisting in the conditions listed below for more than three months is to be classified as a living but non-functioning human beings; in other words, a vegetable-like human:

1. Inability to move unaided.
2. Inability to eat unaided.
3. Urinary and defecatory incontinence.
4. Inability to comprehend moving objects, although the eyes may follow them.
5. No communication reaction beyond response to simple commands.
6. Inability to make intelligible utterances, although still capable of producing sounds.

A person who remains in this state for over three months certainly shows little promise of getting better and may remain suspended in this condition for months or years. The problem is knowing how long to wait before declaring the individual definitely beyond recovery. The difficulty of making a clear pronouncement in cases of this kind is aggravated by occasional, apparently miraculous emergences from the vegetable state, usually after a year or two. In one instance, a patient who had undergone open-cerebral surgery because of an automobile accident remained in the vegetable state for five years, finally to awake after a course of medicinal treatment.

Knowing when a person is irrevocably lost, although alive, is difficult in the extreme. As you say, such patients are not fulfilling their normal social roles. Nevertheless, I believe that society should find the means to meet the economic costs of their treatment, especially because the financial, emotional and physical burdens imposed on their families are immense.

WILSON: Yes, I see your point, but the economic cost is perhaps less important in this connection than the social cost of the facilities required for this community effort.

Specialized roles are developed to care for the sick, and this we cannot, in the normal incidence of sickness, escape or, beyond a certain level, reduce. However we may at least acknowledge that, if through advanced technical means, we considerably increase the numbers of the seriously ill, whose life is maintained only by complicated apparatus and who have little hope, if any, of ever returning to normal life, we incur a social cost – a cost in terms of life – in the increasing numbers who will be needed to devote themselves to sustaining these sufferers. These professionals may, of course, get much personal satisfaction from the humanitarian elements in their role, but they may also, especially as medicine grows increasingly technologized, be overwhelmed by its routine, by its impersonality and perhaps by the eventually hopeless condition of many who are – hope against hope – kept alive for a few lingering months. Apart from the increase in the professional roles, we shall of course make more extensive incursions into the lives of kinsfolk and friends of such seriously ill people. The demands on their emotions and the cost in the anxiety they experience may also be uncertain, and if they are torn by the dilemma that must have afflicted the Quinlan family, we might even say (and I do not judge where the balance is to be struck) that Karen Ann was kept alive at a high cost to the emotions of her relatives, and at the cost of their capacity and opportunity for life-enhancing experience. I raise these points only to indicate what I feel are further social ramifications of the issue you raise.

Turning to the more specifically medical aspects, I believe that many people are in a condition of considerable ignorance (I am certainly among them) about the range of possibilities of recovery of patients in particular types of cases. We have already observed that the medical profession today frequently does operate to norms which, in some respects, are less than wholly patient-centred: doctors are professionally interested in relatively narrow aspects of their cases, and although, in the last analysis, everything that is done is done for patients, some patients might become little more than guinea-pigs for particular techniques that support life (or what, in the vegetable-like condition, passes for life) whilst doctors and technicians consider other possibilities for restoring the individual concerned. My apprehensions amount to lingering doubts and a concern for the dignity of the individual in death as well as in life. I am sure that you will quickly perceive the nature of my concern from the foregoing intimations.

Another aspect of the problem, however, affects the matter of organ transplants. Controversy still surrounds the questions of when an organ donor can properly be pronounced dead so that an organ can be removed without actually endangering his chances of survival. Doctors in Britain have indeed "experimented" with dying people, leaving life support machines functioning after what they term "brain-death" – the point at which organs are removed – to see whether their hearts do, in fact, continue to function and whether there is any chance of revival. They are satisfied that there is no chance of survival after brain-death (as I understand it), but the question must remain whether the removal of organs is in fact congruent with our concern for human vegetables, who may, as you put it, be "beings struggling with all their might to remain alive".

IKEDA: I fear that in many cases they may be just that. The problem once again returns to making a pronouncement of death. In the West, as you point out, brain-death is the determining factor. Japanese doctors, on the other hand, are unwilling to accept this as a certain sign of the cessation of life and still use heart-death as the definitive condition, because they feel that measuring the brain waves of the deep brain stem is difficult and that without accurate measurements of its totality it is impossible to say that the brain has indeed died. In their case, too, the issue is far from clear. As a certain Japanese specialist has said, we do not know the length of the time gap intervening between brain-death and heart-death.

Artificial Insemination

IKEDA: When the ovum is removed and inseminated with sperm cells from the husband and returned to the wife's womb for natural development, family relations remain intact; women who might otherwise remain childless because of blocked Fallopian tubes, adhesions or other abnormalities are allowed the joy of motherhood. Problems arise, however, when a woman's womb is borrowed for the raising of an embryo that will not become her child, when sperm cells from someone else's husband are used to fertilize the ovum, or when an artificial womb is employed.

Although some purely medical problems – protecting the ovum from damage during removal, for instance – remain unsolved, in general, I consider the kind of artificial insemination that I mentioned first to be acceptable as long as the man and wife cannot have children in the normal way.

All kinds of difficulties present themselves, however, if women are allowed to use their bodies as breeding places for other people's children. From the emotional standpoint of the woman who lends her womb, this kind of thing may be completely unacceptable. Moreover, even in the kind of artificial insemination I consider permissible, unless the act is inspired by profound love, the mother and father will be unable to raise the child as they should.

WILSON: On this issue, I find myself entirely at one with you precisely in the terms in which you have posed the problem. Like you, I would rule out the possibility of a woman lending her womb for the servicing of an embryo that will not become her child. I feel that this seems to demean and perhaps even corrupt humankind. On the other hand, one rejoices in the prospect when a woman who, for specific biological reasons cannot conceive of a child in the normal way, can be aided by medical science to overcome an incidental obstacle. One would like to think that all such women might, at the community's expense, be enabled to have children fathered by their husbands and be capable of enjoying the normal relationship of parenthood. In many respects, the case does not differ, ethically, from that of a woman who is enabled to give birth by Caesarian section, and such operations have long been accepted practice.

It might be argued that a woman who is artificially inseminated with sperm from some man other than her husband does no more than many women do nowadays in Western society, in bearing the children of men with whom they live in an unmarried situation or, at times, who are no more than casual acquaintances. It is here that the moral problem arises. What a woman chooses to do with a man not her husband is a matter for her conscience. In general, we still believe that conscience should be educated towards a recognition that it is generally better for all concerned

– the woman, her partner, the child and society at large – if the male-female union is legalized and regularized. We do not punish people in such cases, and we cannot, except by moral education, seek to control what people do in these matters. With respect to artificial insemination, however, there is a possibility of control. Here the techniques of science have to be employed, and they must be used under controlled conditions. We can say, and I believe we should say, that it would be morally indefensible and economically unwarranted to utilize these means to propagate children whose parents are not legally married. To this general principle, I see only one possible exception, about which we might need to reflect further, namely, the situation in which the husband is infertile. Can we say that, as long as an infertile husband not only approves of his wife's receiving sperm from an unknown donor, but also countersigns her application for such treatment, the threat to the marriage should be no greater than that presented by a simple adoption of a young child? I know that adopting, in various ways, is not uncommon in Japan, and I find it difficult to suppose that there is more danger in the father "adopting" his wife's child than in the couple adopting the child of two completely different parents. The husband, who cannot produce vital sperm himself, adopts the sperm of an anonymous donor. As with an adoption, the arrival of a child might, indeed, itself have a beneficial effect on a marriage and, although this should never be the primary goal, it is a latent function that cannot be entirely ignored. Still, problems might arise: a "father" who is himself not entirely emotionally stable might, at some future time, come to see in the child any signs of waywardness, biological defect, moral misdemeanour or intellectual limitation as a result of his adopted son's paternal inheritance. The case may not, however, be worse than that of an outright adoption, when just the same risks are entailed and, at least in this case, the father will have the satisfaction of knowing that he has not deprived his wife of the joy of real motherhood – for which she in turn ought to remain permanently grateful to him.

IKEDA: I agree that, as long as the couple is in agreement on the matter, fertilizing the wife of a sterile husband with sperm from another man is a good idea because it allows the woman to know the "joy of real motherhood". The wife should be grateful to the husband, who can, I believe, if his attitude towards the situation is sound, enjoy his fatherhood as much as if he were actually responsible for the child's genetic composition. In Japan, artificial insemination will probably be more widely used in the future by married couples who once might have adopted a child. At one hospital, initial efforts are being made to select sperm donors who, in addition to being healthy and genetically sound, bear some physical, intellectual and personality resemblances to the husbands of women who are to be artificially inseminated.

Sex Training

IKEDA: Today, we are already seeing signs of the danger of moral retrogression brought about by the wide use of contraceptive measures for the control of population growth. Undeniably, scientific knowledge about contraception is an essential part of education and should be included – as it is in some of the industrialized nations – in school curricula. However it must be accompanied by training in morality in general and in sexual morality in particular. The human sexual act must be based on deep mutual affection. Do you agree with me? What role do you think religion can play in educating young people to the true nature of marital love and sex?

WILSON: In many cultures, and in some cultures for many centuries, the sexes were carefully segregated, and the occasions of their coming together were subject to close social control. Even so, illicit unions and casual sexual encounters were commonplace, and, at some times, in some societies illegitimate offspring may have outnumbered children conceived in wedlock. Yet a "legitimacy principle", that is to say, a preference for legitimate offspring, has been the normal demand of most societies from the primitive to the most advanced, and illegitimate children have generally suffered various social handicaps, whether legally instituted or merely conventionally imposed, because of the breach of moral norms committed by their parents. The ubiquity of the legitimacy principle indicates a profound if unconscious awareness of the potentially disruptive consequences of illegitimacy to the normal operation of the social order. The often vigorous taboos against even innocent sociation between the sexes, the enforcement of sexual segregation, chaperonage and the mythology (largely male) about the opposite sex, are all indications of the effort that has been required to counter the power of sexual attraction.

A much more subtle form of control, centred in the more highly cultivated conscience, developed in some cultures, and in Christian societies perhaps most markedly under the impact of Puritanism. The social control represented by the Church and the agency of confession was replaced by an internalized self-control, as the individual saw himself as directly responsible to a creator-god for his every word and deed. Although such self-control never approached completeness, since some social classes were more thoroughly socialized than others and there remained considerable individual differences in conscience-formation, for a less communally-based society it was a more effective agency than the blanket imposition of the old taboos. As societies grew in scale and as the pattern of life became less and less circumscribed by the local community, the wider range of social interactions led to a situation in which individuals ceased to be known in their personal right: they became more or less anonymous. In such circumstances, self-control was necessarily intensified, since otherwise the social group would have been unable effectively to sustain its regulation of individual behaviour, so much of which now escaped social scrutiny.

All forms of control, however, whether social of self-imposed, invoked as their rationale the seriousness of illegitimacy and the extent of social disapproval concerning it. When birth-control techniques eventually began to reduce and almost to eliminate the risk of pregnancy following sexual encounters, the moral norm demanding sexual continence lost a great deal of its force. The attraction of sexual intercourse, in the pleasure deeply felt in man's biological nature, was now released from the consequence that so often followed in nature. And although man had evolved a long way from the pattern of sexual control maintained by some animals (instincts of strict monogamy or the operation of brute force in the maintenance of sexual monopolies), his own forms of control had come to depend on a strongly felt moral demand, which was entirely social and not biological in origin, linking sexuality to "legitimacy" (i.e. to social approval). When that link was broken, as it was by birth-control techniques, not only was man's moral order jeopardized, but an imbalance in cause and effect was also introduced into the old order of things. Mankind had restrained the force at work in nature, first by group regulation and, retaining the idea of instinctual renunciation as something demanded for the social good, later by self-restraint. With new birth-control techniques, the idea of the social good – at least as far as the risk of consequences was concerned – disappeared from the equation. What was there now to prevent men from seeking as much pleasure as they could obtain, knowing that they had so greatly reduced the risk of untoward consequences?

For rationalists, perhaps this might be all that need be said, but there is another side to the matter. The development of moral conduct based on self-restraint, on the internalization of conscience, and on an ethic of responsibility had, I believe, consequences for the nature of the individual as well as for society. The gradual replacement of force by social control and of social control by self-control, was, in my view, a process of the enhancement of man's humanity and dignity. Fear of social consequences might have been a basis of moral constraint, but eventually it was replaced and sublimated by an awareness by individuals of what human dignity might become when men acquire an inward sense of their own responsibility and integrity. It would be tragic if the elimination of the risk of pregnancy undid what has been a long civilizing process in the individual's self-cultivation, on the mistaken grounds that sexuality is now, like air and sunshine, what the economists call a "free good".

Whenever the individual "gives" himself to others or accords others access to his deep and intimate feelings, there is a cost, a cost that can be requited only by deep and mutual affection. In the demands made of individuals in virtually all human societies that, not merely as a courtesy but also as a necessity of orderly social life, they keep their sexual activities private, there lies a latent and unexplained assumption. That assumption is that when human beings express and exercise their deepest emotions, they, as individuals, are at their most vulnerable – and so, too, is the very fabric of social life itself.

Of all religions, Christianity has been the most explicit in its restrictive attitude to sexuality. Its severe demands concerning sexual regulation rested, however, on premises and expectations that have been shown throughout its history to be too elevated and constricting for the mass of its adherents. In consequence, today, those prescriptions have themselves become more or less nullified, and the exhortations of both Jesus and Paul in these matters are frankly disregarded, even by the clergy. Faced with the inevitability of human sexuality, Christian sex ethics were compromised virtually from the outset. One possible effect of the vigorous attempt to repress sexuality may have been to make more difficult the cultivation of dignified attitudes and relationships between sexual partners, to which the high incidence of sexual pathology in the West may testify.

IKEDA: I suspect that repression of instincts frequently results in pathological phenomena. Buddhism does not attempt to repress sexuality in the case of ordinary lay believers. It is true that earlier Buddhism – especially so-called Sectarian Buddhism – enforced a strict code of celibacy on monks, with the result that natural sexual instincts often manifested themselves in abnormal ways. The five precepts that Mahayana has inherited from primitive Buddhism contain an injunction against adultery, but in this, as in all cases, Buddhist precepts are not imposed unilaterally from without, but are intended as a guide in the process of self-purification. Believers are only bound to obey them by becoming aware of what is best for themselves. This injunction against adultery was no doubt instituted to counter the blind courses into which sexual drives can lead human beings.

You imply that relations between sexual partners can and ought to be dignified. The Lotus Sutra teaches that delusion and wisdom are one. This means that the energy inherent in something like the sex drive can be sublimated into an energy of rich love and mutual self-perfection for man and wife. In other words, sexual desire can become a source of mutual respect.

WILSON: Respect for others and their dispositions; a sense of mutuality; persisting care and concern; and a recognition that man's sexuality should not diminish human dignity, are the basis of a responsible sex ethic. A man's sexual life should be of a piece with his general moral comportment, participating, if in a more profound measure, in the same basic standards of seeking to elevate and not to debase others and to help them discover the finer, more sensitive and sustaining aspects of their physical and their psychic natures. In the face of the vigour of the powerful agencies seeking to do the opposite, in the canvass of purely sensual, casual and hedonistic values by the entertainment industry, the task is now more urgent and more encompassing than ever before.

Christianity may, today, be compromised by the deep hiatus existing between the stringent sexual morality of the Gospels and the everyday assumptions about sex that obtain in Western society. Chastity and fidelity, even though they remain the tacit norms for sexual conduct and even though the majority of people are chaste throughout most of their sexually active lives, are scarcely the proclaimed values in contemporary Western society. Given this situation, religion must accept two roles in sex education. The first continues a traditional role in a contemporary setting: the dissemination of sound, practical advice to make the young aware that the casualness of modern life is their enemy in the whole arena of human relationships; that deep and persisting loyalties, difficult as these become to sustain in modern conditions, are alone likely to bring real contentment; and that human relationships must be based on sensitivity, sympathy and respect, as well as on sexual love. This then, is the educative task. It must be handled with the same type of sensitivity that it commends to others.

The second task is almost political and demands aggression rather than delicacy. Sexuality has been demeaned by the mass media, the voices of which are more powerful, more strident, more insistent, more numerous and more ubiquitous than the voices of all the religions and educational agencies together. It is time for those concerned with religion and with human dignity and integrity to call for the control of the moral content of the productions of the mass media. If teachers must be certificated before they are permitted to teach, ought not similar qualifications to be required of broadcasters? If professional men are subject to scrutiny and enquiry by the ethical bodies of their own profession for any alleged misdemeanour, even in respect of only one case, ought there not to be similar regulation for those whose performances affect millions? If motorists must be licensed and if their licences may be endorsed even if they do no more than drive in such a way that damage to property or injury to persons *might* occur, ought not the men of the media to be subject to a similar system of licensing, since the harm that they may do may be incalculably greater? I wonder if you agree with me that this is an area in which religious leaders have not acted adequately against agencies that are the profound enemies of human dignity and human welfare.

IKEDA: Absolutely. Frequently guilty of publicizing only the sordid side of sexual love, at best, the media concentrate on the pleasures and joys of sex without pointing to the folly and fragility that sometimes play a big part in it. Although, as you know, I am a vigorous advocate of freedom of expression, I think the media ought to emphasize more clearly – especially for young people – the mutual understanding, trust and affection that make love worthwhile and that help partners to overcome life's trials and sorrows and to live both strongly and beautifully.

Contraception and the Population Issue

IKEDA: Although the growth rate of the earth's population has slowed somewhat, the number of people in the Third World continues to increase. In the face of the pressing shortage of foodstuffs on the globe, the population issue is clearly going to remain grave. In the past, wars and epidemics limited population; fortunately their effects are now more restricted and the cruel consequences of these things are no longer sufficient. Contraception is the most promising method of control. Neither the ovum nor the sperm cell can be called a human being, since, genetically speaking, an individual has been created at the moment of fertilization. Destroying the foetus at any stage beyond fertilization is equivalent to taking human life. (Buddhist medicine, based on ancient Indian medical thought, postulates three conditions for pregnancy – sexual intercourse between male and female, the female menstrual cycle and the life that is to be born – and considers the moment of fertilization the inception of the new life.) It seems more rational to me to employ contraceptive measures to prevent insemination than to rely on such drastic steps as abortion, which is, as I have said, the destruction of life and which involves physical danger to the woman. What are your thoughts on the subject of contraception and the population explosion?

WILSON: As you suggest, in the past there were a variety of points at which population was effectively controlled. Infant mortality and death in early childhood were common. The average life-span of those who reached maturity was itself much shorter. War and epidemics terminated the lives of many young adults. Beyond these natural causes in the prevention of over-population, men themselves took steps to ensure that available resources were not exhausted. Among some of the simpler peoples, the elderly simply left the settlement when they perceived that they had become a burden. In other cases, polyandry effectively reduced population growth while, either in connection with it, or by itself, infanticide was a device that societies used to maintain a balance between people and resources. Abortion, which stopped the process of regeneration even earlier and with perhaps less emotional disturbance, was well known in the ancient world. Today science has given us a means that is in every way to be preferred to the emotionally harrowing techniques of the past in which human life was actually destroyed. Contraception must be counted as one of the most important technical advances in man's history. Provided it does not in itself lead to insensitivity in human relationships and providing that the sexual moral order can be sustained by considerations other than those of "getting rid of the consequences" of casual acts, any aids to contraception, whether pharmacological or technical, must surely be welcomed by anyone who takes a balanced view of humanity's needs and progress.

The only regret that we might feel is that knowledge of these techniques has not been disseminated sufficiently widely and rapidly to help prevent the fearful growth of population with which the world is at present faced. Even were we able to ensure the availability of full knowledge of the most effective contraception techniques throughout the world, we should still not escape what I fear will be the devastating effects of growing population. Nor can we suppose that our scientific competence will permit us to find, within a short time, the means of sustenance, food, fuel and the materials for dwellings to cater for the numbers who are now being born. It seems to me that for us to do otherwise than to promote the knowledge of contraceptive techniques would be worse than folly: it would be the gravest lack of responsibility for, and to, humankind.

Abortion

IKEDA: The number of yearly abortions in Japan is said to equal the number of children born. Both here and in other nations where abortion is illegal, voices are being raised in favour of legalization. From the viewpoint of preventing further population growth, abortion seems not only permissible, but also inevitable. From the standpoint of respect for life, however, it is not to be sanctioned. As an advocate of respect for life, I am totally opposed to it in most instances, since I consider it wrong to terminate artificially an already initiated life and thus to condemn it to darkness before it has ever seen the light. Furthermore, abortion is physically and mentally cruel to the mother and, if performed often, can render her barren.

When it can be proved that continued pregnancy or delivery is dangerous to the mother, abortion is acceptable. I cannot agree with the Japanese law in recognizing economic reasons as a suitable cause for abortion. First, other social methods must be taken to improve the mother's economic conditions. Second, if the parents are too poor to have children, they should resort to contraceptive methods, not abortion. Do you believe the Church of Rome is correct in taking a strict stand against abortion?

WILSON: Like many other people in the West, I find the very idea of abortion abhorrent. Like you, I would strongly support a campaign to increase knowledge of contraceptive techniques throughout the world. Our problems arise, of course, when we are faced with pregnant women who are determined not to become mothers and who reject all the implications of that role. In general, I, too, would favour a policy in which women were encouraged to have their babies, even if the mothers subsequently relinquished them to the care of orphanages. In practice, in the West there is still a demand for babies for adoption, and many of these children might find excellent homes and foster-parents. I do not see that abortion can ever be an acceptable policy directed towards the limitation of population. That goal must be sought through the extension of contraceptive methods, which are cheaper, safer, more humane and in the interests of women – to say nothing of what some regard as the evil of abortion towards the human foetus.

Impecuniosity seems to me to be a quite inadequate ground for the approval of abortion. Many very poor families are happy, and many children born to poor parents lead active, healthy and fulfilled lives. In cases where continued pregnancy or delivery would endanger or seriously impair the life of the mother, I do believe abortion to be justified. There are three other possible situations in which I think recourse might be had to this, in itself undesirable, operation, which I regard as a measure of last resort. First, we know that children are sometimes conceived as a result of an act of rape. I know that rape is not a very common crime in Japan; alas, it is a widespread act of depredation in the West. It is horrifying to learn that in some large American cities, rape is so common that the police have become almost indifferent to it, often telling the victims that if they go out alone at night in racially-mixed neighbourhoods (where the incidence of rape is highest), they must be seeking rape. The situation and the attitude of the police are such that women's organizations have affixed stickers to every lamp-post in parts of Philadelphia, beginning with the words, "If you have just been raped . . ." and giving the telephone number of a women's-aid organization. It seems to me to be humane to allow a woman who has become pregnant as a result of rape to have an abortion.

Second, conception sometimes results from incest, which is a covert but by no means uncommon phenomenon in some countries. It is surely socially undesirable (and I stress the social consequences particularly, since the likelihood of untoward biological consequences must depend on the genetic stock of the parties concerned) to insist that children conceived in incestuous unions should be born. Finally, in some cases it might be medically established that, for whatever reasons, a child was likely to be born with a serious deficiency of both physical and mental facilities. The constant care and attention such a child would need could seriously impair the lives of both its parents, foreclosing on their life-chances and curtailing their careers, enjoyment and even creativity. In such a case an abortion, whilst terminating the life of a badly retarded foetus, might allow the parents the chance to try again and to have healthy children. If they commit themselves to a life of caring for one severely handicapped child, they may find the burden so great that they will avoid having other, potentially healthy, children.

IKEDA: I concur that in cases of rape and incest, abortion is a conceivable, absolutely last resort, but insist that it is more important to create social and moral conditions in which neither rape nor incest occurs than to abort the children which result in these situations.

As far as a genetically defective foetus is concerned, I believe that every effort must be made to discover the gravity of the defect. If it is possible to show that it is only slight, abortion should be out of the question. If it is serious, both the condition and its relative gravity must be clearly and immediately explained to the parents, who must then decide whether the wife should carry the baby for the full term. Of course, in this instance, all care must be taken to see that nothing is done to run the risk of a defective foetus. Pregnant women must avoid anything – medicines, chemicals, virus infections, radiation, and so on – that could have harmful genetic effects on their unborn infants.

Comparative Study of the Psyche

IKEDA: It is my opinion that a comparative study of the methods and results of the intuitive Oriental approach to the human mind and the scientific Occidental one, can provide a profounder view of the innermost workings of life than either method is able to produce on its own. For instance, I feel that the Buddhist teaching of the eight consciousnesses, evolved through study and meditation and employed as a fundamental doctrine by the Consciousness-only philosophy and the Hosso sect in Japan, can be compared and contrasted meaningfully with such Western fields as depth psychology, psychoanalysis and psychosomatic medicine. Interestingly enough, the eighth of the eight Buddhist consciousnesses (which, as I have already pointed out, is called the *ālaya-vijñāna* and is the basis of all the other consciousnesses) seems to resemble what Jung called the collective sub-conscious. Obviously a great many difficulties are encountered even in a single instance of comparative study like the one I suggest between the Consciousness-only school of Buddhist philosophy and Jungian psychology. A Christian (if a Gnostic given sometimes to alchemy), Jung based his entire system on psychoanalysis. The Consciousness-only philosophy is a sophisticated theorization of Mahayana Buddhism. The goals of each are different. Whereas Jung was concerned with the sub-conscious as a way of approaching treatment of the mentally ill, Consciousness-only Buddhist thought employs such training regimens as yoga and meditation to illuminate deep sub-conscious levels of the mind.

If the difficulties could be overcome, do you agree with me that comparisons in this field might be significant? I find it fascinating that Jung's encounter with the Orient was a powerful enough experience to send him to the brink of schizophrenia, and think that examinations and inquiries of his situation from the viewpoint of an oriental could shed light on aspects of both East and West.

Working systematically and beginning with comparative investigations of Jung's *animus/anima* and the Buddhist idea of karma and delusion, or of Jung's self and its symbols and the Buddha-nature and its representations in, for example, mandala form, might provide revealing insights into universal human mental functions. What is your opinion of such comparative study?

WILSON: As a sociologist, I am very much committed to the comparative method. If sociology adds anything to our historical, psychological or anthropological knowledge, it does so, I believe, by the procedure of systematic comparison. In principle, therefore, I agree with you that theories of the psyche, techniques of psychic control and empirical evidence about the functioning of the mind and body are all proper subjects for comparative enquiry.

Problems arise in all such exercises. To be profitable, comparative analysis must be well-prepared, rigorous and controlled. With respect to empirical evidence, the primary difficulties are methodological, but with care and patience these can generally be resolved. Techniques, too, can be compared, and their merits can be assessed by quite pragmatic tests, as long as we leave to one side the theoretical principles by which they are explained and justified. If we are concerned with objective conditions, and not merely with subjective states, we can assess techniques as different as meditation, yoga, counter-suggestion, free association or dream analysis in relation to each other. The crucial difficulties arise with respect to theories. Here we face linguistic problems which demand not only translations from one language to another (which are certainly often hard enough), but also communication of the allusions, connotations and resonances carried by language in all matters that are not directly controlled by strictly scientific and mathematical axioms and symbols. Our strictly rational procedures encounter difficulties in the analysis of the non-rational, which features so prominently in psychic phenomena.

Part of the problem relates to categories. Because empirical reference is so difficult in psychic phenomena, the categories that we employ to distinguish states of consciousness are likely to be arbitrary. We cannot unquestioningly assume that the distinctions we make between states or levels of consciousness are necessarily part of objective fact. On the other hand, it is possible that the categories we employ may themselves come to influence not only our perceptions, but also even the actual data. The human psyche is so malleable that it is by no means inconceivable that human beings might respond to, and be influenced by, the types of mental construct that are, initially quite arbitrarily, accepted on *a priori* grounds to be the appropriate basis for categorization. The issues are clearly complex: the pliability of the psyche makes it difficult to assume that our categories represent reliable, constant values. Men are acculturated to the very categories that are then used in analysis, and this in itself affects, or may even determine, the ease and the depth of their responses. Clearly, a comparative analytical exercise demands the resolution of these intricate and complicated issues.

Beyond the categories stand the more general and diffuse bodies of interpretative theory, which usually rest on broad philosophical or religious presuppositions about the origin, nature and destiny of man. In this area comparison is likely to lack rigour, unless a second (or third) order of categories can be evolved that has application – necessarily at a rather abstract level – to the different interpretative schemes. The way in which such a broad philosophical *Weltanschauung* is related to the empirical data and the techniques of therapy must differ from one system, and one culture, to another, and we might need to examine the nature of this relationship. We must also ask whether the broad philosophical underpinning itself actually affects the efficacy of particular techniques of psychological analysis and therapeutic practice. Or might these idea systems be little more than free-floating speculations with intrinsic appeal, which merely organize in acceptable cultural terms a system of thought that legitimizes a psychological system, possibly just as efficacious and valid without such ideational justification? Perhaps I can illustrate what I mean.

Acupuncture is a medical practice that undoubtedly works in many cases. There is, however, considerable difficulty in reconciling the theories supporting acupuncture and those invoked to justify Western medicine. Acupuncture sometimes succeeds where Western medicine fails, but the theories used to explain it are largely incomprehensible to Western medical men. Is there a culturally specific psychological factor affecting the efficacy of acupunctural practice? Or, turning to a different field, there appears to be some convergence of opinion about the experience of phenomena of a para-normal kind, some of which have occurred to people who have been brought back from the threshold of death, or among those who have had powerful experiences of what they consider to be "the supernatural". Yet, however similar the actual experiences appear to be, a wide variety of irreconcilable theories exists to explain them. The theories may sometimes colour the actual accounts of the experiences themselves. Might such theories also occasion these experiences?

IKEDA: The philosophical theories on which such things rest must colour people's experiences of them. You have asked whether there is a culturally specific psychological factor affecting the efficacy of acupuncture. I suspect there must be, since the whole edifice of Oriental (I mean the term in the restricted sense of basically Chinese) medicine depends on an interpretation of the human body that is unlike the one prevailing in Western medical science. As you may know, the Chinese theory is that health and illness are caused by balance or imbalance in the currents of energy and fluid flowing in regular, established courses throughout the body. (Here we already come up against the difficulty of translating terms. The words rendered energy and fluid actually more commonly mean air and blood, both of which give an inappropriate connotation in this context.) Therapy and the medicaments prescribed are varied as this balance alters. The physician diagnoses the case and applies acupuncture (or moxa) at the correct spots on the courses of energy and fluid flow to effect a cure.

This theory of the human body is apparently totally at variance with modern Western medicine. And, as you point out, it belongs to the group of theories that Western men of medicine find incomprehensible. Although it is a product of this Chinese medical philosophy, acupuncture does work sometimes when Western medicine fails. Furthermore, its successes are measurable and recognizable by means of modern Western medical methods. If it were possible to bridge the comprehensibility gap, it might be shown that doctors of both traditions could learn from each other. If this were the case in dealing with physical illness, might it not be the case in investigating the workings – normal and pathological – of the mind as well?

WILSON: A necessary initial step for comparative studies would be the careful analysis of the language employed at the various levels of description, analysis and explanation in each of the different approaches to the study of the human mind. This procedure appears to be essential if we are to effect the transfer of thought structures from one cultural context to another. For this task we need a neutralized or sterilized linguistic code which, however, must be appropriately sensitive to the non-sterile elements in original languages that are likely to be part of our data. One sees that the natural sciences, the data of which is not volitional, volatile and psychologically sensitive, are in a happier position. With their high dependence on entirely objective empirical data they can employ the sterilized language of mathematics, and in consequence the natural sciences transcend specific cultures and are readily internationalized. The social sciences are less readily "translated", since they deal in empirical data that is in itself culturally determined, and for the explanation of which culturally specific concepts must be employed. These concepts may be rendered into other languages and for peoples of other cultures only with difficulty. Making these disciplines more scientific simplifies the task, but at the cost of draining out the specific, localized cultural content of the phenomena they seek to explain. (I leave aside the humanities, since they constitute studies of specific cultural products in the same cultural terms, and as such allow for much less systematic cross-cultural comparison except in loose and discursive terms, as one sees from such flaccid subjects as "comparative literature" and "comparative religion", which lack even the relative rigour of the social sciences.) Philosophy, finally, is very much more culture-bound than the social sciences or than its exponents might care to admit. Since empirical data are not its central concern, it becomes highly dependent on the analysis of concepts and is therefore bound to certain linguistic forms. Thus, what, in a given culture, might appear to be arresting and pene-trating analyses, often fail to carry very much weight when they are trans-lated into another language.

A study of the different approaches to the human psyche as found in the West and in the East might face the difficulties experienced in both the natural and social sciences and in philosophy, but the step-by-step procedure that I have proposed appears to be one possible approach towards the highly desirable type of comparative study that you suggest.

Psychology and Religious Experience

IKEDA: Although each assumes a slightly different viewpoint while contribut-ing to a more or less comprehensible overall pattern, many psychologists –

including James, in his *the Varieties of Religious Experience*, Freud, in his *Moses and Monotheism*, Jung, in his *Psychology and Religion*, and men such as Gordon Allport, Erich Fromm, Erik Erikson and Abraham Maslow – have investigated religious experience in terms of the human personality. Do you believe that study of this kind can clarify the ultimate nature of that experience?

WILSON: Psychological and sociological investigation does, I believe, reveal a great deal about the circumstances of religious experience. By comparing accounts, assessing social circumstances and establishing the particular constellation of psychological conditions of those who undergo conversion or who experience revelation, the social scientific investigator can create a morphology of such phenomena. He may, in some matters, learn more about such religious phenomena than the individuals who actually experience these things. He can do so by virtue of the number of comparative cases that he can review, by reference to the works of others who have written about such things, and by identifying the common elements occurring within such experiences in widely divergent cultures. Just as a medieval historian may, in some respects, know more about medieval society than medieval man himself did, or as the anthropologist may know more about the social structure of a tribe than the individual tribesmen, so an investigator into religion may, in certain regards, penetrate further than the one individual mystic, visionary, convert or worshipper. The fact that he can do so arises from his opportunity to use the comparative method which you yourself advocate. By this means, he can develop lines of general analysis and so produce some sort of broad theoretical framework into which the specific individual phenomena can be fitted and by reference to which they can be, at least in part, explained.

IKEDA: I think I see what you mean and believe that in some instances investigators reach levels of understanding that transcend categories like religion or sect to touch the nature of religion itself in a universal sense. For example, Jung's explanation of the levels of the sub-conscious compares with Buddhist concepts of delusion, karma, and the manifestation of the Buddha nature. In talking about the supreme religious experience, in *Religion's Values and Peak Experience*, Maslow uses terms that, to my ears, have a strong Buddhist ring: spiritual unity, oneness of the object and the world, ability to manifest optimum or maximum ability, sense of creative independence, assurance of free will in connection with the pioneering of one's own fate, spontaneous and abundant expression, and so on.

WILSON: Yes, the investigator may reach a kind of universal bedrock by his analyses of the religious experience, but such an analyst is always working with the data at second-hand. His constructs are second-order constructs, and his theories can only be as good as the quality of the individual reports out of which they are distilled. There is obviously a sense in which the religious individual understands and knows his own religious experience better than anyone else ever can. He may know neither the appropriate categories by reference to which it might be analysed nor the extent to which such experiences are frequent occurrences, either within his own religious tradition or in other cultures and religions. He may have no notion of its sociological significance, but he knows, at first hand, what has happened to him, and in this sense he knows more than any outside investigator can ever know, no matter how wide that investigator's knowledge or how good his theories.

There is an irreducible element in religious experience which must be respected by those who wish to explain such things by reference to psychological or sociological principles. The first step in seeking to interpret religious phenomena is to give opportunities to those who believe and who have had such experiences to express their own understanding in their own terms. Of course, the external analyst may not accept the theories and explanations of religionists as final, but unless he acquires his data from religious people, his own explanations can account for very little. No social scientific analysis, or any other external perspective, dissolves the core of genuine religious belief and commitment.

IKEDA: I agree with that. As William James said, the religious experience is mystical and cannot be expressed in words. Furthermore, located as it is in the innermost depths of the human psyche, it cannot be explained in terms of social-scientific or natural-scientific analysis. None the less, the experiencer wants to share what he has come to understand and, in doing so, may call on the assistance of the scientist's analytical methods to make the content of his experiences more understandable to others. Clearly, the scientist's constructs are necessarily second-hand, lacking the emotion, intuition and willpower that the believer knew while undergoing the religious experience. I concur with you entirely when you say that the scientific analyst must respect the core of the believer's faith and commitment.

Psychotherapy and Buddhism

IKEDA: In general, the trend in psychology today is away from the use of outsiders to bring relief by means of hypnotism, psycho-analysis or Pavlov-type conditioning and towards self-control. Many of the self-control systems show either the influence of oriental practices or a fusion between the approaches of the East and West.

The automatic training system derived by the German psychologist Johannes H. Schultz incorporates hints from yoga and Zen meditation. The bio-feedback system mechanically induces a meditative state of trance. Sensitive equipment gauges changes taking place in the body vessels, makes the person aware of them, and thereby allows him to control them. This is an application of the mutual operational relation between body and mind that is a fundamental tenet of much oriental thought. Fritz Perls, who contributed to the development of Gestalt psychology, studied Buddhism in Japan. Alexander Lowen, who evolved what is called body-energy therapy, uses yoga-like terms when he speaks of the muscular armour that must be eliminated before psychological complexities can be revealed. Many of the breath-control and image-therapy systems used in psychotherapy originated in Buddhist medical methods, and the distinctively Japanese Morita method is founded on the Mahayana doctrine that delusion and Buddhahood are inseparable. Do you agree with me that one of the things which the East can teach the West is sophisticated methods for sub-conscious control of mind and body?

WILSON: Western scientific and medical knowledge has developed along a path that has led to the establishment of a powerful, well-institutionalized medical orthodoxy. The vast majority of doctors, the training hospitals and clinics in which they learn their craft, the whole medical establishment and the technically sophisticated and economically costly organization they control, are all committed to fairly well-defined ideas of what medicine, including psycho-therapeutic practice, should constitute. The cumulative process by which the theoretical structure and practical techniques have developed has been such that radically different procedures and practices which do not grow out of, and so do not so easily fit into, existing theory, are viewed with suspicion and even, at times, with hostility – no matter what their success. In all of this, medicine resembles the natural sciences, in which it becomes increasingly difficult for any one set of discrepant facts to lead scientists – despite their subscription to the canons of scientific method – to challenge the body of existing theory. Since existing theory more or less adequately explains a wide range of associated phenomena, new and discrepant data face major difficulties in that they represent a threat to existing theory within which even minor amendments are not easily accommodated. Theories become institutionalized, and powerful vested interests (which are not necessarily in any sense sinister) grow up for the defence and maintenance of an existing theoretical structure.

None the less, especially in psychotherapy, orthodoxy is less secure than in other branches of medicine, and it is widely acknowledged that quite divergent therapies may all claim some measure of success. In mental health, elements of faith, assurance, awareness and even explanation may be crucial to the success of a given therapeutic method, as orthodox physicians and other would-be healers have long been aware. It seems likely that undue dependence on pharmacological, electric and other therapies may have blinded many medical practitioners to the fact that there may be quite different techniques of physical and mental control, such as those you describe. There are, however, distinct difficulties facing even sympathetic medical men who wish to explore alternative therapies, working as they do within the confines of institutions organized for certain set procedures of medicine and reliant on a highly elaborated code of practice. Given that they operate with a large clientele, one sees how easy it is for them to become dependent on routine techniques based on standard empirical tests. In some respects, a similar dilemma arises in connection with Western methods of psychotherapy, particularly psycho-analysis. Some doctors who might be well-disposed to psycho-analytic procedures have recourse to cheaper, easier, more systematized techniques (particularly those based on the use of drugs) that can be applied more quickly and routinely to a wider clientele, many of whom perhaps lack the developed intelligence that psycho-analytic practice appears to demand.

There is reason to believe that, among practitioners of orthodox medicine and psychotherapy, awareness of the potential benefit of other systems of practice is growing. The very rigidity of modern medical routines and their mechanical application are increasingly criticized. By analogy, one sees how, in the quite different area of self-defence, Eastern techniques of physical and mental control have become widely adopted in the West.

In comparison to judo and karate, traditional Western fisticuffs are crude and clumsy. May not the same be true for psychotherapy? Eastern self-defence arts have spread in the West through voluntary enthusiasm, outside institutional contexts. A similar process of diffusion might be appropriate for psycho-therapeutic methods. Were such techniques capable of wide application, the possibility of eliminating the costly equipment and drugs on which Western medicine depends would make them attractive alternatives. Given the rapid increase in medical costs, anything that would shift the burden from the services of highly trained medical personnel to the application of self-taught knowledge would nowadays commend itself, both for its intrinsic therapeutic contribution, and because it might facilitate the release of resources to deal with other types of illness. The way of life in the West (and perhaps particularly in the United States) has come to operate on the assumption that the unhealthy daily-life practices in which many people indulge (excessive smoking; excessive consumption of alcohol; over-indulgence in entertainment, eating and sex; and neglect of the need for physical exercise and proper rest) can be easily "corrected" by medical attention. Anything that shifts the balance away from dependence on medical cures towards the prevention of ailments must have a significant part to play in the economics of medicine, as well as in the actual development of therapy and disciplined living.

IKEDA: No doubt their purely economical aspects are highly attractive, but preventative and self-control cures are equally important because they restore concern for the psychological aspects of many pathological states at a time when Western medicine, for all its great contributions to human well-being, over-emphasizes the material and mechanical sides of life. In my opinion, oriental religions in general, and Buddhism in particular, have much to teach the West in relation to self-control techniques.

Religion and the Psychology of the Supernatural

IKEDA: How would you describe the relationship between religion and such – now scientifically studied – phenomena as telepathy, clairvoyance, influence on physical objects in distantly removed places and prophecy? What contribution can religion make to the field of psychological study of such supernatural powers? Buddhism teaches that a certain degree of power in telepathy can be acquired through training, although the Lotus Sutra insists that such minor matters are to be forbidden as obstacles in the way of true Buddhist discipline.

WILSON: There are too many well-documented cases of various forms of telepathic or extra-sensory perception for us to dismiss these matters out of hand, just as there are too many accounts of poltergeists and similar phenomena for anyone to be dogmatically sceptical. On the other hand, there appear to be no adequate theories, even at a relatively low analytical level, to explain these experiences and phenomena. What must impress the investigator is the randomness and often the triviality of the demonstrations of such powers, as well as the fact that they remain beyond control and explanation. Few people possess these kinds of power in any controlled way, even though many individuals may claim the occasional experience of having been powerfully affected by some particular mental impression, which is later vindicated by events. Accounts of such things vary tremendously, and, as is often pointed out, those inclined to credit these visions of the future may easily forget all the occasions when strong intimations of some future happening failed to be confirmed.

My own view is rather close to the teachings propounded by the Lotus Sutra: such things might occur, and it might be possible for some people to train themselves to heightened sensitivity of a telepathic kind by some means, but thus far man's abilities in these areas have been of relatively little consequence and have generally been confined to trivial issues. At best, extra-sensory perception has been no more than a distraction from the much more vital and socially rewarding ethical concerns that are central to religion. These phenomena appear to us like some kind of magic, a defiance of normal experience, but it is in the diffusion of an ethic, with its much more universal service to mankind, that the effective saving power of religion must really be discovered.

IKEDA: Yes, the important thing is the diffusion of an ethic or, in terms closer to my own beliefs, the manifestation of compassion and wisdom. We Buddhists believe that calling forth the Buddha-nature inherent in the depths of all life is the goal of discipline. If, along the way, some people – and their number is of course small – manage to attain supernatural powers, this is all well and good. However such powers are not a worthy goal in themselves since, without compassion and wisdom, they can be ill-used. Only when employed wisely and compassionately are they of any true value to society and mankind.

The Occult

IKEDA: Although human beings have always been concerned with – and frightened by – so-called occult phenomena, the recent popularity of motion pictures on the subject probably arises from two causes. The first is curiosity. The second, and more important, cause is the simultaneous fear about and hope connected with the occult, as something inexplicable using rationalistic interpretations of the world. Both the hope and fear manifest a deep level of the human mind – a level that is itself inexplicable in purely rational terms.

Occult occurrences are a part of the traditions of most peoples, although in Japan they have tended to be merely weird – possession by fox spirits and so on – and not tremendously horrifying as they are in the plots of currently popular Western films. I suspect that the more horrendous Western occult stories reflect belief in an omnipotent, exclusive god and his counterpart, a devil wishing to be as omnipotent for evil as god is, presumably, for good. The Buddhist belief in a Law of causation, not an omnipotent, anthropomorphic god, leaves no room for a counter-evil force desiring to control all in an equally omnipotent fashion. Since the nature of the things that people call occult reflects the deep psychological levels where religion is born, differences between the Buddhist – at any rate the Japanese Buddhist – mild occult tradition and the fearsome occult tradition of the West may result from differences in religious interpretations.

WILSON: The strong dualist tradition that is found, most emphatically, in Zoroastrianism, but also in Judaism, Christianity and Islam, is no doubt responsible for the depiction of evil in horrifying and grotesque form. One knows that Hinduism also accommodates malevolent deities, but the polarization of the forces of good and evil in the Middle Eastern and Western religions is very much sharper. As long as men were preoccupied with salvation and particularly with securing for themselves a life of post-mortem bliss, the forces of evil were conceived as exercising an almost entirely repellent power, and the Church itself must bear some of the responsibility for making "the evil one" and his hosts somehow intriguing, even to convinced Christians. The Church came to condemn men for being possessed by the devil or for being in league with him, and a familiar theme in European mythology tells of a man selling his soul to the devil in return for magical power. The very idea that such a choice existed sometimes fascinated men almost as much as it repelled them.

The attribution of evil to all manifestations of the occult and their association with the devil were part of the Church's strategy in seeking to eliminate all non-Christian concern with the supernatural. Paganism – which was merely a collective term for the myriad forms of local religious practice, myth, herbalism, folklore, sorcery and other local magic, conveniently lumped together – was assimilated to the idea of devil-worship by the Church. Witchcraft was vigorously condemned in late medieval Europe by representing witches as agents of the devil, with whom they were said to engage in sexual intercourse. So effective was Church propaganda on the matter that witches regularly confessed to these associations. The force of solemn Church pronouncements led to the assimilation of witchcraft to a general demonology. All sorts of curing arts, spiritism, soothsaying and the rest, became identified with the evil personified by the devil. One consequence of this dualistic division of supernatural phenomena was that many who dabbled in the occult came to believe that they were exponents of an ancient religion with an integrated system of teaching and practices. In fact, of course, the occult has taken the form of only random, localized, unsystematic and diverse practices (no doubt of vast variety) lacking theoretical or intellectual justi-fication. However, because the Church strongly stigmatized all these phenomena as machinations of the devil, in modern times persons drawn to the occult have often been in search of a supposedly "lost" religion. Sometimes, as in Britain, this ancient religion has been identified with fertility rituals and druidism or, as in Germany, with Aryan racial myths. By intimating that the devil might counterfeit Church rituals or even recite scripture, the Church encouraged the idea of an evil parallel organi-zation, and perhaps all this induced some occultists to organize themselves more effectively.

As Europeans learned more of other religions, particularly in the last century, and as the Church castigated those relations as "of the devil", the traditions of those religions were sometimes assimilated in occultism. The mystical traditions of non-Christian religions were explored to discover the arcane secrets of the universe, and a widening compendium of electric occultism was drawn from such sources as the Cabbalah, Sufi mysticism, Tibetan religion, tantric magic and congeries of other mystic arts. Societies and cults came into being, and some of them even attained worldwide membership, so that, at the fringes, they influenced the course of religious history – as in the influence of the Theosophical Society on the revival of Buddhism in Ceylon.

Theosophy is a relatively sophisticated concern with the occult, even though it has spawned many cult movements that have been both less intellectual and more disposed towards the acquisition of so-called magical arts. The lesser arts are those of clairvoyance, exorcism, conjuring of spirits of the dead and the practices of witchcraft covens (which sometimes include sexual initiations and – perhaps the fault of the Church – mockery of church rituals). At higher levels, occultism promises the possibility of travelling back centuries in time; of making instantaneous flights to mystic, or solar, regions; of attaining invisibility; and of procuring desired partners for actual, or mystical, sexual acts. As we can readily see from modern comic books and science-fiction films, the appeal of such fantasies is widespread. Another element that may encourage some forms of occultism probably arises from one of the paradoxes of our social experience. Society is a construct of everyone's ready contribution to the tissue of mores and conventions by which our lives are governed. Yet, that body of custom is normally presented to us, and realized by us, as something absolutely objective, something as factitious as the external world. All sophisticated people are aware, however, that the fabric of custom is sustained only by a continuous process of subscription to it by all (or almost all) members of society. They know that society is made up of many individual acts conforming to social norms and that we are engaged together in the maintenance of an elaborate façade of morals and manners. (Of course, societies could not exist without such a structure, which guarantees regularity and order, but that is not my present point). Because men half-see that what appears to be external and objective depends on individual subscription and conformity, they perceive the possibility of another order, perhaps of a world not bound by custom and convention where they are released from the variety of inhibitions necessary for everyday life. I believe that the Satanist cults and some branches of occultism and witchcraft covens appeal to people who yearn for release from normal society, at least from time to time, and who seek the excitement of becoming involved, in apparently legitimized circumstances, in practices and relationships that would normally be socially proscribed.

IKEDA: I understand your point, but you seem to be discussing the occult almost exclusively from the standpoint of the Christian church and its prescriptions of mystical activities outside its own bounds. Colin Wilson, in his book *The Occult*, offers a wider interpretation of occultism that I think can lead to a fruitful field of discussion. He speaks of the X-function, which, though not the occult in itself, is the power-giving key to the occult experience and describes it as a universal perception. According to Wilson, the X-function enables us to understand actual existence and brings about a fusion of our conscious and unconscious spirits. He goes on to say that the X-function is innate in human beings, but has been pushed into the depths of the sub-conscious and forgotten as men have striven steadily to rationalize their way of thinking. If the X -function is the key to the occult experience and if it enables human beings to perceive the true nature of existence, it – and therefore the occult too – must be related to a broader mysticism. The X-function can be interpreted as a key to the mystical experience which, though capable of narrower interpretations, in its widest sense means a unity between humanity and the divine (universal).

Friedrich Johann Heidlerr has said that, in contrast to the Islamic-Judaeo-Christian religions, which are fundamentally faiths of prophets, Indian religion is profoundly mystical. And this statement includes Buddhism as one of the religions evolved in India. It is interesting to notice that, in contrast to the Christian Church, which vigorously condemned all non-Christian magic and mysticism as plots of the devil, Buddhism has been more lenient.

Yoga is one of the most famous mystical religious disciplines of India. Like most of the other religious leaders of his time, Shakyamuni Buddha trained in yoga under its two most outstanding exponents, Ālāra Kālāma and Uddaka Rāmaputta, and attained a high level of skill in it. At a later date he abandoned it as useless in the search for pure wisdom. After giving up yoga, however, he went on to develop his own system of meditative concentration, which he employed only as a means and not as a goal. As the incantations and magical spells of the *Atharva Veda* patently demon-strate, magic and supernatural powers were highly revered in ancient India. They were attained only by people who had reached high states of spiritual development through yoga meditation or ascetic austerities. Shakyamuni is said to have attained such states but, once again, never to have thought of them as goals in themselves. While not condemning them, he realized that supernatural powers, like all things, are neutral and good or bad depending on how they are used. In this case, as in the one we discussed in the preceding section, such powers are of use only if applied with wisdom and compassion. This attitude accounts for the way Buddhism has embraced – in the form of tutelary deities – the gods of other religions. From the Buddha's standpoint, the gods, like all other things in the universe, are subservient to a Law and are therefore not to be feared since they are by no means absolute in their powers. I think this explains why Buddhism has never taken the Christian Church's stance in assimilating "paganism" – or, as you say, a collective of the myriad forms of local religious practice – into the idea of evil that, in the form of a devil, must be opposed and put down.

Mahayana inherited the tolerant attitude of the Buddha and therefore, as I have said elsewhere, facilitated the accommodation of Buddhism among the deities of the many lands into which it moved – for instance, both the ancestral and nature divinities of indigenous Shinto have been included in Japanese Buddhist thought, some as good guardians and some as hell-bound beings who can, however, be saved from suffering by the power of the Law that finds its greatest expression in the *Sutra of the Lotus of the Wonderful Law*.

To summarize, the Christian fear of non-Christian religions forced the Church to take steps against what it called paganism and thereby to become – albeit unwillingly – the creator of a vast array of occult and mystical phenomena that Christians are taught to hate and fear as the work of the devil. By taking other religions' gods into its fold, Buddhism has generated much less occultism. What has been generated is viewed with much less dread in Buddhist cultures than witches' covens and Black Masses have been in the Christian world.

PART VI

The Wider Ethical Perspective

Innate Good and Innate Evil

IKEDA: The question of man's innate goodness or evil has been viewed in different lights by men of religion and philosophy for centuries. Whereas Confucius thought man was innately good, Hsün-tzu regarded him as innately evil. The Christian doctrine of original sin seems to indicate sympathy with the standpoint of Hsuñ-tzu. In contrast with Jung, who opted in favour of innate good, Freud leaned in the direction of innate evil. Abraham Harold Maslow is decidedly in favour of the idea that man is innately good.

Buddhists believe that all life, including the highest condition, which is called Buddhahood, simultaneously includes both innate evil and innate good, and that it is therefore essential constantly to attempt to extend and reinforce the good while suppressing and controlling the evil. Since suppression and control must be carried out from within, each individual must attempt to cultivate the power to combat his own evil.

Morality is generally thought of as the way to control one's innate evil. However it tends to be an intellectual matter, and human evils involve emotion more often than reason. I believe that religion, which delves deeper into human life than the rational mind, must be the source of the inner strength to control evil and facilitate life on a high moral and ethical plane. Do you agree with my standpoint?

WILSON: Good and evil seem to me to be essentially relative terms, to such an extent that I find it difficult to envisage human beings as innately good or evil without postulating a normative context within which their dispositions might be assessed. That normative context is invariably social, for it is in society that moral categories are established and that moral precepts are conveyed to each individual, giving him a sense of proper and improper desires and deeds. I do believe that the individual is born with strong impulses for self-gratification, which include not only the demand for sustenance, warmth and love, but also sexual appetites and the recourse to aggression, particularly when frustrated in the pursuit of other desires. Such impulses must sometimes run counter to the needs and demands both of other individuals and of the orderly regulation of social life, and in this sense these impulses are readily designated as evil, since the interests of society demand that they be suppressed, contained or channelled. I see social life, and hence psychic life, as a matter of the containment of tensions – containment which, in the best circumstances, can be effected to such a degree that the individual himself may be unaware of the potentiality of such tensions. Thus, I find it difficult to designate man as good or bad in any absolute sense, although I think it self-evident that man's inclinations are often directly contrary to what society requires of him.

Education is very largely the process by which the individual acquires civilized attitudes and dispositions that govern not merely outward comportment (in the observance of manners, styles and conventions), but also inward integrity (one's sense of right, duty, obligation and honesty). We can say that the individual takes in a socially determined sense of himself. Society – or its best exemplars – becomes his point of reference for his own comportment. He learns to regulate himself by those same norms that are externally maintained in general social intercourse. As you can see, I find myself very much in the same position as the one you describe for Buddhists. Whilst society maintains a framework of control, the highest degree of civilization is attained only when individuals can internalize social norms and maintain their own self-control.

Moral prescriptions are indeed often justified by intellectual arguments, although perhaps you will agree that moral norms, as such, are arbitrary and justified in part because they constitute a system of stable expectations concerning the way in which individuals will behave. The human desire for self-gratification is rooted in the emotions and constitutes a complex search for a wide variety of desired objectives, some of which, such as the esteem of colleagues, good reputation and acceptance as an exemplar, merge with much deeper-laid emotional demands for love at all levels, and not only in its higher, more cognitive, aspects, nor merely in the affective expression of deep regard, but also in its most physical form. Moral regulation in society is, in effect, the education of the emotions for the individual. Unfashionable although the word might be (at least in the increasingly permissive West), discipline is the keynote. In the nature of morality, however, nothing can be forced. As you imply, discipline must be at least partly self-imposed, and there is reason to believe that, in all the more advanced societies of the modern world (and perhaps in some in the past), self-regulation has necessarily been the main source of moral order. In his early life training, the individual learns how and in what respects to discipline himself.

The education of the emotions and the acquisition by individuals of values that conform to general social demands are clearly a subtle process that begins in very early life. Some of the fundamental responses may, I believe, be implanted before either reason or religion is invoked: the child takes in a set of interdictions and makes them part of his own psychic response to situations. When, however, he must later resolve more subtle moral problems and when he needs to justify his own moral attitudes or to appraise the moral framework of social life, he will need to have recourse to other value systems and to their intellectual or religious legitimations. Reference to such higher value-systems may furnish him with convictions about morality that are derived from (or at least reinforced by) meta-physical ideas or some transcendent sphere of reference.

The ascription of morality to a religious source has been common in man's history: whole societies have subscribed to such ideas and, even when a society is officially secular (as is the United States) or in practice virtually secular (as is true of many modern states), individuals continue to regard their morality as originating in, and as being legitimized by, the traditional religion. Needless to say, the total agglomeration of customs that make up the moral practice within any society has roots in folk culture, but these have usually been amended by subsequent religious teaching, which has embraced a more universalistic ethic or which (as in Islam) has added many precise regulations for individual comportment. Out of these *dicta* and *scripta* a system of morality evolves. Such systems are not born fully formed, of course, and they contain elements that become defunct, unresolved contradictions and unattainable exhortations. Religion has been the most powerful reinforcement of morality. Westerners are acutely conscious of this, since Christianity explicitly underwrote a moral system and both Catholic and Protestant churches vigorously made morality virtually their chief concern for centuries. Not only were Christians given a set of divinely prescribed rules to obey, but also the emotive power of religion was utilized to awaken sentiments that brought home to every Christianized individual his need to be on constant guard concerning his behaviour and his inner thoughts. The idea that in behaving immorally one was betraying one's god, causing him suffering when he had sacrificed himself for sinners, was added to the fear of endangering one's own soul as strong emotional reinforcements for good behaviour.

I imagine, however, that you use the word *religion*, as a Buddhist must, in a much more metaphysical sense than is required by Christianity (with its emotionally harrowing story of man's rejection of God). Buddhist morality is rooted in a system that is objectively stated and impersonally operative. It becomes a part of a system of principles by which the world – perhaps the universe? – operates. Such a philosophy appears to postulate good and evil as objective categories. Each act brings its consequential effect, characterized as good or evil. Is this goodness or evil therefore determined according to some pre-existent scale of values? Clearly, if such a scale of values is subscribed to, there is immense reinforcement, particularly for those who are intellectually capable and emotionally stable, and who are thus able to envisage the long-term balance of causes and effects of moral dispositions. For those less intellectually alert, less emotionally in control, less disposed to live for the future than for the present, such a scheme may permit them, in the short term, to shrug off the demand for moral excellence. In this case, of course, we should say that their religious obligations are not understood.

IKEDA: As you said at the beginning of this section, good and evil are relative, especially when they are defined as observance or violation of social codes, which obviously vary from period to society. Buddhism does, however, adhere to one set of what could be called pre-existent values in that it regards as absolute evil the depriving of any other creature – including non-human creatures – of life and happiness, and the preservation of life and stimulation of good fortune for others as absolute good. This is vividly illustrated by the parable-like stories – which I have mentioned elsewhere – of former existences of the Buddha in which he is depicted as sacrificing his own flesh to feed a starving female tiger to enable her to suckle her cubs, and giving himself to an eagle as food in order to prevent the eagle killing and devouring a dove. The evil of depriving others of life and good fortune and the good of altruistic behaviour for the sake of others are immutable in all times and societies.

There are people who find a kind of sadistic happiness in killing. It might be argued that, on the basis of our defining evil as depriving others of happiness, we Buddhists would be committing absolute wrong by trying to force such people to desist from taking life. In this instance, depriving the person of the temporary pleasure he derives from sadistic killing does him great good in the long run since it lightens his load of evil karma. Such a situation might be compared to the cruel cures needed to break drug addicts of their physically and mentally harmful practice.

All living creatures are in the dilemma posed by the need to take life for food in order to go on living. If such killing is evil, it must certainly be less evil than killing for pleasure or out of hatred or the taking of life for no useful purpose. Put in the embarrassing situation in which, while condemning killing as evil, we must take life to survive, we must always examine our motivations and always, as you say, discipline ourselves in order to suppress impulses that might stimulate us to take life for reasons other than necessity. As I have pointed out, Buddhism teaches that all human beings are innately capable of both evil and good and that the important thing is to suppress our inner evil and cultivate our inner good.

WILSON: Religion has, I believe, generally been a source of inner strength, enabling men to withstand temptations to evil and providing them with reasons for seeking to live life on a high moral and ethical plane. There are, however, extraordinary differences among societies with regard to the level of moral demand, and among men with respect to the measure of moral attainment, and I wonder if we might invoke religion as the explanation of these? There are differences in moral performance among people of different Christian denominations that might be attributable to religion *per se*; for example, Roman Catholics make a much more than proportionate contribution to the incidence of delinquency in a country like Britain (although, it is true, other sociological variables may be involved). The generally high moral performance with which Quakers are usually credited may relate to the degree of personal autonomy their religion has encouraged. There are differences among nations: the United States, with a much higher rate of church membership and church attendance, has a much higher per-capita incidence of crime than Britain. Church attendance and membership may offer only limited evidence of the state of religion, of course, and crime may not be the best index of immorality. Yet this is evidence of some kind. Although it reveals a much higher level of moral and ethical comportment in public than any Western country, Japan is often described as a highly secularized country in which, despite nominal allegiance, many people are said to have only very superficial religious attachments. How can we explain such evidence?

IKEDA: Lacking your wide experience of many nations and their religions, I am not in a position to offer a definitive answer. My personal opinion is that the disparity between such things as church attendance and membership and a low level of public morality results from the failure of churchgoers to internalize and truly assimilate the lessons of their religion. Human beings tend to obey orders as long as a powerful force endorses them. When the Church represented the palpable power of God, Christians may have obeyed its dictates. Now that the Church has lost this power, Christians may tend to think that the observance of outward forms acquits them of religious responsibility and liberates them to behave as they like outside Church doors. The personal autonomy the Quakers encourage is no doubt associated with a sense of greater personal responsibility to carry out the moral teachings of Christianity.

Japan is indeed a secularized nation in which the internalized major religious traditions, Shinto and Buddhism, exercise no influence over public morality. The controls that account for our "higher level of moral and ethical comportment in public" as you call it, probably derive from powerfully operative, long-established customs, internalized religious traditions and the concern people of a homogenous population (perhaps not originally homogenous but homogenized in the process of history) have for reputation.

Unity with the Universe

IKEDA: Man has many different kinds of desire – instinctive drives; material greed; and the hunger for power, dominance, fame and glory. Modern civilization, which enables mankind to live in greater affluence than ever before in all history, strives to satisfy these desires. In the rush for this gratification, other more laudable desires – for instance the desire for love and compassion, and what I called the religious desire – are often shoved into the background or overlooked entirely.

By the religious desire, I mean the longing, which is, I believe, common to most peoples, for identity with the fundamental source of all things – the desire to be at one with the great universe. Although, as I have said, modern civilization underplays matters of this kind, we ought to make use of the religious desire in ways that enrich human life on more than superficial levels. What are your ideas on this subject?

WILSON: The hiatus between all that the technological order can provide and the fundamental values of human life becomes increasingly stark in the modern world. We are led to suppose, more by the often only half-informed men who produce the mass media than by the scientists themselves, that scientific progress is ever-continuing and that new techniques and discoveries will soon satisfy all our wants. No one would wish either to decry the remarkable things that have been achieved by advances in the natural sciences or to abandon the many conveniences that new technology has introduced into everyday life, but we need to be reminded, as you make clear, that there is an aspect – in some ways the most vital aspect – of human life that depends on qualities and resources that lie within individuals themselves and that technology can do absolutely nothing to create or augment. Human compassion and love (and to this I would add sensitivity) are profoundly cultivated human virtues that simply cannot be simulated by science and that technological development tends to ignore and, at times and perhaps incidentally, to stifle. The technical is necessarily the impersonal, but there is a point at which, if I may put it ironically, life must be lived at a personal level.

Ultimately, the most rewarding facets of life for practically everyone, no matter what their material circumstances, their enthusiasm for technical innovation, or their commitment to the idea of being "modern", are all found at the personal level, in the bosom of the family and in the shared activities of a sensitive and mutually constructive human relationship. Science and technology have at best a limited and indirect contribution to make to this type of satisfaction; religion surely has more. At its highest levels, religion moulds and transmits human values and provides interpretations for life experiences. The objective facts of human existence do not explain themselves. Life must be interpreted and evaluated if it is to be controlled, and religion, far more fully than science, functions to provide the widest context of meaning and the interpretative reconstruction of experienced reality.

IKEDA: I agree, and it seems to me that contemporary mankind has lost the basis for the interpretations and evaluations which the religious view of the world and of humanity once provided. In the modern era, for a while at any rate, faith in technology and nationalism played the part religious faith played before its power to affect human thought and action waned. However, their influence was not destined to last long. Nationalism, in the name of which mankind has fought two global wars in this century, is now viewed with extreme caution, especially in the so-called free countries. Few people today would be willing to say – as people once did – that anything done in the name of the national state is just. Similarly, the scientific and technological progress in which people in the nineteenth century placed great hope, has clearly led mankind to the drastic crises we currently face.

It seems to me that, in the latter half of the twentieth century, the majority of people – at least in the industrialized nations – either base all judgement on their own personal desires and interests or, from a sense of impotence, despair entirely. Self-interest and hopelessness have taken the place of faith.

This phenomenon is less pronounced in regions where religious feeling and a strong sense of communality have persisted from the distant past and in areas which, though socially modernized, remain agricultural and to an extent rural. It is in the cities where the trend I have described assumes greatest prominence. For this reason, I think a very strong religious desire – that is a desire for some kind of spiritual foundation – can be found among many of the world's urbanites.

WILSON: Many individuals do not, of course, depend directly on a religious creed as the foundation of their sense of meaning and purpose. Some are capable of forging their own sense of values, of critically re-evaluating the intimations that come to them from the religious and cultural traditions of their own society. However such re-interpretations themselves arise within a context – a context in which the time-dimension, the inheritance from the past, is as significant as the environmental dimension. To re-interpret this statement, the individual must already have some received intimations about life, its goals, attributes, origins and values, and he will derive these initially from the culture of his society. Within that culture, no matter what his own predilections may be, religion has played a significant part.

Nowadays, particularly in dynamic and highly heterogeneous societies, such as the United States – in which there is no one settled and continuing culture and within which many individuals lead highly disoriented lives (unsure of their values or purposes; vulnerable to the winds of fashion; shopping, without intrinsic character or commitment, in a supermarket of displaced cultural artefacts) – we can readily see that the threat of mental, social and civic disorder grows at a pace which eventually threatens the peace and stability of the lives even of those who do still possess cultural roots. Science, which in its internationalism becomes increasingly *a*cultural, can do nothing for people in this situation. Indeed, in some respects, particularly in the speed with which it forces processes of technical, and hence of social, change, it is itself a factor producing the accelerating disarray of social norms and mores. Wholesome human relationships necessarily feed on cultural intuitions, depend on the cultivation of sensitivity and on the disciplining and ordering of the affections; in our modern circumstances such patterns are not easily established or maintained. Primitive and instinctive sexual impulses, shallow hedonism, the cult of the neoteric are all fostered as appropriate to the life-style of modern man. Over and against these cultural currents, which are now stimulated by the powerful industries of entertainment and advertising, there are few barriers which might help men to resist the tide. For many men, religion still represents one such support in warding off the deleterious effects of cultural and social anomie. Perhaps for this reason, in the Western world, and especially in North America, there is some evidence of a shift of support towards the conservative churches and to religion avowedly committed to the moral prescriptions of the past.

IKEDA: I suspect the shift can partly be explained on the basis of an awareness of the harmful influences which resulted from the abolition of such moral prescriptions. To be sure, their lifting had the desirable effect of greatly broadening human freedom, but at the same time it has had the undesirable effect of expanding material desires as well.

The moral prescriptions of past religions were imposed from without; and I believe that, in the modern world, commandments and restrictions forcibly applied from outside are practically meaningless. For one thing, many people are free to travel where they like and change their domicile at will. If they find restrictions imposed in one place distasteful enough, they can escape them merely by moving to a different location. To make restrictions truly binding would demand depriving people of freedom of movement and in this way would create a set of prison-like circumstances that most of us would find intolerable.

Consequently, to meet the needs of modern man, a religion must not try to clamp down rules and laws from without but must induce its adherents to cultivate, from within themselves, the wisdom and independence to control their own desires and impulses.

Surely internal control of this kind, based on no concrete rules but on the best urges of the power of life, is the true realm of religion? This is what I have in mind when I speak of oneness with the great universe – or manifesting in one's own being the Law that is the source of all things. The attainment of this oneness with the universe – which in Buddhist terms is called the attainment of Buddhahood – provides human beings with a transcendent morality which enables them to think and act in ways consonant with the best of their natures.

WILSON: Beyond its concern as the voice of moral consensus and social stability, religion has the function of providing men with well-articulated expressions of goals that transcend everyday experience and social well-being. Men often wish to be, in a phrase that Westerners sometimes use, "in tune with the infinite", at one in their own being, and reconciled to ultimate realities. Understandably, such a desire, which may be felt by only a minority and perhaps even then only intermittently, is expressed in different ways in different cultures. As you yourself phrase it, it is a wish to be at one with the great universe. Some Christians would call it a real relationship with Jesus, and others might refer to it as a deep inner peace of mind. This search for union with the fundamental or the ultimate aspects of being is, I believe, a profound and perhaps in some ways a universal human disposition. The desire for complete absorption is found in lesser forms in the human appetites, including sexual desire. In religion it is sublimated and elevated to a point where it can be expressed only in metaphysical terms. In itself this leads to its being beyond the comprehension of those who, as Max Weber put it, are "religiously unmusical", but it is regarded as the apex of spiritual aspiration by religious teachers and devotees, whether expressed philosophically as by Gotama Buddha or mystically as by Saint Teresa of Avila. From such striving, it is widely maintained, stem those benefits by which religion profoundly enriches human life.

We cannot ignore the difficulties which remain. In all advanced countries, many peoples who desire personal spiritual enrichment and perhaps even the spiritual consummation to which we have referred, as well as the lesser benefits of moral consensus in society, none the less find it impossible to accept intellectually the propositions on which religious belief rests. Others who believe that, in the long run, religion might be of value to them are deterred from committing themselves because they are not prepared to forgo short-term pleasure for long-term benefit. Perhaps these two considerations represent the major hindrances to the attempt of religious leaders to call forth men's spiritual and religious desires.

The Control of Desire

IKEDA: Desire is a vital source of creative physical and spiritual energy and, as such, can be the cause of either great good or great evil. Christianity interprets instinctive desire as animalist and reprehensible, and some schools of modern Western philosophy set up a profound opposition between instinctive desire and reason, and insist that the former should be either controlled or eliminated. Theravada Buddhism also advocates the elimination of all desire. I consider such attempts threats to the continued existence of life itself, which is partly supported by desire. Mahasanghika Buddhism teaches that, when permeated with altruistic, practical striving for the compassionate salvation of others and the improvement of society, desire can be sublimated and controlled.

Without doubt, instinctive desire which is allowed to run rampant in such forms as greed for power and dominance, is a threat to life. However the desire of a controlled, enlightened, compassionate self can be highly valuable and creative. Mahasanghika Buddhism teaches that such controlled, sublimated desire can be achieved through union of the small self of the individual human life and the great self that is the universal source of all life. What is your opinion of the Mahasanghika prescription for controlling desire?

WILSON: Theravada Buddhist teaching presents a difficult paradox for Westerners. To elimate desire is obviously to extinguish life – at least, life as we know it (that in itself might be the attainment of Nirvana). The extinction of all desire is a conceivable aim only for very few people in the modern West. Whilst it has traditionally sought to repress animal passions and the demand for self-gratification as one of its paramount concerns, Christianity none the less recognizes that men must be motivated in some way in order, not to destroy desire, but to channel human energies for the attainment of certain specified goals. The true Christian's principal aim might be said to constitute enlightened, long-term self-interest. The Christian has to be concerned, above all else, with his own soul. A subsidiary aim, at times apparently incidental to the primary pursuit of individual salvation but an aim that, in the interests of social order, the Church has often emphasized, is that of conduct conducive to the social good. This subsidiary goal of social well-being has at times even been predominant and, when deviant Christians have sought to assert the orthodox view that social benefit is purely incidental, authority has stepped in to support socially beneficial heterodoxy against individualist orthodoxy (the treatment of the orthodox Calvinist, Anne Hutchinson, in New England, is a case in point). In practice, long-term enlightened self-interest, working out one's own salvation, and the Christian commitment to "good works" are offered as the twin pillars of Christian purpose by the major Christian denominations.

Like other religions, Christianity has (or has had) an ascetic strand in its tradition, in which sensual hedonism has been rigorously subdued. Christian ascetics cannot, however, be described as having no desires in the Theravada sense, or even as seeking their eradication. Rather, the Christian ascetic channelled his passion to goals such as union with God, the attainment of mental peace, or the penetration of a higher state of consciousness. The sublimation, cultivation and education of human aspirations may be an area of common ground between Mahasanghika Buddhism and Christianity.

IKEDA: Yes, that common ground can be recognized. Another area of similarity between at least one sect of Buddhism and Christianity is belief in post-mortem reward in a paradise. The faithful are promised that they will be taken to Heaven if they believe in Christ and abide by his teachings. In the Pure Land sect, the faithful are promised the reward of re-birth in his paradise in the west if they merely call on the name of the Buddha Amida (Amitagus) who is, incidentally, mentioned as an imaginary Buddha in the teachings of Shakyamuni. Whereas, ideally, Christians strive to purify their aspirations and lead good lives to be worthy of their crown in "Heaven", followers of the Pure Land teaching, in their eagerness to attain bliss in the world to come, have all too often developed a loathing for this world and all efforts to improve it.

WILSON: There may be a variety of ways of purifying the aspirations, and the effectiveness of each must have something to do with prevailing social conditions. Clearly, the agencies for educating and controlling men in a largely agrarian society in which, throughout their lives, men live in small communities may not be effective when men live in an urban society, play impersonal roles, and spend their time in social contexts in which technology and bureaucratic order dictate a wide spectrum of their social behaviour. Judaeo-Christian morality was forged first among a nomadic, then among a settled agrarian and pastoral people, and finally in the context of a colony under foreign domination. As a result, it may not be so readily adapted to the circumstances of contemporary living. Where rules are specific, concrete and made for a context in which strong personal and familial ties obtain, they are likely to have less than total applicability when social conditions have radically changed. Christianity stipulated an exacting morality for face-to-face communities, and many of its prescriptions pertain to intimate relationships within a family, a kin group, or a village. Rules of this kind are not so easily transferred to mass society. How does one "turn the other cheek" or "forgive seventy times seven" when the miscreant is a large bureaucratic corporation, a government department, or a role-player who, if one complains of his behaviour, will say, "Don't blame me: I am only doing my job"? Controlling desire in modern conditions, whether that desire is for vengeance, status or material gain, is not so easily affected by reference to highly specific and concrete examples that lack cogency and relevance in changed social circumstances.

IKEDA: This is a very interesting point. You are quite right that injunctions related to everyday life are frequently difficult to transfer from one society to another. In its eagerness to rid human beings of all desire and delusion, Theravada Buddhism overlooks this and establishes various elaborate codes of concrete day-to-day behaviour. Some of them, like the instructions to male laymen to take no life, not to steal, not to indulge in wrong sexual practices, not to lie and not to drink intoxicants are easy enough to follow almost anywhere and at almost any time. The ten rules for female lay believers, the 250 precepts for monks, and the 500 for nuns, on the other hand, were largely pertinent only to the Indian way of life at the time when they were drawn up. The same is obviously true of the many rules evolved by independent groups during the age of Sectarian Buddhism.

The Mahasanghika and later Mahayana tradition, however, has been to work within a large metaphysical framework for the development of fundamental wisdom that enables the believer to lead a good, moral life under the customs and conditions obtaining in each social environment. In other words, Mahayana precepts have dealt with matters of practical faith and the cultivation of the wisdom to deal correctly with any and all concrete social situations.

WILSON: If religiously prescribed morals are to be effective, they have to be expressed in terms of abstract generalisations, so that they can be applied in widely divergent circumstances. Today, exemplary Christians tend to pay less heed to the specific injunctions contained in their scriptures, either because these do not apply (such as the items that I cited earlier) or because they are now regarded as trivial (such as the New Testament injunction, "above all things, swear not"). Rather, they seek out the most general propositions that can be derived from their traditional morality, since these can be applied in modern circumstances. Christianity, however, lacks the coherent metaphysical structure of Buddhism, and the construction of a systematic moral code has required prolonged and contentious effort by Christian theologians, whose disputes still continue, even though Western societies now pay little heed to the moral pronouncements of theological pundits.

Both Mahasanghika Buddhism and Christianity have the goal of disciplining human passions that, if left uncontrolled, might lead to anarchy and chaos. This appears to be true not only for the baser instinctual impulses of men, but also for such relatively more refined but egocentric goals as status-striving. Even the search for social mobility can produce confusion about social norms and can disrupt the orderly operation of society, as the sociologist, Emile Durkheim, long ago illustrated: he regarded such striving as a case of boundless desire. For many who hold essentially civilized values, it is not the Theravada goal of stalling all desire (which most men might find unattainable), but, as you intimate, the attempt to channel desire, on which the future of civilization rests. The term "social control" is no longer fashionable with sociologists, even though they originally developed the concept, but control is not repression, and human consciousness must, in any case, be moulded. The Hegelian notion of man unfettered and free from social constraint is as much a miasma as the idea of man free from all desire. If men are to lead satisfying lives, they need an enduring framework of predictable social order. I believe that such a context is better produced as a result of moralization, of the internalization of received values, and of the careful, but not uncritical, study of the intimations of tradition, rather than by the abrasive operation of the crude, mechanical and electronic devices. Yet, if moralization were to be abandoned as the process by which we attain social control in society, as might become the case in an increasingly technological world, should we not in all probability become the victims of just such techniques of manipulation?

Sex for Pleasure

IKEDA: The interpretation of sex as a source of pleasure divorced from procreation leads to sexual activities beyond the normal pattern and in this way may be effective in retarding the growth of the world's population. However, it may have untoward effects on fundamental human reproduction and life styles. Some religions abhor all sexual pleasure that is not reproductive. I believe that the issue deserves closer scrutiny and that sex for pleasure should not be condemned unless it is in some way harmful. What is your opinion on the subject?

WILSON: The nexus between the animal (including human) yearning for sexual gratification and reproduction is, in nature, a crude mechanism that functions to ensure the continuance of a species. It is always beset by intense passion and struggle, as exemplified in such animal patterns as territoriality, sexual rivalry, monopolization of sexual rights (among animals with herd instincts, and even among men in instances such as medieval Muslim harems), and in the disputed control of children. The early stages of modern medical advance reduced infant mortality, thus providing the search for sexual pleasure with the unanticipated consequence of rapid population growth. Before modern techniques of birth control were developed, over-population (in relation to resources) was checked by random starvation through famine; by the high incidence of disease; and by a variety of socially prescribed devices, none of which would now commend themselves to us. These included the voluntary abandonment of the settlement (and hence the suicide) of the elderly among the Eskimos; the practice of female infanticide in many parts of the world (sometimes in association with polyandry); the exposure of children, and particularly of the malformed, in the ancient world; and abortion. Each item, as I have listed them in a regressive scale, extinguished the life of the individual at an earlier point. We might also include, as another incidental item that unintentionally worked to the same end, the practice of voluntary celibacy, to which not inconsiderable sections of the population of some societies committed themselves – for example, the priests, monks and nuns of medieval Europe. Alerting society to the dangers of over-population, Malthus recommended pre-marital chastity, postponement of marriage and restraint within marriage as the appropriate preventative measures.

The greatly increased effectiveness of birth-control techniques from the late nineteenth century onwards permitted more and more people to plan the size and spacing of families, and opened up the prospect of extensive modern public policies of population planning. Public authorities, of course, can do little except offer prospective parents the carrot or wield the stick, on the one hand, by way of special benefits and social honour, seeking to induce people to have more children (as in Nazi Germany and at times in France) or, on the other hand, cajoling people to stop having children (as, in recent decades, in India and, at times, in China).

IKEDA: Implementation of such plans is always difficult and seldom successful for a number of reasons. The length of time, difficulty and expense of rearing infant human beings to adulthood frequently colour attitudes towards family size, especially in the industrialized world. Human infants are more helpless than the offspring of most other animals and require years of nurturing before they can function effectively on their own. This is true even in nations where a primitive life style persists, although under such conditions, the process of maturation is abbreviated and accelerated by the comparatively unsophisticated demands made on human beings, and by the need for the young to contribute to the general family well-being by working in some way or another as soon as possible. The need for extra helping hands – as well as sexual pleasure *per se* – no doubt in part accounts for high birth rates in places like India and China.

If an extended period of maturation is essential to life in primitive societies, it is all the more important in sophisticated industrial nations where children must acquire a much broader spectrum of skills and knowledge to equip them to function successfully with their fellows. The difficulty and expense of providing them with the requisite training and education probably help account for the lower birth rates in nations like France, Germany and England.

These two considerations – the need for more and more young people to help gain sustenance and awareness of the need to limit family sizes in order to train children adequately – have ironically stimulated officialdom in some over-populated nations to impose restraints on childbirth or, in other more developed nations, to attempt to stimulate the birth of larger numbers of children.

If birth-control plans are to enjoy any degree of success at all, they must not be forcibly imposed. A far better way is to improve the standard of living and education within a society to the extent where birth-control measures will be autonomously applied by the people themselves.

WILSON: Whether processes of public or private family planning are effective or not, the clear implication of all attempts to control the *consequences* of sexual activity (as distinct from urging sexual restraint) is that sexual gratification in and for itself, and without regard to procreation, is at least tacitly acknowledged as a perfectly legitimate goal and, some would say (although not, of course, the Roman Church), a human right.

IKEDA: Yes, an increasing number of people have come to think of sexual gratification as a perfectly justified goal in itself. Of course, in the cases both of attitudes towards birth control and feelings about sex for pleasure, different people adopt different stances. Some people engage in sexual relations solely for the sake of procreation. Some women consider sex their duty as wives and prospective mothers. However, in general pleasure plays a large part in sex for humans and, especially in the industrialized nations, the urge to gratify the desire for such pleasure not infrequently results in unwanted pregnancies, with their potentially tragic consequences.

Given the nature of the human animal and of society in much of the modern world, an emphasis on the pleasurable aspects of sex is probably inevitable. The important issue is not suppressing natural human desires but inculcating rules of morality that prevent desire from breeding tragedy.

WILSON: We are, in the nature of the case, somewhat ignorant about the patterns of sexual activity in various cultures and time periods, but there is no doubt that the possibility of sex without conception has removed one of the powerful constraints supporting chastity in those societies – societies influenced by the Judaeo-Christian-Islamic tradition, for example – in which chastity was socially demanded of the unmarried. Moral rules are not always enjoined on teleological grounds, but for centuries the risk of untoward pregnancy was a powerful reinforcement for Christian sexual prohibitions in the West, particularly for women. The elimination or, at least, the very appreciable diminution of that risk opened the way for many people to challenge traditional Christian sex ethics.

The Roman Catholic Church has continued to abjure sexual activity that is not intended to lead to procreation. Yet even that Church has engaged in casuistry on the matter, as the use of the "safe-period" method makes apparent. Other Christian churches have steadily relaxed their strictures. The Anglicans have moved from a position where, in 1916, the bishops made "an unhesitating judgement" that the use of artificial methods of birth control was "dangerous, demoralizing and sinful" and "unnatural", to a virtual acknowledgement that sexual activity is one of the joys of companionship in marriage. Nevertheless, all the major Christian denominations, together with Judaism, continue to demand that sexual intercourse should be confined to married partners, and all of them take it for granted that casual sex outside of marriage – which is, of course, by definition, undertaken solely for pleasure – is morally reprehensible. In this they may have the weight of sociological evidence on their side. For while extra-marital sexual encounters may be pleasurable for the participants, should birth control techniques fail, the consequences might well be harmful for the offspring of such liaisons. This has been particularly true in the West, where illegitimate children have often been the prime example of the victims of that disposition pronounced by the god of the Old Testament of "visiting the sins of the fathers upon the children". There is, however, a wider possible source of harm. Casual sex, or sex outside regular stable unions, might be shown to have some, albeit indirect, consequences for marriage itself. If men could easily obtain one of the chief benefits of a stable partnership outside its confines, this might lead to the abandonment of the institution of marriage. Whilst, for the individual, this might appear a form of liberation from something that is currently often represented, at least frivolously, as a form of bondage, the longer-term consequences for the stability of society might be serious. The other functions that marriage fulfils might not be so easily superseded, and one sees that the sexual division of labour, as it is conventionally understood – the advocacy of the feminist movements notwithstanding – is a well-adapted form of domestic economy which appears to function well for society at large.

The longer-term consequences of the disjunction between sexual activity and procreation still have to work themselves out in the wider sphere of societal organization, although other complex patterns of inter-relationship between social institutions support the institution of marriage and the persistence of the nuclear family. There may be an incidental benefit in the older advocacy of moral restraint in sexual matters – namely, the control of self-indulgence, the inculcation of patterns of discipline, and the sublimation of instinctual procreative urges into creative endeavour in the fields of the civilizing arts. In some societies, these necessary dispositions of restraint may have been stimulated and sustained in the individual by other agencies and mechanisms, but I am inclined to believe that, at least in Western society, the moral attitudes that were enjoined towards sexuality may have provided an archetypical form of moral response providing the model for other areas of social comportment. If this has been the case, then a radical change in attitudes towards sexual morality, such as the open and explicit approval of sex for pleasure, might lead to a weakening of other moral injunctions. Whether, given the new technological order of modern societies, moral restraint might be adequate for the orderly regulation of society is a question that I have raised before.

IKEDA: I agree entirely that traditional sexual morality has a stabilizing effect on areas of society other than sex itself. The Buddhist precept against wrong sexual activity – that is, adultery – is based on belief in the importance of support for marriage and the family. This system and the morality associated with it are essential in modern society, in which, as I have said, the current tendency is to stress the pleasurable aspects of sexual activity. Marriage and the family not only serve as the basis for many other social structures, but also create the environment without which the cultivation and education of offspring would be impossible – or highly difficult. Because children need both parents if they are to grow into fully rounded adults, the family system based on long-term union in the form of marriage is essential. I must add, however, that I do not countenance the use of political or any other kind of superordinate authority for the imposition of the family system.

Sexual Ethics

IKEDA: The conservative in both East and West blushes at the boldness with which the mass media treat sex. Although, on the surface, the reactions of both the liberal and conservative camps in Japan and the West resemble each other, they actually differ in an interesting way. Christian morality long imposed strict controls on sexual expression on Western nations, and the current outburst of liberalism is probably a reflection of the struggle between innate human longings for freedom and old, externally imposed restraints. Until the late nineteenth century, however, the Japanese were permitted great freedom in sexual matters. It was only when the nation began to copy the West in culture and technology that the government exerted itself to control such things in order not to lose face in relation with (at least ostensibly) highly moralistic Western countries. In other words, the government told the Japanese people, "You must not allow yourselves to be permissive in sexual matters since permissiveness is condemned in the West." Ironically, today the Japanese who advocate greater sexual liberalization argue, "We should be more permissive in these things to keep up with the permissive West."

The important point in this connection, however, is this: sexual ethics belong to the mental and spiritual world of the men and women involved;

external authority should not interfere or impose restraints, except in cases in which actual harm is likely to result.

The Christian religion is well within its rights to teach its own version of sexual morality, but I cannot understand why it should emphasize the topic and persistently interfere in private matters of this kind to the extent that has caused some people to abandon the Christian faith in disgust. To what extent does Christianity stress sexual ethics? Does liberalization in this field pose a danger to Christianity?

WILSON: Within the overall scheme of Christian morality, sex has always been an issue of the greatest importance. It would not be an exaggeration to say that sex was the linch-pin of the Christian moral system as it came to be taught by the Church. The universal interdictions on incest and murder within the group were proclaimed, together with injunctions of honesty, truth-telling, and familial and group loyalty, but sexual continence was, from the time of Saint Paul, a preoccupation of the utmost significance. As I suggested earlier, I believe that sexual comportment became a model for a wider class of moral behaviour in Christendom, providing a basis for the internalization of a wider range of moral norms, particularly through the influence of Puritanism, when these intimate and personal issues became the touchstone for the individual's conscience. A man was charged to watch his very thoughts, lest he commit adultery in his imagination. Thus, sexual self-control became a basis for the form of individual conscience-formation that played an important part in shaping Western man. With less dependence on group control and conformity than, for example, has perhaps been traditional in Japan, the individual behaved according to an internalized set of moral constraints, which were based in disciplined attitudes to personal sexuality.

Such a process of intense socialization depended on striking a delicate balance if appropriate self-denial and self-discipline were not to lead to severe repression. At the social level, a different balance had to be struck between public and private moralities. Anglo-Saxon society, particularly in the Victorian period, depended on a considerable level of hypocrisy. Public virtues were paraded, even if in private some individuals absolved themselves from the demands of a moral code that they publicly endorsed and upheld. It would be easy to condemn such hypocrisy, but in certain social arrangements hypocrisy may be an important lubricating oil for life. When demands become very exacting, hypocrisy becomes important as a way of encouraging public compliance without disheartening men too much by the private difficulties which compliance presents.

IKEDA: I see what you mean about hypocrisy being a social lubricant. The Japanese system fully recognizes the importance of such a double standard of judgement and employs two words to indicate our attitude to the difference between what is claimed openly (*tatemae*) and what is actually done (*honne*). For instance, the *tatemae* is that prostitution has been abolished from the nation. The *honne* is that female attendants in private rooms in Turkish-bath establishments indulge in prostitution. Officially, such places are baths and, from the legal standpoint, above stricture. Officially, Japanese males have one wife each, although it is by no means uncommon for people with the means to support one or more mistresses. If the legal spouse gives tacit consent, all the better. If she does not, the philanderer must find ways of concealing the presence of his paramour.

We human beings are imperfect. Spotless moral performance is usually impossible to expect. However, in relationships with legal spouses or extramarital sweethearts, the most important thing to aim for is the self-control necessary to prevent causing any other person injury or sorrow.

WILSON: In all societies, moral norms are pitched at a level that exceeds the performance of some men; otherwise there would be no need to have norms which are formally enjoined and persistently reasserted. When norms exceed performances, they may function gradually to raise the levels of performance. Men live in part on their pretensions but, at least occasionally, must live up to those pretensions, which become the means of enhancing the moral quality of social life generally. It seems to me an important pretence that men should behave towards each other as if each one of them did in fact sustain the moral norms of society at all times. (The pretence and hypocrisy that characterized nineteenth-century Britain may have become necessary with the slow development of a well-differentiated public life separate from private life. Public life became moralized to standards exceeding those which could always be sustained, hence the age was one of ostensible and at times ostentatious public virtue, combined with private peccadillos. In the twentieth century, we have seen the steady demoralization of the public sphere with the institution of impersonal roles and technical procedures.)

The functions of pretence may be discerned when pretence is destroyed. Thus, among groups that live on such terms of enforced intimacy that normal morality becomes difficult to sustain, anyone who tries to maintain a higher moral tone may be ridiculed or ostracized. This occasionally occurs in military units where, because of formal discipline and the dependence on social control rather than on self-control, it is easy for everyone to assume that all concerned are in some sense "against authority", and so against even normal decencies. In such circumstances men allow their private departures from the formal code to become public within the group, and the lowest common denominator dictates the moral tone. Hypocrisy is eliminated, but so are standards. Without the formal assumptions of high levels of widespread moral compliance life can become a rubbish pit.

The point that I am making, perhaps too obliquely, is that, given the important place ascribed to sex within the traditional code of Christian morals, as the model for the internalization of other moral norms, one cannot regard sexual standards as having traditionally been matters solely for the men and women concerned. Christianity made sex a pivotal point for the conduct of a Christian society as such, and regarded the possibility of harm arising from irregular sexual liaisons as something that might affect the entire social fabric. In other societies, sexual issues may have remained outside the sphere of public concern, and other social mechanisms may have operated to ensure the maintenance of adequate levels of social control.

Except for the Roman Church, the Christian churches have greatly moderated their attitudes to sexuality, and some, whilst counselling sex only within marriage, acknowledge that stable unions exist between unmarried people and even that homosexual relationships can be wholesome. Although Christian doctrine is, today, very much disputed, even within the churches, the popular idea of Christian morality is perhaps the point at which the churches are most strongly integrated into contemporary Western society. Not only the devout laity, but also many lapsed Christians who together constitute the so-called "moral majority" endorse Christian ethics, including perhaps very prominently, sexual ethics. The more liberal clergy, who preach relaxation of standards, often find themselves resented by a public little inclined to religion but still attached to much of the traditional Christian morality.

IKEDA: I see what you mean, but my point is related to the important place ascribed to sex in traditional Christian morality. It is true that Hinayana Buddhism includes a precept about wrong sexual acts in its codes for ordinary lay believers. Relations between the sexes were much more strictly controlled for monks and nuns. Mahayana Buddhism, on the other hand, concentrates more on self-improvement for an understanding of the universal Law and underplays matters of sexual ethics, although, in its case too, at least in the past, monks and nuns have been expected to live up to moral codes very similar to those of Hinayana Buddhism.

(In later times, in Japan, since it was felt that high positions in temples should be hereditary, it became customary for Buddhist priests to marry and raise children. This custom persists today.)

Since, in its pursuit of enlightenment to a great truth, Mahayana has not stressed sexual ethics, in Japan matters of this kind have largely been regulated by Confucian teachings. In Japanese history, Buddhism, Confucianism and Shinto have coexisted for ages in a kind of symbiotic relation. Confucianism had for its domain relations among lord and vassal, parent and child, elder and younger brothers, husband and wife, and friend and friend. Shinto prayers were thought to bring safety and good harvests in agricultural endeavours. Buddhism was wrongly thought to be concerned solely with happiness after death.

As I have said, however, Buddhism concentrates on enlightenment to the universal Law (or Life) and self-improvement in accordance with such enlightenment. Ethical and moral behaviour naturally evolve as a consequence of self-improvement but are not a primary concern. This is not to say that Buddhism advocates sexual licence. Morality is relative, varying from culture to culture. Any religion's attempts forcibly to impose on another culture alien ethical moral standards can only stimulate rejection of the religion itself and the negation of its powers to do good. For this reason, teaching basic, universal truth and giving only secondary emphasis to matters of ethical codes – in the way Buddhism has usually done – seem to promise greater advantages to all parties than overstressing points of morality that are, at best, relative. This is why I asked whether Christianity is not mistaken in giving sexual morality a high priority.

Sin

IKEDA: Sin is stressed more in Judaism, Christianity and Islam than in Buddhism. Buddhism has a concept of sin, of course; but according to its teachings a bad deed brings its own retribution without the intercession of an outside punisher. A Buddhist who does something wrong more or less knows what to expect; a Christian cannot know what punishment his arbitrary God will inflict and therefore suffers great anxiety over even minor infractions of divine regulations. Perhaps awareness of sin inhibits transgressions, but it can also lead to cruel psychological suffering and even desperation. Believers in arbitrary gods who punish resemble the subjects of a fickle tyrant. Buddhists, who live according to a universal, just Law which prescribes punishment proportionate to the malefaction, are like people living under a constitutional government. What is your opinion of my views and of this contrast in approaches to sin?

WILSON: According to traditional Christian ideas, God would punish all unrepentant sinners at some future time. (That time remained uncertain, varying with different eschatological schemes: punishment might occur immediately after death or might be reserved to the end of the present dispensation when, according to the scriptures, an elaborate procedure of judgement would take place.) Conventionally, most Christians believed that after death unbelievers and unrepentant sinners are consigned to hell, a place of eternal torments, or at least to purgatory to "work off" their burden of guilt. Among Roman Catholics, the idea of divine intercession was widely entertained. The intercession would be made either by Jesus or through the advocacy of the Virgin Mary or the saints, for the mitigation of the severity of God's punishment. Protestants emphasized the vicarious sufferings of Jesus in bearing the sin of ordinary mortals who, through faith in him, might escape punishment. For those outside the Church there was no hope. In the Middle Ages (and perhaps more recently), some Christians certainly experienced great anxiety over even minor infractions, and some went to extraordinary lengths to mortify the flesh and to suppress every tendency towards self-indulgence. These dispositions have much diminished in modern times: today's Christians are much less preoccupied with personal sin than Christians of the past.

In Western countries, a different conception of evil has developed in place of sin. Evil is now widely seen as less a matter of personal wrong-doing than as the result of failure in the social system, the so-called malfunctioning of which is said to cause some men to suffer deprivations which, it is alleged, induce them to commit anti-social acts. Punishment is no longer regarded as the remedy: instead, what is advocated is some type of therapy. Morality has thus, in part, been "politicized", with wide categories of thought and action being labelled as evil. Public policy is in part blamed for such evil – in such matters as sexism and racism. Since Western societies are largely secular, the essentially religious concept of sin has largely dropped out of account for most people.

Even among those who remain Christians, the emphasis, at least in the major denominations, has shifted away from concern with sinfulness and punishment to a much more other-directed religiosity. Few Christians today envisage God as particularly punitive in disposition and certainly not as a fickle tyrant. One can trace, particularly in the nineteenth century, the growing emphasis on the god of love and the decline in conceptions of him as a stern judge or a criminal investigator. Within the major liberal Protestant denominations, the re-conception of the divine economy occurred long ago. The term that you use, "constitutional government", is by no means inappropriate for what is implied in practice, and – despite the burden of the scriptures to the contrary – in the way Christians actually behave. When pressed, any Christian who retains a vestige of literal belief in the Bible must, of course, concede that it remains within God's power to behave arbitrarily. His omnipotence cannot be gainsaid. In reality, the spirit of the times, the rule of law, the ideas of rationality and faith in natural justice have all conditioned the way in which Christians have come to expect their deity to behave.

IKEDA: I see your point, but what I actually had in mind was less the practice of Christians today than the fundamental Judaeo-Christian interpretation of God and his justice, as set forth in the scriptures. Your remarks have, however, answered my question by suggesting that modern Christian thought might be receptive to the Buddhist approach to this issue. No doubt, European rationalism would be prepared to accept the principle of cause and effect as an explanation for the punishment of evil more rapidly than it would the idea of a capricious authoritarian god. Should rationality fail, Christians must fall back on traditional beliefs as explained in their scriptures. For this reason, and because these beliefs probably still exert a great, even if only partly consciously realized, influence on the daily lives of many Christians, examining such basic tenets as that of an omnipotent and punishing god is worthwhile.

Religion and Morality

IKEDA: Religions influence society and derive much of their strength from moral precepts and ethical standards, which may be either an integral part, or only an indirect result, of the given religion's doctrines. Sometimes, however, moral or ethical precepts become outmoded and no longer suit the needs of society. When this happens, the religion that persists in attempting to impose anachronistic moral requirements is likely to face popular resistance.

Without setting forth direct social moral codes, Buddhism concentrates on revolutionizing the inner world of the individual. Its social effects are the outcome of such inner revolutions. Consequently, specific moral and ethical standards may be worked out in accordance with the actual conditions and needs of the society in which they are supposed to work. Ideas of morality in India and South East Asia differ greatly from those in China and Japan, yet Buddhism has thrived in all these regions. What are your thoughts on the relation between religion and morality?

WILSON: It has often puzzled me when Christians are at pains, as they sometimes are, to subordinate the moral aspects of Christianity to what they see as more fundamental, namely, the specifics of belief and worship or church commitment. For religion to be religion, as distinct from magic, it must embrace prescriptions of universal applicability and rules for personal comportment and social order. It must, that is to say, have a moral prospectus. I entirely concur with you when you say that morality is the form that a religion's social influence must take. If religion is concerned with "what to believe in", it must also be concerned with "rules to live by". Religion becomes a social reality as its members' beliefs find expression in everyday life. The way to the highest religious goal is in leading a certain sort of life. Whilst religions may canvass an idea of "salvation" as a future state to be achieved, in practice what religions always provide, in a more encompassing sense, is a condition of salvation here and now. From a sociologist's perspective, salvation can only mean the sense of present well-being, even if that well-being takes the form (as it does in Christianity) of a *present* reassurance about one's *future* circumstances. Present reassurance is reinforced by the prevalence of conditions of predictable order in everyday life. If religion persuades men to behave in decent ways to each other, to minimize aggression and to cultivate sensitivities, fellow-feeling and human-kindness, then it provides salvation, at least in the only form in which it can be realized within man's this-worldly experience.

You suggest that the involvement of religion in the life of a given society may produce a negative effect on the maintenance of faith, particularly when that religion's moral emphasis is no longer congruent to the life of a given society. I must confess to having been more struck by the opposite effect: when moral interdictions and prescriptions have been heavily underwritten by religious sanctions, morality has sometimes suffered when belief in religion has declined. In such a situation, the risk is that, being tied to a specific religion, moral injunctions lose their force when faith in that religion itself weakens and when society becomes secularized. I do not believe that a secularized society need be a less moral society (and certainly not that secular individuals are necessarily less moral than the religiously committed), but, in the West, the loss of moral consensus has certainly accompanied the decline of Christianity, and secularization has not occurred in a way which would allow a secular ethic to be effectively canvassed or sustained.

I realize that excessively severe moral injunctions may weaken faith in the religion imposing them, although I think that there is some evidence to show that people often dodge their moral obligations even while persisting in their faith, relying on the offer of mercy and vicarious effort institutionalized in their religion (whether in the Amida Buddha or the Virgin Mary and Christ) to mitigate the consequences of their derelictions. For instance, although the Roman Church has maintained its form of moral interdiction of all artificial methods of birth control, we know that a very large percentage, perhaps a majority, of Roman Catholic women in advanced societies actually practice birth control in ways their Church proscribes as immoral. We know that in a country like Chile, although many people acknowledge that divorce and remarriage is immoral, none the less, and even with the connivance of the clergy, people evade the religious law by obtaining from the Church annulments of their marriages in order to be free to re-marry with the blessing of the Church. Recently, we have seen that, although the Church teaches that abortion is sinful, the majority of the Italian electorate, including, of course, many devout Catholics, has actually voted in a referendum to retain the laws permitting abortion. The reason for such abandonment of moral obligation and the rejection of religious counsel on moral matters may well be that many people no longer see these moral injunctions as consonant with their needs. Religion may have lost support for its moral stance, but we cannot ignore the three other developments that I have enumerated: first, that some men continue in their religion even though they have abandoned the attempt to maintain religiously-sanctioned morality (whether by quietly disregarding it or by noisily contesting it); second, that, because of involvement with the modern world, religions have sometimes amended their own former moral positions; third, that the decline of religion may itself have led to the decline of moral consensus.

The effective moral thrust of any religion comes from what has been called "an ethic of responsibility". The individual may behave morally because he obeys specific rules, but rules, as we have already noted with respect to the origins of Jewish and Islamic moral structures, become situationally conditioned and cease to be applicable in changed cultural contexts. Dilemmas increase for both the faithful Muslim and the faithful Jew as these religions are transplanted to cultures remote from their regions of origin. In some measure, the same problems arise for Christians, but Christianity contained the seeds of a much more universalistic and adaptive ethic in which the individual might judge for himself how to apply generalized rules to particular cases and contexts. In this respect, the operation of Christianity in moral matters is not dissimilar from what you say of Buddhism. A powerful Christian injunction says of the law, "the letter killeth, but the Spirit giveth life", indicating the importance that is attached to the internalization of the sense of the law rather than to meticulous, and perhaps mechanical, performances. To say this is to ignore neither the numerous prescriptions for personal comportment in Christian teaching nor the way in which the Church has sometimes powerfully influenced governments to enforce Christian morals – as in the prohibition of birth-control appliances in Catholic Ireland.

Christianity itself, of course, has undergone periodic processes of internal change as it has had to adapt to new conditions, and these have sometimes demanded the transformation of individual consciousness which you might even consider in some ways to be analogous to an inner revolution. The heightening of moral awareness among the Puritans, Pietists and Evangelicals provides instances of just such re-intensifications of an ethic, primarily concerned with inducing a heightened sense of responsibility within the individual himself instead of relying on agencies of social coercion. Of course, the Christian faith has never left moral judgement exclusively to the individual: there have always been objective standards, even if they relate to propositions couched in very general terms, concerning which reforms and revival movements have sought to make the individual more conscientious. In practice, Buddhism may leave more room for individual discretion, and it has been more easily adapted to diverse cultural contexts. Christianity has always tried, sometimes in a narrow and bigoted way, to impose its specific moral demands on alien cultures, regarding its role as that of Christianizing – by which is meant moralizing – all societies. It has been a more powerful vehicle for directed cultural change than any other religion, although an assessment must take into account its organizational structure as well as the ideological underpinning of its ethic.

Equality

IKEDA: Most of the higher religions teach the equality of all men. (Religions that insist on the superiority of a single class or race cannot become universal unless they alter or abandon this doctrine.) Although, ideally, equality is desirable, in fact it does not exist. Inequalities pervade the entire world. Overlooking them is tantamount to approving – at least tacitly – the very real differences that separate people from each other, and thus to weakening attempts to eliminate class, racial and religious prejudices.

For this reason, religions that insist on universal equality must accompany this insistence with actual efforts to remove inequalities among classes and other groups if they expect their ideal to have real meaning. Shakyamuni's attempts to eliminate the caste system in ancient India lend weight to the Buddhist teaching of equality. Some of the cries for equality made by many other religions today, however, impress me as lacking substantiating action. An ideal that is no more than an ideal loses its significance – even as an ideal. What are your feelings about religious advocacy of equality and current class (and other) inequalities in the world?

WILSON: The idea that men should enjoy equality of rights, facilities, and conditions is, as you say, entrenched in the higher religions. The Christian Church has always recognized that equality does not obtain in the world, however, and has supposed equality either to have been possible only in a primeval condition of bliss (before "the Fall" when man, through sin, forfeited paradise) or to become possible again in some future dispensation, when God will resurrect the faithful and establish them in a post-apocalyptic society that Christians believe will prevail for a millennium. The Church fathers held that, although men were equal according to God's natural law, in the conditions prevailing in the period between the Fall and the Resurrection the world was governed at best only by relative natural law under which inequalities characterize society. Having abandoned perfection and surrendered paradise, man must learn how to manage in a corrupted system. The role of the Church in this interim dispensation was to mitigate the harsher realities by urging the rich and powerful to be merciful to the poor and the poor to be patient, putting up with their lot until God restored the faithful to their lawful estate after the second advent of Christ.

There are theological difficulties in this prognosis, but it can be seen that the Church has never abandoned the ideal of equality, even though it has not felt capable of establishing conditions of equality in this world. Church leaders have thus been able simultaneously to justify and to condemn inequality, saying in effect that, whilst it could not be avoided, it ought to be moderated. Today, the churches generally condemn racial inequalities, although only two decades ago an Archbishop of Canterbury could declare with respect to racial differences that while all men were equal in the love of God, they were not equal in the sight of God. Slave-trading, despite both periodic papal pronouncements against it and its elimination in medieval Europe, developed and grew between Africa and the New World, where slave-owning continued in the Southern states until the American Civil War, and was vehemently defended by local Christian leaders. Castes have never existed in the West, even in the muted form of the differences between *eta* and other Japanese, but the Church readily accommodated itself to the system of feudal estates of medieval times. In general, the churches have not preached against status differences, and the episcopal churches made such differences basic to their own church structures, regarding the social order almost as a divinely instituted extension of natural order. The Church has generally supported the ruling authorities, legitimating them in their power, wealth and status. There is, of course, a counter-force in Christianity, and dissenting movements have generally arisen to assert a more radical case for social equality.

In recent times, some Christians have become more concerned about equality, particularly racial equality, not only in the United States, South Africa and other societies of mixed settlement, but also in Britain, where liberal citizenship laws for a time extended the right to take up residence in Britain to the peoples of her former empire. The issues are not so much the basic matter of formal equality before the law, which is guaranteed, as widespread feelings of racial discrimination and hostility. Here, religious movements might do more to eliminate the (often mutual) sense of racial antagonism than can be achieved by coercive legislation, although the tendency even within denominations of mixed racial adherents is for different racial groups to worship separately.

IKEDA: Yes, I realize that this is true. However, if I may be permitted to digress slightly, this tendency to separate worship can be overcome. Our organization has active branches in the United States, and our membership there is multi-racial. Most people who come to us realize that equality is a major tenet of Buddhist philosophy and soon feel at home with the way all our members, no matter what their race, participate in services and activities together. Even those people who, at first, find it impossible to divest themselves of old race-connected feelings are generally won over to the Buddhist way before long. The key to our success in this is our reliance on discussion groups – in contrast to formal services in which the predominant relation is between the worshipper and a deity instead of among worshippers. In discussion groups, everyone shares experiences and gradually comes to know and understand everyone else. It is understanding that generates the environment in which equality can be maintained – even among races that harbour traditional mutual animosities.

WILSON: Leaving aside the specific issue of race, it may be said more generally that the ideal of equality is not easily translated into a code of action. Absolute equality is beyond our reach. Men are born with divergent talents, and these eventually attract differential rewards, so leading to differences of wealth and status. Even in socialist countries, the talented – artists, musicians and intellectuals, for example – enjoy considerable privileges. Equality of opportunity, widely proclaimed as a principle of education in Western democracies is, after all, the opportunity to display one's talents and so to create inequalities. Were it even possible for equality of opportunity to be established, the differences among individuals in cultural and genetic endowment would soon be realized in new patterns of inequality. Such random factors as birth order, the death of a parent, illness and pre-natal influences, affect the individual's capacities, and the institution of equality of opportunity could only allow these items to produce new inequalities.

The principle of equality before the law, with respect to human rights in freedom of belief and speech, and so on, prevails as the rational base-line in terms of which cultural diversity may find opportunity for expression, but that expression in itself can never be a matter of strict equality. Wherever the individual can be treated rationally, as a unit, the principle of equality can be applied, albeit at times with difficulty. Where the actual quality of the individual is at issue, differences will persist. Religion deals with men as equals in certain respects, but religion is also sensitive – perhaps more sensitive than any other social institution – to the qualities of men, to their strength of purpose, generosity of spirit and openness of heart. In these respects men cannot be treated as homogeneous units. Certainly, in the West, where the uniqueness of the individual is strongly asserted, such differences have been of primary spiritual importance.

IKEDA: I certainly concur with your statement that we are all different and that equality cannot therefore obtain when the quality of the individual, not his nature as a rationalized unit, is of uppermost concern. Indeed, over-looking our qualitative differences leads to a lessening in respect for the individual and his freedom.

As you said in your opening remarks on this subject, human beings ought to enjoy equality in terms of general rights and conditions. This means that, in the greater view of such things as the love of God or the truth of the Buddhist Law, all men are equal. The Lotus Sutra explains the egalitarian impartiality of the Buddhist Law by comparing it with the rain, which falls alike on all parts of the earth, though each individual plant puts forth leaves, flowers and fruit according to its own distinctive characteristics.

Ideal impartiality is not always either possible or desirable. As the Buddhist scriptures state, the parents of seven children love all their offspring equally until one of them falls ill, when partiality to the comfort and care of the sick child is perfectly in order. Since ideal impartiality is impossible in the real world of politics and society, I should like to recom-mend this kind of compassionate partiality. I should like to see govern-ments show concern towards the unfortunate and help them acquire the ability to stand on an equal footing with their fellows.

All men are, as you point out, born with divergent talents. Although total equality is impossible, it is up to our authorities and social systems to create the next best thing: an environment in which each individual has the same opportunity to develop and employ his talents for the sake of his own and the general well-being.

Religious Freedom

IKEDA: Freedom of religious faith, together with freedom of thought and conscience – among the most important human rights – has been won in the West with great sacrifices; and it is our duty to guard it jealously. Yet I believe that freedom of faith should include both the right to embrace any religion one chooses and the right to conduct missionary activities to carry that faith to other people.

Some nations permit only the former while prohibiting the latter (or, worse, allow missionary work against religion and forbid it in its name, as is particularly noticeable in the socialist nations).

Unless the two rights are granted simultaneously, maintenance and future growth of religion are difficult. If publicity against, but not for, religion is permitted, religions will gradually die out. Do you agree with me that human religious conscience can only be maintained when both the right to believe and the right to proselytize are granted?

WILSON: Any concept of democracy surely implies that man's beliefs should be free from attack and should have equal standing with anyone else's. By extension, democracy requires that everyone should have an equal opportunity to learn about the faith of other people and to examine such faiths for himself. This implies that people who follow a religion should be free to present their beliefs to a wider public if they so wish. It may be the collective wish of a people to ensure certain facilities for a particular religion or a traditional way of life, but no people is really free, whether there be an officially endorsed religion or not, unless all men have the right to publicize their ideas.

The steady advance in religious freedom in Western countries in recent times has extended to some sects that demand considerable concessions for their practice − for example, in the matter of exemption from military service, in the right to refuse particular forms of medical treatment, or in being exempted from work on days that they regard as holy. Some of these concessions were granted only slowly in countries with entrenched Roman Catholic majorities and in relatively secular countries like France, but now, even in countries at the periphery of the Western democratic tradition − Portugal, Spain, Greece and Argentina, all of which have had right-wing and hence usually religiously intolerant regimes − some extension of religious freedom has now been generally accorded. Today, paradoxically, it is in left-wing countries, despite their nominal commitment to democracy, that freedom of thought and speech is most inhibited. In such countries, the censorship of ideas is spuriously justified only by the sophistry of proclaiming proletarian consciousness to be true consciousness and by making Marxism-Leninism into a substitute religion.

Although the official prohibition of missionary activity severely hinders the dissemination of religious knowledge, there is evidence that despite prohibition, religious ideas still circulate and commitment is still covertly maintained. Religion has a long record of success under conditions of persecution, and in some socialist societies it appears that, because of the absence of any political alternative to the regime, religion gathers support as the primary, and perhaps the only, focus of allegiance other than the state. Religion may even become a surrogate for a political opposition, as the one activity in which there is some expression of independence of, if not actual dissent from, the state. I am inclined to think that, without denying its importance as a purely religious phenomenon, the persistence of commitment to the Roman Church in Poland is partly an expression, conscious or unconscious, of passive resistance to the socialist party and the state. This is one explanation of the radical difference between the diminishing religiosity (as expressed in church attendance) in Western Europe, where religion is free and competitive, and the very vigorous involvement in religion in Poland (and in Poland more than in other Eastern-bloc countries because the Church there has been, historically, a symbolic surrogate for nationalism).

IKEDA: In both the East and the West, religion does have a long history of success under conditions of persecution. However this is not to imply that religion thrives only in adversity and languishes under conditions of freedom. (I suspect it is materialism and the influence of scientific rationalism, not freedom and competitiveness, that have brought about a decline in religiosity in the West.)

The specially privileged position of Marxism-Leninism in the socialist states makes the Christian religion seem attractive to a small group of people. Since religious education outside the framework of Marxism-Leninism is forbidden in these countries, knowledge about the teachings of Christianity must inevitably become less and less available. This means that the good counsel and advice that religion has to offer on the ordinary affairs of everyday life are lost, with a consequent loss of an important aspect of the general spiritual culture. (Of course, over-protection robs Marxism-Leninism of its vigour and value and thus deprives political leaders of ideological underpinnings.)

For this reason, I insist that true religious freedom must permit missionary work, allowing people to air and explain their thoughts and beliefs, since only such freedom makes possible continual examination and stimulation and, of course, growth and development.

WILSON: Restrictions on missionary activity makes it difficult for new religious ideas, or ideas that are not a variant on the indigenous tradition, to gain a hearing. Thus, whilst such radical Christian sects as Seventh-day Adventists and Jehovah's Witnesses and such somewhat less radical groups as Pentecostalists and Baptists have, in spite of bans on their literature, had considerable success in Eastern Europe, it might be much more difficult for a religious movement from another culture — and I am thinking of

Buddhist, Hindu or Islamic movements – to make headway in societies with a specifically Christian tradition. Similarly, the restrictions on missions in some Muslim countries and in India and China discriminate against Christian groups more than against movements with some link to the old indigenous religions. Although restrictions on missions, and even on religious meetings, make certain manifestations of faith difficult, they operate differentially on different movements. Variants of traditional religions may receive some fillip from official censorship; movements disseminating radically different beliefs may find it difficult to win any initial purchase. This appears to be the case because only a variant of a familiar religion can function as a focal point for the concentration of symbolic dissent.

Just how effective anti-religious propaganda is seems to be an unresolved issue. Evidence about the Soviet Union suggests that although, over the course of the years, secularization has occurred there, this development has been less the result of militant atheism than the consequence of structural changes in Soviet society that are, in some respects, not dissimilar from those changes to which secularization is attributable in Western countries. If this is so, then one must say that religion *per se* (or at least religion that is strongly linked to the indigenous tradition) will not necessarily decline because of hostile publicity, but might even react vigorously against such attempts at restraint. On the other hand, religious decline may occur because religion loses its relevance when social conditions undergo rapid processes of change.

Whatever the effects of government policies towards religion, it is my view that religious freedom is a fundamental requirement before any society can be described as free. Only by open debate, the right to explore and criticize ideas, can men work out their own salvation. On such rights all other human rights depend. The right to discuss ideas; to communicate what one believes to be beneficial, right or necessary; and to canvass the support of others is implicit in the right to choose what to believe and how to practice. I entirely agree with you that without freedom of religion and the right to disseminate one's faith there can be no rights of conscience and no genuine democracy.

Tolerance

IKEDA: Followers of a religion – especially of religions with distinctive doctrinal systems – are generally convinced that they have attained the real truth. Some religions are more tolerant than others, but most insist on their own unique orthodoxy.

We followers of the Buddhism of Nichiren Daishonin believe that other religions have discovered parts of the truth but that the teachings of our faith bring all the parts together in an inclusive teaching. We therefore think that error in other religions and philosophies arises from interpreting parts of truth as the whole. We believe that our truth (that is, the whole truth) is unique and real; if this seems intolerant, we are none the less convinced that we are right.

Certainty of the absolute nature of one's doctrines is fundamentally different from intolerance aimed at depriving others of the rights to their views or at forcing others to conform to views they do not embrace. Religious discord almost always arises from this kind of intolerance.

I believe that assurance in one's faith is natural but that tolerance must be exercised in attempting to spread that faith. In other words, no matter how superior a religion, secular force must not be applied to impose it on other people. What is your opinion of my view that this is the only compatible way between assurance in the truth of one's religion and religious tolerance?

WILSON: Religious toleration was established only very slowly in the history of Christendom. Accustomed, from their very early days, to persecution, once they became a state religion the Christians were quick to visit persecution on others and continued to do so for many centuries. Despite the command to love one's enemies and the exhortation of the virtues of meekness, humility of spirit and forgiveness, Christianity, as organized in the Church, proved to be implacable and relentless in its pursuit of pagans, heretics, dissenters and those committed to other religions. Christianity was an exclusive faith brooking neither criticism nor opposition. Some stirrings of attitudes of tolerance can be found in the Renaissance, but this was tolerance within an intellectual milieu rather than tolerance for the irreligion of the masses or for the schools of conscientious dissent and, until the seventeenth century, the Christian record is one of unreflective certainty and almost unmitigated by tolerance.

Those guilty of religious intolerance, whether Christians, Muslims or others, have usually been utterly convinced of the rightness of their cause and have even persuaded themselves that their very intolerance was exercised for the long-term good of their victims and was necessary if those victims were to have any prospect of ultimate salvation. Not infrequently, religious self-righteousness and other, political and economic, interests have converged. The Middle Eastern religions furnish abundant examples of men who, in the name of religion, have perpetrated cruelty and inhumanity for covert political ends.

Although Protestantism gave an impetus to the extension of religious toleration, securing a measure of religious freedom in some countries by the end of the seventeenth century, I believe that it was only the creation of a new multi-religious society that really ensured that religious freedom would become the norm in Christian countries. That new society was, of course, the United States which, because its people were drawn from divergent religious traditions (albeit mostly from within the Christian spectrum of faiths) and because many of them were religious refugees in search of liberty, was obliged to become a secular society dedicated to providing conditions of religious freedom. In many ways, the United States became the forerunner of other states in guaranteeing that men might believe and worship according to their own individual judgement. The religious form of organization known as the *denomination* (in contra-distinction to *church* and *sect*) was created in America. Denominations accept the legitimacy of each other, recognizing what is sometimes called the "plentitude of faith" *within* the Christian tradition. Denominationalism does, however, also steadily lead to the diminution of doctrinal distinc-tiveness, to mutual acceptance and even to indifferentism.

To single out the United States is not to ignore instances of religious tolerance in other societies. However, the United States deserves pre-eminence because it self-consciously espoused tolerance in the face of a religious tradition in which exclusivism had been the strong concern. In other traditions, where there has been no explicitly monotheistic commit-ment, intolerance was less likely. Many Asian rulers have behaved with exemplary tolerance towards peoples of other persuasions. There is, how-ever, a difference between conscious and actively promoted toleration and the indifferentism that can obtain within a polytheistic or syncretistic tradition, where simultaneously held, mutually contradictory beliefs are tolerated, almost in the conviction that the more religion there is, of whatever kind, the better.

In the modern world, religious freedom is guaranteed only where the state pursues a conscious and deliberate policy to ensure freedom of conscience for all citizens. The rights of minorities are protected, and there is a free exchange and diffusion of ideas. Although members of each religious movement may feel, and feel strongly, that they alone have the truth, their only guarantee of being able to operate without interference is for each group to recognize that other groups take exactly the same position. If they anathematize each other, they may destroy the framework of order and tolerance without which none of them could survive. Thus there is, as you suggest, a delicate balance to be struck. No religious movement can be asked to derogate its own position or claim for itself less than total allegiance from its votaries. (Lesser claims are certainly made by mainline Christian denominations and perhaps among other established religions. The denominations operate as superficially differentiated organizations, with different "brand names" for virtually common products – a condition of virtual religious oligopoly.) On the other hand, no religious movement can afford so to disparage others that it induces a climate of hostility. Much less can it afford, for its own benefit, to seek the interference of secular authorities in the religious life of other movements – lest, in course of time, that same weapon be used against its own people.

Theory and Practice

IKEDA: Since the initial phase of modern civilization. Western philosophical tradition has bifurcated theory and practice and has stressed the former. In the Orient, on the other hand, theories have generally been accepted as true or wise only when they have arisen from practice. Particularly in Buddhism, theories with no relation to actual practice have largely been abandoned. Close links between theory and practice in teachings are one of Buddhism's most salient characteristics. Buddhist practice is always an inward-oriented discipline for the sake of the improvement of the individual. What is your opinion of the need for consistency between theory and practice and of the effects of inward-oriented religious discipline?

WILSON: In the Western tradition both philosophy and theology have become highly specialized theoretical disciplines. The growth of specialization and the tendency of all subjects towards academicism have been a pronounced feature of the educational development of the Western world. Certainly, today, no one in the West looks to philosophers for practical guidance, and it is a commonplace that professional philosophers are often utterly impractical people. Nor, in general, are their commentaries on social affairs – lacking as they often are in empirical evidence and analysis – of much consequence for the solution of political and social problems. The same is true of theology, the concerns of which are often remote from those of even devout laymen. Although theologians do, in some measure, influence religious practice, the effect of their thought is often indirect and by no means uncontroversial. Laymen are frequently suspicious of theological pronouncements and innovations in theory and liturgy.

Empiricism and pragmatism do, however, find full expression in Western society, and science and technology have developed only by empirical procedures and pragmatic tests. That the natural and applied sciences have become entirely independent of theology and, in a very considerable measure, even of philosophy, is a matter of historical fact. Scientists do not make much direct recourse to philosophical propositions in their work: they proceed by techniques and procedures that are now entirely endogenous to their own disciplines. This autonomy of the sciences is by no means irrelevant to the loss of religion's prestige. For many people, religion today appears to be impractical and irrelevant and so has been abandoned. Alternatively, many of the new religious movements that are enjoying some measure of current success, do so, it appears, because they offer what is claimed to be practical therapy for contemporary problems.

Although it specifies certain standards of required performance from its adherents, Christianity has tended towards the communication of a very generalized ethic. In this sense, Christianity also looks for its greatest effect in its transformative power in the lives of individuals. This is particularly true of Protestantism, but it is by no means absent from the tradition of Catholic piety or even from the new Charismatic Renewal movement. It would be difficult to say that Christian theology is entirely consistent with Christian practice, and there are, indeed, so many varieties of each that a general assertion is impossible. The tendency within the faith has been towards an inner orientation of fitting the individual with those resources that make him more adequate in the contemporary world.

Justification

IKEDA: When a sect that considers itself the proponent of the religious truth breaks away from a larger religious body, the parent religion usually opposes the split and dissension over orthodoxy arises. Sometimes the two parties resort to violence or political coercion. This was the case in medieval Christianity, when victory for the secular powers supporting a given religion constituted justification of the religion itself. The victory of the Athanasians over the Arians was connected with the power of the Roman emperor, and dissension among the Catholic Church and among the various Protestant churches took place against the background of equivalent dissension among secular rulers supporting various religious factions.

In the case of Buddhism, on the other hand, sects that have arisen in India, China and Japan have usually tried to settle their differences among themselves without calling on either violence or secular authority. Is the Christian way the only one to justify a religion? Why have the Buddhists succeeded without resorting to force?

WILSON: A strong commitment to non-contradiction in belief is at the heart of the historical tendency of Christians of different persuasions to anathematize each other and to resort to force. There has been a strong and sustained thrust within Christian theology towards the perfection of an internally consistent, coherent, systematic and unitary body of doctrine. Given the arbitrariness of revelation, such an endeavour has been a taxing exercise in reconciling the diverse sources of Christian ideas. There are some well-known problems: for example, the ill-reconciled schemes of eschatology; the mysterious, which is to say, intellectually incomprehensible, doctrine of the Trinity; and the differences between literal and symbolic interpretations of the scriptures. Christians assert the omnipotence and omniscience of God, but even here a problem arises: if God is all-knowing, he must already know what will happen in the future, but such knowledge precludes the possibility of his ever changing his mind, which seriously impairs the claim to omnipotence. With all these ill-' adjusted claims, it is not surprising that Christians should have disputed their own teachings to so great an extent. A misplaced phrase or comma has sometimes been enough to set contending parties at loggerheads. From shifts of emphasis, differences have arisen in the whole ethos of particular denominations and in the cultures that they have influenced, as can be illustrated from the Calvinistic assertion that, although man has free will, God has already determined the destiny of each soul, to the Arminian reversal of the balance, in saying that whilst God's foreknowledge cannot be denied, the primary issue is the individual's opportunity to choose salvation. The difference in mood between such Calvinistic cultures as those of Holland and Scotland and populations influenced by Arminianism, like the English working classes of the nineteenth century, is striking.

The political authorities in the West have traditionally sought religious justification or legitimation. Kings made claims for which transcendental support was vital. Popes and bishops crowned kings and claimed, in return, secular coercive power in support of their religion. Church and state stood closely associated. Such associations have not, in other religious traditions, led to the use by the state of its coercive power in the cause of sectarian rivalries, – for instance in Thailand, *brahmin* Hindu priests are used for the coronations of kings who rule over *Buddhist* kingdoms and who are themselves Buddhists. It is the association of the state with a monotheistic, exclusivistic religion that apparently leads to secular power being mobilized for religious ends.

The time when Christians had access to such power has, however, now gone. Modern Western governments are extremely unwilling to be drawn into religious disputes. Even in those countries where there is an "established" church, enjoying protected privileges, church authorities have little, if any, political influence. Governments seek to avoid religious affairs, ensuring rights of freedom of conscience and assembly to all religious groups, unless a movement operates in an illicit way. Church leaders themselves would, today, not want to invoke state power, since they recognize that religion cannot be imposed by force.

Buddhist sects have certainly shown far more tolerance towards each other and towards followers of other faiths than has ever characterized Christianity. Buddhism has, of course, been less closely identified with secular authority, and even where governments have supported Buddhism, as did King Ashoka in India or the Tokugawa Shogunate in Japan, the fact that the Buddhist ethic has never been canvassed as an exclusivistic faith has mitigated the ardour with which it has been supported by secular powers. Shakyamuni did not excoriate the deities that men worshipped, but merely incorporated and subsumed these inferior conceptions of religious duty into his own more elevated system. Buddhism has also traditionally lacked the centralized organizational power that the Christian Church inherited from the collapsed Roman Empire, and thus, organizationally, was never in the position to promote one consolidated obligatory creed (supposing that any Buddhist had ever wanted such an opportunity). Finally, one must revert to the fact that Christianity inherited much of the Greek preoccupation with a coherent, logically articulated, doctrinal system. Although all religion necessarily deals in ambiguous categories and non-empirical referents, one must be impressed by the attempt of the Christian theologians and schoolmen to produce a deductive system of theology including all forms of knowledge and excluding no branch of creation. The intellectual intolerance of unreconciled elements, or ill-coordinated issues, manifests the same spirit as the general Christian preoccupation to encompass all men within the one universal Church. The very words to which Christians have such swift recourse – catholic, universal, ecumenical – are explicit claims that Christianity is relevant to all mankind. The struggle to accommodate revelation to reason, and to present one definitive theological system, assumes the global significance of the task. These dispositions represent not merely random symptoms of Christianity, but constitute a veritable syndrome of a latent structure of assumptions that conjoin intellectual monism with religious intolerance of diversity or deviance. The medieval Christian attempts to unify faith and to embrace the world within the Church were not the only ways in which religion might be justified, but they were implicit in the entire constellation of Christian purpose and ethos.

IKEDA: I see what you mean by saying intolerance is part of the overall Christian ethos, and in my opinion this is so because of the unique and absolute omnipotence attributed by peoples of the Judaeo-Christian-Islamic tradition to God. There can be no questioning the dictates of such a god on the plane of human reasoning. Similarly, by extension, such of God's vicars on earth as popes and kings acquire or have bestowed upon them an aura of infallibility and omnipotence that is open to no questioning whatsoever.

As I have said before, the absence of a deity with an arbitrary, human-like personality who is the source of revelations that must be obeyed without dispute has led Buddhists to reason and discuss among themselves in a mood of mutual tolerance in the general desire to arrive at truth. The Buddhist scriptures themselves are written in the form, not of divinely delivered revelations, but of dialogues and discussions among Shakyamuni and his followers. This same tradition of discussion, without the decisive interference of secular authority, has persisted throughout the history of Buddhism and has usually, although I must admit not always, made possible peaceful resolution of disagreements.

The Imposition of Religious Restraints

IKEDA: Although the teachings of the founder of a religion are usually clear and simple, as the organization founded on them expands and ages, the limits to which doctrinal restrictions are enforced tend to spread. For instance, early Christianity gave no thought to whether the world was flat or round; by the time of the Renaissance, asserting the spherical nature of our planet and the idea that the earth moves round the sun had become major heresy. In the early period, Buddhist teachings consisted of such simple instructions as the Five Precepts and the Ten Good Precepts – which taught that one must not kill, steal, and so on. In later times, however, the number of rules that monks had to abide by rose to 250; (there were 500 for nuns). As Buddhism became firmly established, hunters suffered social ostracism because their work involved taking life. Ironically, religious doctrinal restrictions reduced the hunter to virtually as wretched a state as that of the animals he hunted.

In my opinion, the religious man ought not to force the doctrinal restrictions of his faith on others but ought to seek to ingrain in himself the fundamentals of his religion. If he himself is true to his faith and if that faith is convincing, he will win the respect and possibly the following of others. Do you agree with me?

WILSON: The process which sociologists know as institutionalization appears to be inherent in all religious movements. Pristine vigour, simplicity and charismatic appeal give place, over time, to routine and complexity, to the growth of a bureaucratic structure and to the inauguration of rules. A successful religious movement, sooner or later (usually sooner) becomes an integrated organizational structure. Certain typical developments occur: a hierarchy of officials who make their careers in religion; regulations about promotion; a division of function (departmentalization); the elimination of duplicated effort, the routinization of training and the production of catechisms, forms and set procedures. A movement increasingly comes to rely on structured procedures and responses. New situations and dilemmas call forth the need for commentary and elaboration of the direct and straightforward original statements of faith, and so the process that you describe follows its steady path.

The transformation of a spiritual ethos into a body of legalistic rules is a pattern of change that has been common to all the great religions, and words that originally denoted religious groups have entered our language, usually as perjorative terms, to encapsulate these characteristic orientations: legalism is *pharisaic*; scholarship is *talmudic*; sophistry is *jesuitical*; scrupulous concern for purity is *brahmanic*; moral censoriousness is *puritanical*. As you have implied, the elaboration of rules becomes a dead weight on religion: rules are often sustained by special classes whose expertise lies precisely in interpreting regulations, as among the *ulama* of Islam, or in ensuring purity in minute form, as with the *rabbis* in Judaism.

The enforcement of religious obligations has been common when a particular religion has gained dominance in a given region, most vigorously with the exclusivistic religions, of course, but sometimes in other cases, when public opinion has been mobilized. It would have taken a bold villager who, in either a Catholic or a Hindu village, ignored the sanctity of particular religiously symbolic objects, at least until recent times. To have due regard to sacred cows or to genuflect at the door of a church were part of the mores of everyday life and were thus imposed on local people. Of course, people are skilled at avoiding or evading situations in which duty is enforced, but we must acknowledge the penetration of custom by traditional religions as a form of social enforcement of religion.

IKEDA: And I think that, in their nostalgic longing for the good things of the past, people today sometimes forget the extent to which religious enforcement played a part – and not always a pleasing part – in the lives of our forebears, in East and West alike. It is doubtful whether many of the people who enthusiastically take part in re-creations of past festivals would be content to live in its entirety the life of the people by whom those festivals were originated. (Knowing no other way of life, the people of the past probably suffered less under the restrictions imposed on them by religion than would a modern man – with his entirely different education and world view – were he to be miraculously set down in the environment of times gone by.)

The basis of much of life in the past and of most systems of manners and mores was religion. The priests and others who conducted the religious ceremonies that were vitally important to society derived not only great influence, but also considerable wealth from their positions. The people devoted part of their hard-earned harvests to the priesthood, which in turn assumed formalized duties and, forgetting its essentially elevated mission, became a specially privileged class. This development did little good for the ordinary people and, furthermore, had lamentable consequences for the priesthood and indeed for religion itself.

WILSON: Wherever religion has effectively influenced men it has, inevitably, become infused into the customs of everyday life and this has often given priests a considerable degree of social influence. At times, religiously prescribed injunctions have been imposed on particular societies, particularly in matters such as the prohibition of alcohol or the stipulation of diet, or regulation of the hours at which business can be conducted. It would be easy for a rationalist to demand that such codes be swept away, but one must recognize the value of providing a framework of predictable order and a tissue of custom. Social mores arise from many sources. Religion is perhaps as good a source for them as any other and, in so far as the customs it enjoins conform to a more elevated ethic, it may be a better source than the random accretion of rules drawn from many diverse episodes of a community's past history and the borrowings from its neighbours.

These considerations notwithstanding, religious leaders have sometimes found it difficult to resist the temptation, in favourable circumstances, of prescribing social and moral rules in society. They have regarded it as an encouragement to faith to make men obey, imposing on those who are not committed, or not much committed, as well as on the genuinely devout, at least the outward and visible signs that might, so some supposed, promote the growth of an inward and invisible grace. Such compulsion can only be exercised when a religion has attained social dominance, attained maturity and become socially entrenched. At that point, its leaders may be more concerned with maintaining stable practice than with the urgent proclamation of truth. It occurs when the radical vision has dimmed and conformity, rather than voluntary religious virtuosity, has become the predominant preoccupation. Leadership in settled and well-established religions calls for different qualities from those required in the early period, when a movement is still a challenging departure from normality.

The wider public grows innured to established religion, manifesting at most only mild respect or mild resentment for its representatives and certainly rarely, if ever, recognizing in them the stimulus to re-dedication and the life of devotion. Indeed, the hierarchies of long-settled religions do not often aspire to have this effect, and they normally regard those who too vigorously assert the fundamentals of simple faith with suspicion. As a religion is institutionalized so it tends to become dominated by a class of minor officials, occupying specific posts which the division of religious labour creates. These busy themselves with the minutiae of religious order, frequently at the cost of any wider spiritual vision. They are the career men, who prefer safety to challenge, and routine to spiritual vitality. How to inspire these men in the lower echelons of hierarchy with heightened spirituality, whilst preventing them, on the one hand, from challenging their own superiors or, on the other, from sinking into routine operations, is one of the perennial problems of all persisting religious institutions and organizations.

IKEDA: Earlier on you suggested that religion may be a good source for social mores. I understand this to mean that it is advisable for religious organizations to extend their influence beyond the field of simple faith and dogma to other regions of human experience, perhaps including ethical, political and economic ideals and ideologies. I agree that this is true, with reservations. People who may be averse or indifferent to the dogmas of a religious sect may be initially attracted to it because of its participation in such, strictly speaking, non-religious activities as peace drives. Once associated with the group on the basis of this interest, such a person might come to experience deeper, more spiritual satisfaction from the association as he gradually comes to learn of the group's fundamental articles of faith. (Incidentally, I must say that most of the religious sects in Japan today apparently attract membership on the basis of associations other than purely religious ones.)

Expansion into non-religious fields is not without its dangers. No matter how pure a group's motivations and no matter how closely its action is related to its fundamental articles of faith, extensive non-religious activity always runs the risk of severe criticism from without. Furthermore, when a religious body places great stress on such extra-curricular activities, the enthusiasm of its members for the fundamentals of the group's faith may diminish.

The situation is particularly vividly illustrated by instances in which religious organizations assert certain special ethical or political ideologies. Whereas people in harmony with its ethical and political position may be attracted to the religion, those out of key with it may be repelled. Since a religious organization is a closely woven fabric, rejecting its politics is tantamount to rejecting the religion and everything connected with it. When rejection of this kind is severe and powerful, events such as the European wars of religion can start, as you have said, over highly trivial matters. Jonathan Swift satirizes this kind of thing in the episode involving bellicosity over how a boiled egg should be shelled in the Lilliput section of *Gulliver's Travels*.

As I said in my original comment, the optimum way to ensure that religion's influence on social mores is wholesome without being forcibly imposed, and probably the best method of keeping lower-echelon career men of religion from misplacing emphasis in their activities, is to guard the purity of the fundamental faith. If this is done, the activities of a religious sect may safely ramify into many fields in a spirit of tolerance for the liberation and benefit, and not for the oppression, of mankind.

Religion and Social Values

IKEDA: Estimation of the effectiveness of a religion must take into consideration organizational structure, social relations, personnel components and social environment. Of course, the nature of a religion's fundamental teachings is of paramount importance.

One example of the way a teaching can lead in the wrong direction is the Pure Land Buddhist sect, which in twelfth-century Japan taught that merely calling on the name of the Buddha Amida brought post-mortem salvation and the bliss of eternal life in Sukhavati, the Paradise of the West. Shakyamuni actually mentions the Buddha Amida, but only as a figurative illustration of the vastness and eternity of Buddha compassion and never as a specific Buddha in whom human beings ought to put faith. In twelfth-century Japan, when strife and natural disaster made life miserable for much of the population, many people actually killed themselves to escape the horror of their existences and to attain the bliss of Amida's paradise. In short, a religious teaching became an indirect stimulus to suicide.

A religion which leads to such tragic consequences is suspect. I insist that it is of great importance to estimate the effectiveness of a religion on the basis of its fundamental teachings and their interpretation of the facts of life. In addition to an accurate view of what conduces to human well-being, for true validity, a religion must be able to come to grips with the intellectual issues of its time and stimulate responses from a wide segment of the population. What criteria do you set for judging the effectiveness of a religion and its doctrinal contents?

WILSON: In one form or another, the effectiveness of religion has been a subject of still unresolved debate. Presumably, we mean by *effectiveness*, first, influence over people's lives; second, the capacity to achieve certain specified goals; and third, consideration of the desirability of those goals in terms of some other, external criteria. Let us, for the moment, leave aside the additional items that you mention – organization, social relations and the quality of personnel. Religious teachings as such have sometimes exerted a powerful, perhaps decisive, influence in social affairs. You give as your example the effect of twelfth-century faith in Amida Buddha which led many to suicide. Let me mention another instance: the Circumcelliones of the fourth century in North Africa were so impressed by the blessings to be achieved through martyrdom that some of them invited non-Christians to kill them so that they might claim the special state of grace in the after-life which they believed was reserved for those who "died for Christ's sake".

These are dramatic cases, of course, but the extreme nature of such responses indicates that, in many less dramatic and less terminal matters, religious beliefs have had their effects on social life. They may not always have been foreseen, of course, and sometimes men become convinced of certain ideas against the counsel of their leaders and pursue them to points never originally envisaged. The periodic reassertion of the imminence of the second coming by Christians has sometimes awakened expectations of an early transformation of life and society, to hasten which some converts have engaged in revolutionary action: there are abundant examples from early Reformation Europe, and from Africa and Melanesia in more recent times, to show how uncontrolled expectations of an apocalytic event can lead men into grotesque and harmful behaviour. Even among a more sophisticated public, at times religious belief persuades men that faith matters more than life. Adherents of various Christian sects – Pentecostals, Christian Scientists or Jehovah's Witnesses – refuse certain forms of medical treatment, and some have died rather than receive it. All these cases, then, are the effects, but not the intended consequences, of religious belief.

IKEDA: Consequences, intended or unintended, may have both good and bad influences, which are often the basis on which society judges a religion. Shakyamuni mentioned the Buddha Amida, but it is by no means a logical outcome of such a passing mention that people should kill themselves to find happiness in Amida's paradise. As I said earlier, Amida is introduced into the Buddha's teachings by way of an illustration, like a character in a novel. Suicide in his name is about as sensible as donning a yellow vest and putting a bullet through one's head in the name of Goethe's Werther.

Teachings can also have good effects that their author perhaps does not intend. For example, before revealing to his followers the true way to attain enlightenment, Shakyamuni pronounced the doctrine that all things in the world are transient and that nothing has a permanent existence. Among his disciples, some persons of great perspicacity were able to understand the meaning of true enlightenment and to strive to attain it on the basis of this teaching alone, though no doubt such was not the Buddha's actual intent.

WILSON: Religious teaching's capacity to inspire men to attain particular well-specified goals can be easily demonstrated from history. The transformation wrought by the Protestant ethic indicates the effectiveness of religion in diffusing a specific value orientation to a wide society. There are other examples: the influence of Methodism in re-shaping much of the ethos of working-class nineteenth-century England or the fervour with which Islam has, at various times, inspired whole populations to a new sense of social identity and destiny.

The actual measure of religious effectiveness is a more difficult matter, and here the additional factors, such as organization and quality of personnel, come very much into account, while the conduciveness of the social context has been so stressed by some writers that they have made religious teachings purely epiphenomenal – a response to the felt needs of men living in particular social conditions. Obviously, if it is to be effective, a teaching must strike resonant chords in a particular milieu, but to say this is not to neutralize the importance of ideas and beliefs as such. When an entire population is transformed in its ethos, life-style and values, ideational elements must be at work, and those elements have most typically been religious beliefs and morality inspired by religion. Certainly, perfectionist religions, such as Christianity, do not achieve their ostensible goals in full measure. The code of moral conduct is too exacting to be realized, and even though whole populations have sometimes been deeply affected by religion, perfectionism precludes complete goal-attainment.

IKEDA: Yes, and demanding perfection when it is impossible leads to frustration and despair. Very few human beings are capable of perfection, and religions require an element of understanding – like the Buddha's compassion or the love of God – that will inspire constant effort for the gradual, if never complete, achievement of an ideal goal, within the security of the knowledge that errors and failings are forgiven and can and must be corrected.

Of course, in their wilfulness and selfishness human beings sometimes take advantage of the compassion of the Buddha and the love of God to perform all kinds of evil, safe in the belief that, at the final hour, they will be forgiven. In other words, many aspects of religion – including elements as important as compassion and love – are subject to various kinds of interpretations, including the purely personal as well as other interpretations related to the historical age and social circumstances.

WILSON: We are talking here in very broad terms, and we both appreciate that systems of religious teachings undergo interpretation and re-interpretation and are subject to shifts, and even reversals, of meaning. Such changes are no doubt induced by particular social contexts: by climates of secular thought, by the competition of other religions, by changing economic structures and by a variety of other influences. No system of documentation, catechization or ritual repetition can ensure that a body of doctrine will not, over the course of time, undergo a change of meaning. In the past, religion has at times set the tone of intellectual discussion, presenting problems that men have earnestly debated, even if, at later times, those issues have seemed trivial and inconsequential. The debates of medieval Christian scholars mixed important philosophical issues and the attempt to establish categories with questions that were themselves pure products of metaphysical imagination and could be approached only by speculation. Such questions have now been abandoned, as have many of the issues on which the definition of heresy turned. Men were sometimes burned for beliefs that were merely variants on orthodoxy, on subjects that are, today, inconsequential. Modern theologians sometimes take the erstwhile heretical position on some of these points. Religions generally claim to offer truth that is universal and ageless, but it must be apparent that every religion is highly relative to the age and culture in which it gains allegiance.

Presenting men with value-orientations that transcend what may be described as their mere interests is a task in which religion is always engaged. Interests relate to the maximization of economic and material well-being and are the basic concern of materialistic philosophies, of which Marxism is the chief example. Religion offers a transmutation of ordinary experience, a re-evaluation of life and its purposes, in which certain transcendent values are canvassed as worthy of devotion in their own right, not because they accord with interests in the narrow economic sense. It advocates a higher path and offers counsel about how to follow it. It is never solely concerned with immediate benefits and is never merely instrumental or utilitarian – otherwise it is magic. The ethic of the higher religions is always in some sense arbitrary, claiming to derive from some super-empirical source of experience, but these ethical systems have much in common, including an emphasis on self-surrender and service to others.

Such high goals can, of course, deteriorate. Religion can depreciate into the narrow legalism of set forms. Symbolic meaning can be dissipated, and inspiration can descend into routine, even when elevated language continues to be used. In some respects, religion is always in need of renewal, demanding recurrent re-dedication of energies if it is not to atrophy. Renewal is needed because the goals of religion are ultimates. They are never finally attained. Religion's business is to keep men travelling hopefully, rather than to organize their arrival. In the transformation of experience, religion confers meanings, regulates emotions and communicates values. For this reason, its language is always ambiguous, denoting but simultaneously evoking and evaluating. Whereas science excludes the emotive and the evaluative in order to operate more effectively at the cognitive level, religion is inevitably committed to operating at all levels at the same time. The scientist may be content to try to demonstrate the empirical facts and how they are related to an empirically based theory, but the religionist must also know how the facts are to be evaluated and what, of his emotional resources, it is appropriate should be summoned in response to them. Because life is full of decisions, men need more than cognitive knowledge: they need interpretation, and interpretations entail emotional response and a sense of values. It is at these levels that the profundity of religious doctrine is discovered, and it is for this reason that religion participates in a wider spectrum of experience than do other systems of knowledge.

The Growth of Science

IKEDA: Although scientific technology has made astounding progress and is likely to go on doing so, not all aspects of its growth are laudable. Developments in the dangerous field of armaments and the greedy employment of technology to the extent that the natural environment has become gravely polluted are certainly to be deplored. Though some people insist that research in arms development stimulates growth in other fields, I suspect that the same growth could be stimulated through specialized, non-military study.

All scientific development has both good and bad sides. Modern conveniences make life easier but they debilitate as well. For instance, some school teachers complain that reliance on electric sharpeners has produced a generation of youngsters who cannot sharpen pencils with a knife. On a more serious level, who knows what disastrous results tampering with man's genetic make-up could have for future generations? Do you believe that, in the face of such threats, men of religion should speak out against unbridled scientific technological progress? Or do you consider outspokenness in this field unwarranted meddling?

WILSON: Science is now thoroughly institutionalized in modern society, in universities, special research establishments and in industry. It is high time that its powerful, diverse, and ramifying influence was subject to some form of social surveillance and perhaps even control. Science affects the lives of all of us, even of those people in pre-literate societies who have no voice in determining just what influence science should exert in their lives or on their societies. Clearly, scientists may need a very wide measure of freedom for the prosecution of their work, but that freedom should be counterbalanced by an ethic of responsibility. No one doubts that most scientists are, individually, thoroughly responsible people, but science itself is now so internally diversified, its fields so finely sub-divided, and its activities so completely institutionalized – largely at public cost – that perhaps the time has come for a scientific ethic of responsibility to be given formal, permanent and public expression.

Is it beyond the bounds of possibility that an ethical code to regulate the uses made of scientific knowledge might yet be instituted? Ethical codes are operative in the practice of the professions of medicine and law, at least in Western countries, and although one sees that the regulation of science is much more complicated, these codes might provide rudimentary models or at least reference points, for the ethics of science and technology. The scientist works much less on a direct client-practitioner basis than do doctors and lawyers. Their work is more finely divided into specialisations, and depends more heavily on co-ordinated team work (although similar trends are occurring in medicine, too).

The diversity of science and its multifarious prospects of advance suggest that scientists alone could neither evolve nor operate an adequate ethical code. To be effective, such a code would need the support not only of the consumers of science and technology, but also of representatives of the general lay public. The code would need to be both supra-political and international to be truly effective, and one sees at once that its institution would present considerable difficulties and demand the co-operation of many levels of government. There are, however, international agencies that might provide the nucleus for such a body, from the United Nations and UNESCO to organizations like the one administering the Nobel Peace Prize. It is clear that such an agency must not be purely political or diplomatic, and would itself need to be infused with an ethical spirit transcending that which normally prevails among politicians, whose interests, after all, are often the rather short-term concerns of the well-being of their own constituents for the period between elections.

IKEDA: Absolutely. We in Japan are painfully aware of the harm that can be done to the environment when politicians pander to industrialists – the politicians' major backing – who combine science and technology for the sake of their own financial aggrandizement.

However not all industrialists are guided solely by greed, and not all religionists act totally altruistically on the dictates of disinterested consciences. Consequently, the agency you envision would have to be manned by people from many fields, ideally people as little governed by their own material interests or those of their close associates as possible. In selecting a staff, as in most other things, perfection is unachievable; but we must strive to do the best we can. Small sub-committees of people with specialist knowledge would probably be essential to digest and assimilate the technicalities of difficult issues since debate among the uninformed would be meaningless.

WILSON: As you suggest, an agency to develop and operate an ethical code for science would need to be disinterested, detached and objective. It might need to have ultimate recourse to more than merely moral power, which could involve it in the realm of politics. It would need the advice of technical sub-committees, and the services of a properly constituted administration. Despite all this, it would have to operate at a level transcending both politics and the technicalities of science and, above all, it would need to remain the master and never become the servant of its own bureaucratic hierarchies. Its personnel would need to be men of the highest integrity, capable of withstanding the efforts of all sorts of pressure groups – industry, the media, governments and cranks. Its composition could only be of well-tested, public-spirited individuals, among whom I should expect to see religious leaders.

The type of ethical council that I propose would in itself institutionalize the regulation and control of science and technology. Its concern would be to preserve the rights of freedom of scientific enquiry, whilst at the same time considering the social and ethical consequences of the application of new techniques. Its point of control is likely to be less over the individual scientists and more over scientific institutes, research foundations, governments and – perhaps most important of all – industry. The very existence of such a body would encourage increasing public concern about science and would provide an opportunity for religious leaders and others to bring matters of special ethical concern to the attention of this agency. Among these might be the justified public concern at the cost of some government-supported scientific ventures, of which space research is the outstanding example. In a world in which millions are facing starvation, it would be appropriate for a well-constituted public forum to consider whether scientific expenditure of the kind involved in space research is justified.

Man and Nature

IKEDA: Destruction of the environment, sickness caused by pollution, and other ills of our times offer mankind a good opportunity to revolutionize attitudes towards nature. In many parts of the world, movements for the conservation of the environment have started and, in some cases, have already borne fruit. Their scale is, however, still too small. For the sake of the kind of plan that is required to salvage our natural environment, agreement and cooperation among many more people is essential. In effect, all peoples everywhere must always remember that man must live *with* his natural environment and must never damage it for the satisfaction of his own greedy, egoistical desires.

Obviously a schism between nature and man, who for his own profit wishes to exploit and conquer nature, is at the bottom of modern scientific civilization. (Pursued still further, this schism can be seen to have arisen in Judaic monotheism.) As the scale of environmental pollution has grown, the detrimental effects of human actions have become clear. The science of ecology, which attempts to show that we must live, not in opposition to but in harmony with nature, has resulted in conservation movements that are now spreading all over the world; for these movements to reach a maximum audience, each individual human being must awaken his inner self to an awareness of oneness with nature. This in turn necessitates the cultivation of sufficient psychological strength to crush the greed inherent in all life. Religion is the only way to bring about an essential inner revolution and thus to conquer greed and ego. In my opinion, the Buddhist philosophy of the oneness of man and his environment can be of great value in this respect. What are your thoughts on man's relation to his environment?

WILSON: The whole thrust of man's scientific efforts and now, increasingly, of his endeavour in the social sciences has been to establish control over nature. To a very considerable degree, man has succeeded in producing a man-made environment, in which all the features that provide the background to his day-to-day living are the artificial products of his own devising. The mass of men live in cities, all of which are built by men. Pre-stressed concrete rises around them, almost rivalling nature's hills and valleys. He moves less and less by his own power and increasingly by mechanical devices, and he can transfer himself from any natural or social context to another at will. His food is refined and manufactured, watered by irrigation, or stimulated by chemical fertilizers, and often remote in consistency and nutriment from that afforded directly by nature. Even the temperature in which he lives is controlled by central heating or air-conditioning. He has constructed a human environment quite different from any that could have existed when men lived closer to nature. Instead of small communities of total persons, face-to-face groups in which each individual was known thoroughly (in respect of past, kin, associations, dispositions, character and talents), modern associations of men are conglomerations of role performers, anonymous people playing their parts in a complex structure of functional relationships. The human environment becomes as artificial and man-made as that of the physical context.

Yet, ultimately, beyond all the contrivances, the basic dependence on nature remains. Similarly, behind all the elaborate systems of devised relationships, there remain human individuals, many of whom are desperately seeking the warmth and affection of close human relationships and the security of community in an increasingly impersonal world. There is, as you observe, a strong, if not always articulate, demand among men to return to nature, to preserve its life-enhancing qualities, and to experience increased harmony with a more basic physical and human world. Paradoxically, attempts to make this return often involve recourse to techniques that are themselves scientific or social-scientific.

IKEDA: That is both very true and very ironical. Eager to get back to nature, people take vacations in air-conditioned automobiles, travelling over roads that cut through the natural scenery and for the construction of which hills and forests are destroyed. In their cool cars, they arrive at air-conditioned mountain-top hotels or restaurants, through whose glazed picture windows they gape out at the beauty of nature as they eat over-refined, over-processed foods. Then they get back in their air-conditioned automobiles and return to the cities.

In the workaday world, as well as on holiday, human beings depend on technology. They move from floor to floor in buildings by means of elevators or escalators and then frequent sports centres to counter the effects of lack of exercise. This would be totally unnecessary if they walked up and down steps more often or if, when on vacation, they used their legs instead of their automobiles and breathed the fresh sea or mountain air instead of artificially cooled air. Intimate contact with earth, stones, trees and the rest of the outdoor environment would constitute an invigorating return to nature, not just a trip through space both in and to artificially controlled interiors. If more people realized that contact with nature means not just seeing, but also tasting, touching and smelling, more would be willing to do something about the pollution of our environment.

WILSON: Yes. In different terms, science and human organization are our own inventions, and even when we seek to undo their untoward effects, we are often caught using their methods and techniques in order to re-capture the non-scientific, communal (not consciously organized) world that, through science, we have lost. We use science to put back vitamins into food de-natured by our scientific methods. We introduce new chemicals to counteract the effect of other chemicals that we have introduced into the soil or into our own bodies. The same phenomenon occurs no less at the social level. A few years ago, during the period of student unrest in American universities, a group, desperately seeking a quality of human relationships that has been lost in the immensely impersonal context of a big university campus, designated itself as "the committee to establish community". Committees are self-conscious devices and do not establish communities: the very bureaucratic processes that had destroyed community were now resorted to in an attempt to restore it.

The various agencies, whether governmental bodies or pressure-groups of concerned and well-intentioned citizens, are unlikely to effect much by way of restoring the congruence of man to nature or of re-establishing community among men. I agree with you that only if there is a widely diffused ethical concern, which individuals deliberately make part of their own consciousness and seek to transmit to their children, is there a chance of any re-creation of the balance between man and nature. What you call an "inner revolution", I might dub "internalization", but I think that we both mean the acceptance, at the deepest level, of humane value-orientations. The way in which values are diffused throughout a society relies on subtle processes of cultural adaptation. Certainly, new value-orientations cannot be decreed by governments, as has been evident in the experience of the Soviet Union. In an official Soviet report made some years ago, observations were made on – among others – two neighbouring villages. In one village, the inspector found that production quotas were not fulfilled, roads were in ill-repair, the people were often drunken and dirt and disorder prevailed – these people had a high record of Communist Party membership. In the other village, there were high levels of production, well-maintained roads, an absence of alcoholism, cleanliness and order – these people were said to be ideologically unsound: they were Baptists. Official ideologies receive lip-service, but a genuine change of consciousness and life-style must proceed from inner values to which men have subscribed voluntarily, and which are taken in and "made one's own".

IKEDA: You are quite right. It is easy to give orders and pay lip-service to ideologies and slogans, but putting what the slogans advocate into actual practice is more difficult. Often people who are most strident in their preaching are very negligent in their practice. Though there is something vaguely comical about the American college students' forming a committee to establish something that no committee is capable of establishing, in many other fields of concern human beings often adopt a similarly paradoxical approach. In the past we have had wars to end wars; that is, wars in the name of peace. Now, in the name of peace, we engage in nuclear-arms races. As I said earlier, we destroy nature in order to get back to nature. Perhaps a large part of man's tragedy derives from the inability to – as you put it – internalize the value-orientations to which he pays lip-service, and which he professes to believe in. The internalization of correct ideas and values is precisely what I mean by the human revolution. And, as I am sure you will agree, bringing about such a revolution in each individual human being is the task of religion.

WILSON: There is no doubt in my mind that the most effective agency for this process of socialization and acculturation is religion. It may indeed be the only agency that can effectively disseminate values of this kind. Institutional arrangements do not, we must now recognize, produce the effect which a naive Rousseau-like optimism supposed. Good institutions, in and of themselves, do not make good men (even supposing that there is agreement on what constitutes good institutions). There must be, also and perhaps primarily, a widely distributed social consciousness of what must and must not be done: in short, there must be a culture in which nature is regarded in a light quite different from the one that has prevailed in Western traditions.

　　To disseminate values that restore the congruity of man and nature might, as your comments imply, be a task for which the religions of the

Judaeo-Christian-Islamic tradition are ill-adapted. "Man above nature" is a powerful Christian conception, and the corruption of the real world, and of the social world, is an idea deeply entrenched in these religious traditions. In Protestantism, this orientation flowered into the demand that man should master nature, and this disposition was highly conducive to the development of science and technology. Many Christians are, today, very much concerned about ecological problems, but perhaps the most active groups of this persuasion owe relatively little to Christian conceptions. It may, indeed, require a re-diffusion of new values to awaken the mass of the population to the untoward consequences of man's dominance over nature (including his dominance, for example in birth control, over human nature). If it can supply those values and awaken men to the damage and danger occurring in the destruction of the environment, Buddhism might have a vital role to play in saving mankind from itself.

The Future of the Family

IKEDA: With the improvement of facilities to care for the elderly and rear the young and the increasing dislike young couples feel for living under the same roof with their parents, the old-fashioned, multi-generational family is becoming a rarity – at least in industrialized nations. Furthermore, the importance the family *per se* has in society has diminished to the extent that some people are actually worried about the continued existence of the institution. I have heard that young unmarried women can bear children without worry in some Western countries, since institutions will take care of and raise unwanted infants. This is undeniably better than abandoning illegitimate children to the fates they must face elsewhere in the world, but what is your opinion of the influence this situation must have on the awareness of parental responsibility?

Even in the wealthy nations, how long will society be willing to bear the financial burden of such institutions – which are patently impossible in developing nations, the budgets of which are already strained without this luxurious expense?

It is far more important to note the decline of the all-round educational effect children enjoy when they share a home with more experienced, older brothers and sisters and with affectionate parents and grandparents. The time will come when the value of the multi-generational family will be seen to outweigh whatever annoyance accompanies living with elderly people.

What is your forecast of the future of the family and what role do you think religion can play in restoring to general awareness the psychological and emotional value of the multi-generational family?

WILSON: Because of the unprecedented speed of social change in the twentieth century, the modern individual's experience of the world differs radically from that of his parents or his children. So quickly do new developments occur that even within his own lifetime the individual finds that his early-life training ceases to be an adequate preparation for the new phenomena he encounters. Throughout the world, and at ever widening levels of society, people now encounter new knowledge; meet new types of demands; become involved in new patterns of social organization; have to learn, for their work, in their households and for their leisure, about new techniques, new appliances and new procedures. Today's man discovers that he is recurrently in need of re-education. Whereas in the past, the individual learned in childhood the rudiments necessary for the type of life he was likely to lead and found subsequent learning to be a cumulative process, building up into a fund of experience, now the element of cumulativeness is much diminished. Experience is often a hindrance, attaching one to out-of-date measures, and un-learning and re-learning become everyday necessities.

The consequence of all this for the family is that, whereas once the experience of one generation was transmitted to the next and knowledge of the past (often of the past of that particular family) was the most vital knowledge of all, establishing for individuals their own sense of identity, today, in all the increasingly important technical departments of life, past knowledge is increasingly regarded not merely as obsolete, but also as an encumbrance.

IKEDA: In a very real sense, the past itself is an encumbrance, a plexus of bonds tying us to all the things and people that have gone before us. This bondage is not necessarily bad. A tree is oriented towards the future in that it grows skyward, puts forth new leaves and flowers and bears fruit. However its roots are bound firm in the soil, and it is through those roots that the organism receives the nourishment which makes future growth possible. An understanding of the past and our relation to it requires effort. I observe in the young people around us a revived interest in history that would signify willingness to make such effort if it were not, as is apparently the case, a matter of mere curiosity. The young still adamantly refuse to be bound to the things of the past in everyday affairs – this suggests the threat of instability.

Without making the effort to learn about past traditions and without submitting to a certain amount of the bondage such knowledge entails, young people are like trees rooted in sand. They will topple easily. People whose relations with the past are profound are like trees whose roots are bound in firm soil. Such trees can both grow towards the future and derive nourishment and stability for the strength to withstand the buffetings of rough weather.

In brief, the past is a bondage that we should all welcome for the strength and richness it brings. Instead of wanting to flower and bear fruit in isolation from preceding human history, young people ought to make the effort to assimilate what has happened in the past and employ it in the creation of the future. Such public institutes as schools can help young people see this.

WILSON: Yes, but at the public level, the schools, which are devoting more time to technical subjects, are increasingly abandoning education in history and in the cultural heritage of their own country. Where the human disciplines are still taught, they are often taught in an increasingly technical spirit (one hears, in England, of teachers of drama who are much more interested in television-camera techniques than in the content of plays). This public loss of cultural knowledge is reinforced by the loss of inter-generational transmission of values within the family.

The seriousness of all this is that, no matter what the capacities of the new technology, certain vital areas of life of necessity depend on the diffusion of moral attitudes, and moral wisdom is not subject to the process of recurrent obsolescence that characterizes technology. The widening gap between the generations seriously undermines the process of moralization of the young, and this in turn deprives them of due sensitivity to human and cultural values. Understandably, their experience inclines them to suppose that all problems can be solved by the application of the findings of the natural sciences.

Given the effects of social change and the exigencies of modern living, the multi-generational family ceases to be a viable pattern of human sociation. Other agencies, and particularly those of the state, step in to fulfil the functions that the family once discharged. This is true in the case of the care of the elderly, which was once automatically the responsibility of their children. This process of transfer of functions from family to state is cumulative and interactive. The state seeks to provide a service that is much less often being undertaken by young people. Having moved in, it is then expected by young couples to take on more and more of the burden, and so the provision of welfare services multiplies and comes to be taken for granted. From being a "long stop" to protect those who have no children or who have become too ill to be cared for at home, the state steadily becomes a "mainstay", regarded as the agency responsible for caring for old people.

The social services of the modern state multiply at very great economic cost, as specialists in "caring" take over from ordinary people who no longer care or who have forgotten how to care. The development of role specialization in tasks once regarded as no more than human nature towards kith and kin is a commentary on the times in which we live. Why cannot ordinary people regard the frailty and suffering of kinsfolk (short of the need for medical care) as their own concern, rather than having to hand even slightly difficult cases over to experts? My remark in parentheses indicates the difficulties, however. The family may be able to do much less than the expert. Even non-pathological suffering is now an area in which new techniques may yield more relief than can be afforded by family care. Such experts and expertise increasingly intrude into the lives of those who, through age, infirmity, accident of birth, parental deprivation or neglect, or other malfunctioning of the normal pattern of family life, need attention if they are to have a chance to live life "more abundantly".

All of these services are, as you note, economically costly. It is almost as if younger people have decided to sacrifice income (in taxation) in order to pay for services, rather than use their own time to provide these services themselves. Ironically, just at the time when "do it yourself" has become so popular in all manner of household handiwork, "don't do it yourself" has almost become the slogan for choice in the matter of family responsibilities and the task of caring. The choice reflects our modern preoccupation with personal autonomy, the desire to be unburdened by others and to control our own time and pleasure. If that choice indicates the failure of moral responsibility, it also suggests how much we expect that whatever must be done can be done by the application of new techniques, and the often quite unwarranted assumption that new and specific techniques are better than old, diffuse concern. In the contemporary West, there is a growing reaction against the proliferation of welfare services, if only on economic grounds. What is much less frequently recognized is precisely what is lost when moral responsibility is abandoned in favour of technical competence.

IKEDA: The loss is tremendous. Nichiren Daishonin once said that the treasure of the body is more important than a treasure in the storehouse, but the treasure of the heart is most important of all. Welfare facilities can take the place of children by supplying economic assistance – the treasure in the storehouse. Trained personnel can care for ailing elderly people – the treasure of the body. Only affectionate children and relatives can give old people the love they need most – the treasure of the heart. I believe that the collapse of the traditional family is to a large extent the outcome of our having forgotten the importance of the treasure of the heart.

A similar forgetfulness exerts influences in many other fields of modern culture. People no longer regard the past as a source of nourishment and a basis for the creation of the future because they concern themselves solely with material wealth and technological advance (the treasure in the storehouse) and pay little attention to the treasure of the heart. In other words, we lose a great deal when we allow moral responsibility in any field to be abandoned in the name of technical competence.

WILSON: Technology is a cumulative phenomenon. It develops in ways that recurrently render older methods obsolete. Moral wisdom is not like that. It must be learned slowly, and there are no short cuts. The young can quickly learn new techniques: moral, social and spiritual values can be acquired only slowly. Furthermore, and this endorses your point, such values are acquired largely from association with older people in the family and in the community. As the family breaks down and as local residential districts cease to be real living communities, the process of moral trans-mission is disrupted. In all the areas in which moral and social cohesion are at stake, education requires the stability of relationships, the availability of example, and the sense of continuity of commitment that can occur only in the context of natural communities. Obviously, there are costs in such relationships, but that is an intrinsic element in moral learning. The young must acquire a sufficiently long-term moral time-sense to know that the inconveniences of living with the elderly may be but a requital of the inconveniences that older people suffered in bearing and rearing the young.

The family has now lost many of its erstwhile functions. It has become a more ephemeral institution, remaining a social entity only for the relatively short period of breeding and raising children, who then hive off, leaving the residual married pair, unless death or, increasingly, divorce intervenes. Unsolemnized (although not necessarily less durable) unions increase, and even the biologically predicated division of labour and its contingent domestic economy are now undermined by the techniques that have given mankind – perhaps one should say, specifically, womankind – control of the incidence of births. Technology has invaded the structure, functions and ethos of the family, and its weaknesses as an institution are evident. Yet, we know of no adequate alternative to the family and its decline is undoubtedly closely associated with the growth of a wider variety of moral and social trends, from adolescent hooliganism and vandalism, even (in the West) to the bloody-mindedness of some trades unionists.

Only thorough sociological analysis will enable us to recognize the social forces that undermine it, but given these forces it is unlikely that the family will ever be restored to its former role. On the other hand, it is equally difficult to envisage its total demise. We could certainly organize the bearing and rearing of children in institutional contexts, but we know that such alternatives produce children of lower intelligence, diminished motivation and a less responsive emotional repertoire. The desire for parenthood persists and virtually demands familial organization.

The family and religion have, in many respects, been intimately associated institutions, both of them rooted in the local community. Religion everywhere legitimizes family relationships, consolidating the sense of continuity between older (and often dead) generations and the young. The forces that undermine the family are those that militate against religion: technology offers itself as the alternative knowledge to moral and spiritual wisdom. Modern society has few real conservatives (the parties which call themselves such are usually deeply committed to *laissez-faire* economics and to the *laissez-faire* morality contingent upon it). Those who espouse ecological conservation, who criticize "big government" and multi-national organizations, and whose motto is "small is beautiful" appear as yet to be unaware of the erosion of family functions and values and certainly represent no common religious perspective (where they are religious at all). Yet, family life has deep symbolic significance, often invoked by politicians who, however, have little conception of the forces threatening it. If religious leaders were to commission research sensitive to the problems of cultural transmission and its impediments, a public that has perhaps grown somewhat cynical about political promises might respond readily in ways that support the values of family life.

IKEDA: I suspect they would meet with such a response and that they would be able to reinforce that support. After all, in most parts of the world, religion has traditionally been a mainstay of the family system and has stressed relations with the past. (The first of the two Chinese characters with which the word religion, *zongjia* in Chinese and *shūkyō* in Japanese, is written means ancestral.)

Parent-child Relations

IKEDA: In the past, relations between Japanese parents and children were governed by Confucian principles of filial piety. Just as the emperor demanded unquestioning obedience from every one of his subjects, so the head of the house – father or husband – demanded total subjugation on the part of all women and, of course, children too. This version of Confucian morality is what made it possible for militarists to send young men, trained from childhood to be obedient to authority and do as ordered, to their deaths in World War II. After that war, however, Confucianism was tossed out the window together with other old ideas that had led Japan to defeat, and with it went the emphasis on filial piety. The new democratic system of education stresses the personality and rights of children and forbids authoritarian control and suppression. Children now regard parents with much less awe and are much less docilely obedient than – at least ideally – they once were. Furthermore, the level of material well-being in contemporary Japan is higher than in the past. Couples usually have few children, whose wants and needs they are financially able to satisfy fully, but the press of business and daily life is so great that they have insufficient time to discipline their offspring and find themselves powerless to rectify the situation when, as is not infrequently the case, pampered, uncontrolled young people run wild. Materialist codes of values are no doubt causing similar problems in most of the industrialized nations of the world. In Japan, at least part of the problem in controlling children today arises from the discrediting of the old Confucian principles of filial piety and the failure of the Japanese people to find something to take its place. Has the decline of Christianity in the West had a bad effect on parent-child relations? What social consequences do you foresee from less stringent parental control?

WILSON: Filial piety as such has not been an explicit demand of Christianity in recent times, even though Christians are expected to observe, with Jews, the third commandment of the Decalogue, "Honour thy Father and thy Mother . . ." The unquestioning obedience that Confucianism instilled into the young has never been part of Western tradition, however, so that changed attitudes to parental authority have probably been less abrupt than in Japan. In the West change has been associated with new ideologies of child-rearing, with the intensification of individualism, with the demand for personal autonomy and with the general decline of the sense of responsibility to the wider community. Technical change has given the young the means to escape family influence (whether by motor-cycles and cars or through television and discos). Their social experience has been transformed, and a permanent but ever-changing youth culture has become part of their everyday life. Because they pick up technical "know-how" quickly, they do not perceive that moral sense can be acquired only slowly, and they tend to derogate parental values simply because so often parents are, technologically, "has-beens".

Parents today undoubtedly treat children very differently from the way in which they were treated even as recently as 40 or 50 years ago. The assumption that even quite young children are already moral beings allows parents to absolve themselves from the often arduous task of providing moral training, and it exculpates them should the child run into trouble. The phrase which parents often use nowadays when an adolescent decides on some questionable course of action is, "It's his life", by which they mean, "I am not responsible". Obedience is less expected than formerly, and the very word begins to sound authoritarian and archaic.

The new attitude to children emphasizes permissiveness for their creative dispositions to emerge and find expression. It began as a sensible reaction against the repressive attitudes of the Victorians towards children, who were "to be seen and not heard". The reaction has gone too far, and that it may result in much worse forms of psychopathology and the erosion of cultural values is now widely acknowledged, even by parents who find themselves unable to stand out against the trend. Children become demanding and self-determining. With values derived from the mass media and reflected in their own peer group, many quickly become materialistic little hedonists. The economic causal nexus, of the high and uncommitted income of the young and the need of manufacturers for high turnover in the consumption of ephemeral, hence wasteful, products, need not concern us here. (For example, in the field of entertainment, young people increasingly dictate the only kinds of facility, activity and styles that are made available.) Since they are indulged at home, the same demand for indulgence persists in the wider sphere of everyday adolescent life, and we may take this as one of the consequences of less stringent parental control.

The requirement that elders be respected and obeyed is virtually universal in traditional cultures, and Christianity, which sacralized such mores and customs, reinforced the sense of filial duty for many centuries. It must be remembered that Christianity is a "son" religion. Although the family is sanctified in Christian mythology, it is not a supreme value: the true believer in Christ is, indeed, exhorted to leave his family. In Christianity the focus is on the son and, perhaps increasingly in recent times, on the father's love of the son. With such an orientation, it is perhaps understandable that Christians as such have made few protests about the shifting balance in parent-child relations.

Index